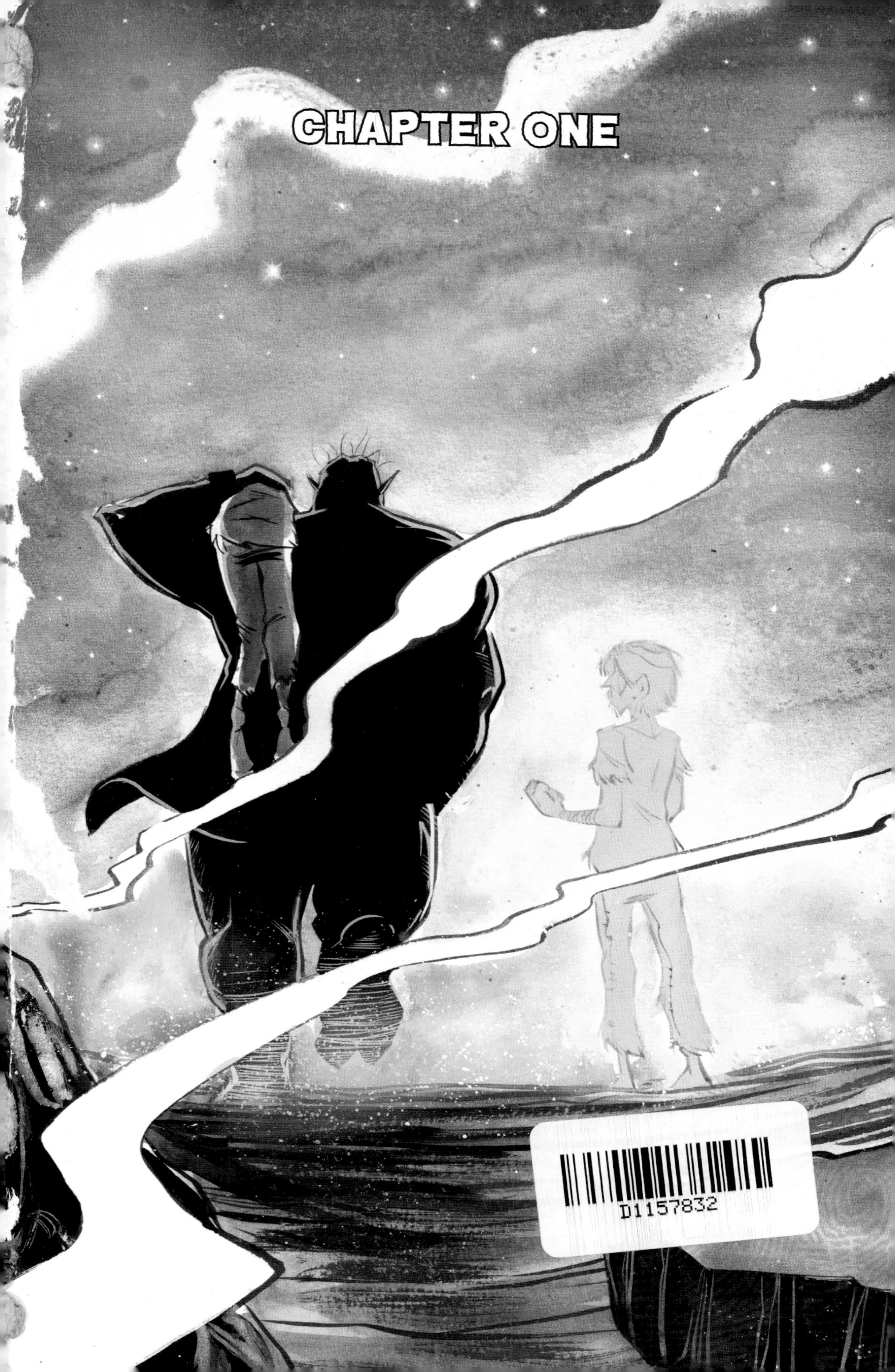
CHAPTER ONE

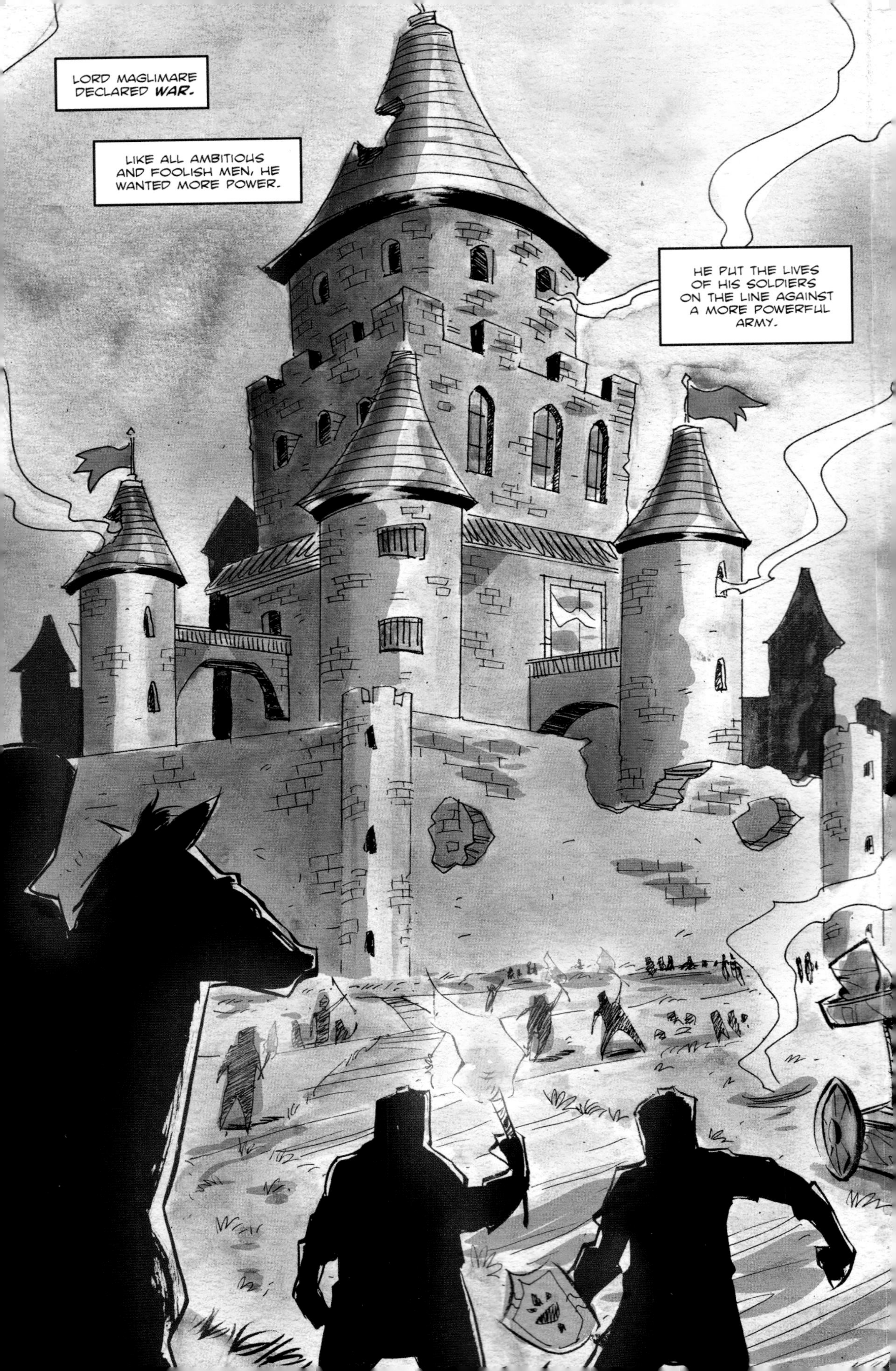
LORD MAGLIMARE DECLARED WAR.
LIKE ALL AMBITIOUS AND FOOLISH MEN, HE WANTED MORE POWER.
HE PUT THE LIVES OF HIS SOLDIERS ON THE LINE AGAINST A MORE POWERFUL ARMY.

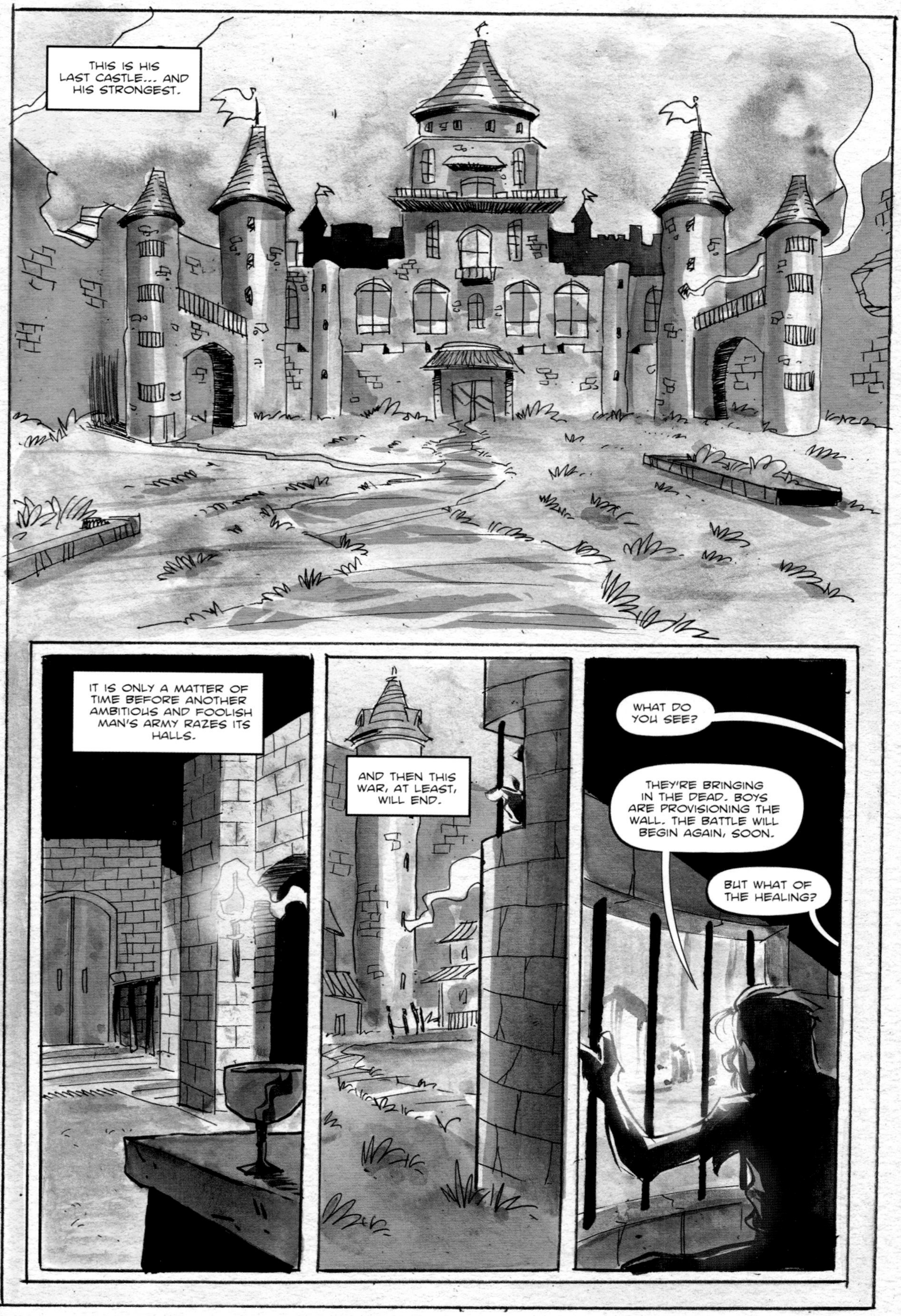
THIS IS HIS LAST CASTLE... AND HIS STRONGEST.
IT IS ONLY A MATTER OF TIME BEFORE ANOTHER AMBITIOUS AND FOOLISH MAN'S ARMY RAZES ITS HALLS.
AND THEN THIS WAR, AT LEAST, WILL END.
WHAT DO YOU SEE?
THEY'RE BRINGING IN THE DEAD. BOYS ARE PROVISIONING THE WALL. THE BATTLE WILL BEGIN AGAIN, SOON.
BUT WHAT OF THE HEALING?

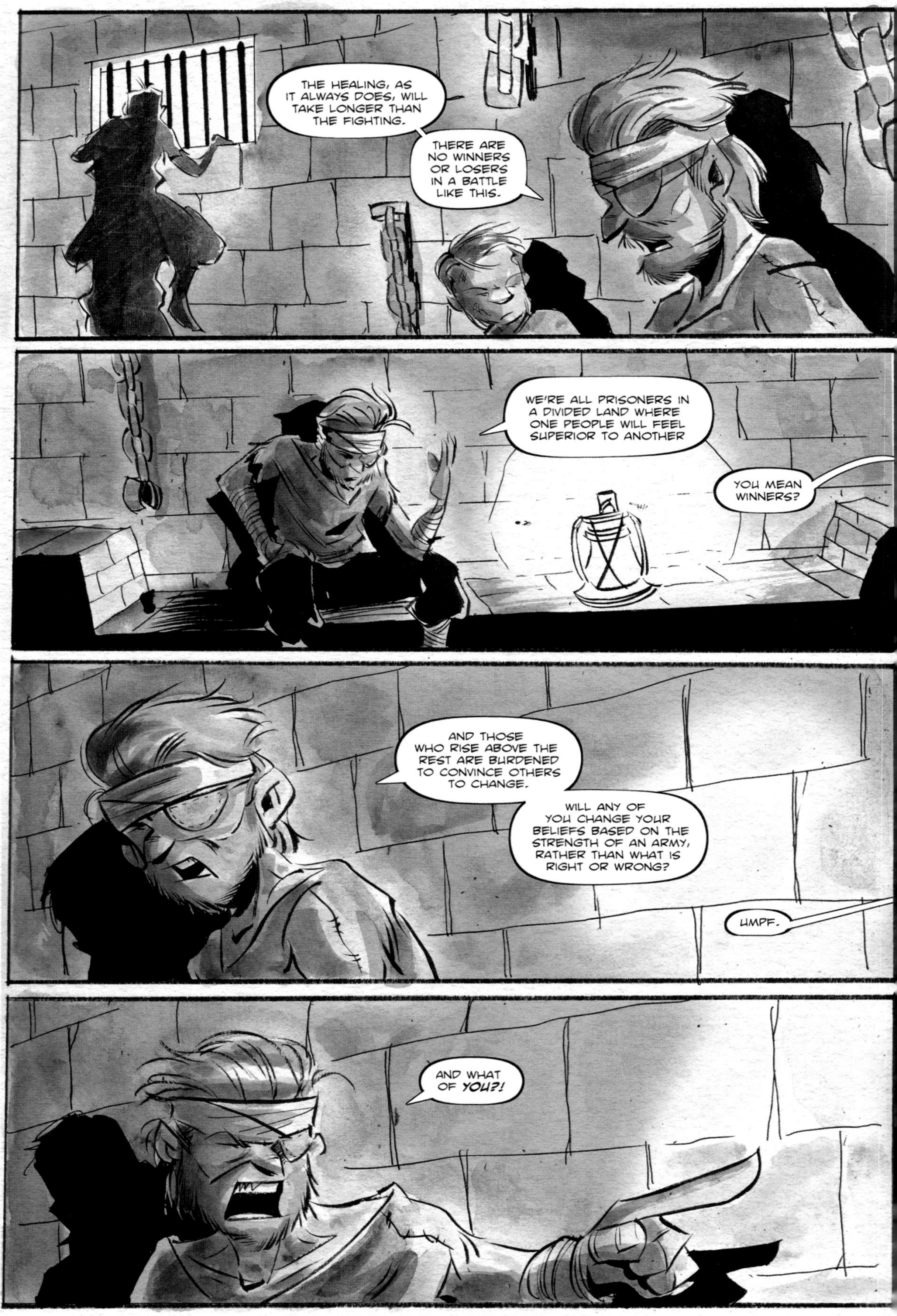
THE HEALING, AS IT ALWAYS DOES, WILL TAKE LONGER THAN THE FIGHTING.
THERE ARE NO WINNERS OR LOSERS IN A BATTLE LIKE THIS.
WE'RE ALL PRISONERS IN A DIVIDED LAND WHERE ONE PEOPLE WILL FEEL SUPERIOR TO ANOTHER
YOU MEAN WINNERS?
AND THOSE WHO RISE ABOVE THE REST ARE BURDENED TO CONVINCE OTHERS TO CHANGE.
WILL ANY OF YOU CHANGE YOUR BELIEFS BASED ON THE STRENGTH OF AN ARMY, RATHER THAN WHAT IS RIGHT OR WRONG?
UMPF.
AND WHAT OF *YOU?!*

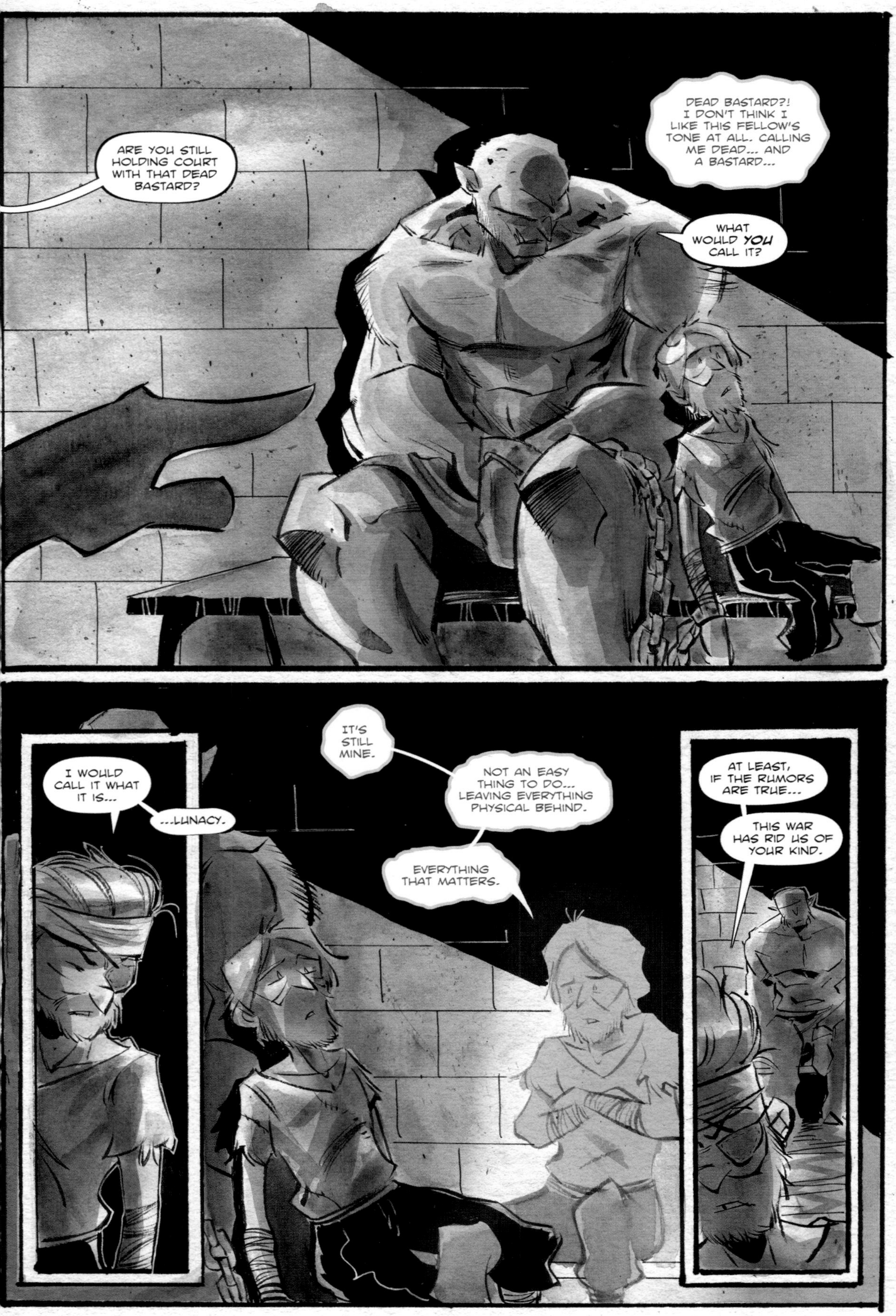
ARE YOU STILL HOLDING COURT WITH THAT DEAD BASTARD?
DEAD BASTARD?! I DON'T THINK I LIKE THIS FELLOW'S TONE AT ALL. CALLING ME DEAD... AND A BASTARD...
WHAT WOULD *YOU* CALL IT?
I WOULD CALL IT WHAT IT IS...
...LUNACY.
IT'S STILL MINE.
NOT AN EASY THING TO DO... LEAVING EVERYTHING PHYSICAL BEHIND.
EVERYTHING THAT MATTERS.
AT LEAST, IF THE RUMORS ARE TRUE...
THIS WAR HAS RID US OF YOUR KIND.

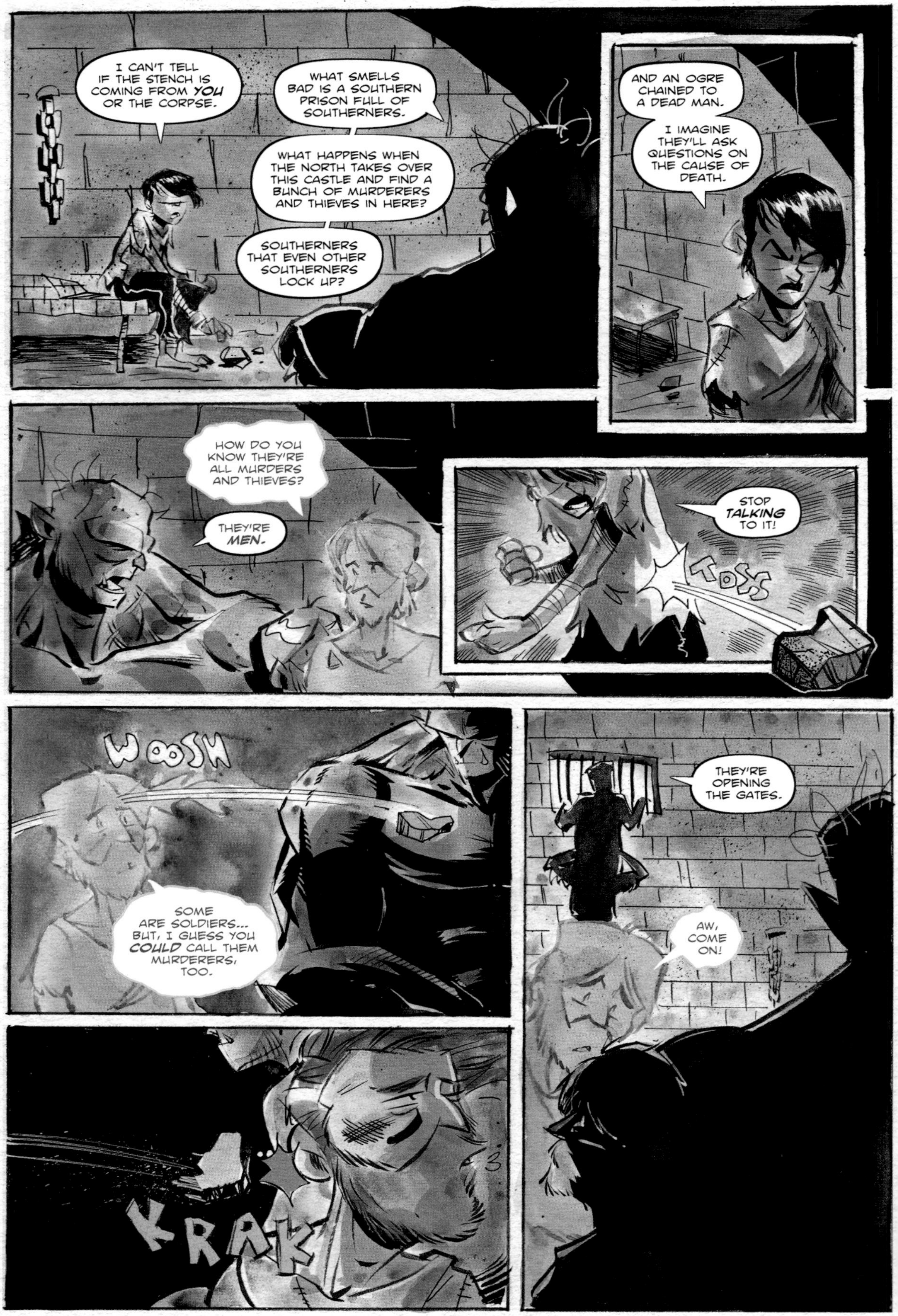
I CAN'T TELL IF THE STENCH IS COMING FROM YOU OR THE CORPSE.
WHAT SMELLS BAD IS A SOUTHERN PRISON FULL OF SOUTHERNERS.
WHAT HAPPENS WHEN THE NORTH TAKES OVER THIS CASTLE AND FIND A BUNCH OF MURDERERS AND THIEVES IN HERE?
SOUTHERNERS THAT EVEN OTHER SOUTHERNERS LOCK UP?
AND AN OGRE CHAINED TO A DEAD MAN.
I IMAGINE THEY'LL ASK QUESTIONS ON THE CAUSE OF DEATH.
HOW DO YOU KNOW THEY'RE ALL MURDERS AND THIEVES?
THEY'RE MEN.
STOP TALKING TO IT!
TOSS
WOOSH
SOME ARE SOLDIERS... BUT, I GUESS YOU COULD CALL THEM MURDERERS, TOO.
THEY'RE OPENING THE GATES.
AW, COME ON!
KRAK

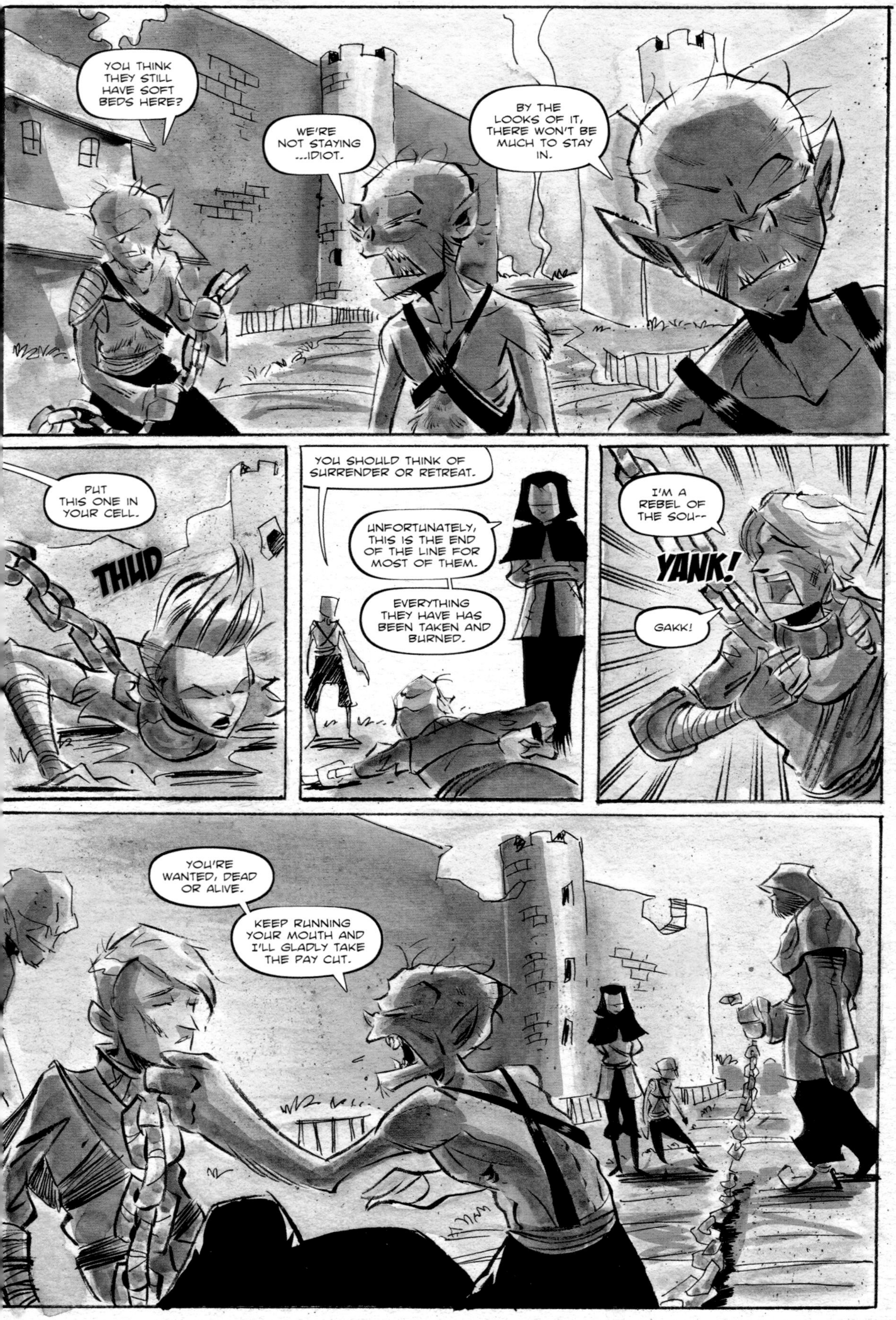

YOU THINK THEY STILL HAVE SOFT BEDS HERE?
WE'RE NOT STAYING ...IDIOT.
BY THE LOOKS OF IT, THERE WON'T BE MUCH TO STAY IN.
PUT THIS ONE IN YOUR CELL.
THUD
YOU SHOULD THINK OF SURRENDER OR RETREAT.
UNFORTUNATELY, THIS IS THE END OF THE LINE FOR MOST OF THEM.
EVERYTHING THEY HAVE HAS BEEN TAKEN AND BURNED.
I'M A REBEL OF THE SOU--
YANK!
GAKK!
YOU'RE WANTED, DEAD OR ALIVE.
KEEP RUNNING YOUR MOUTH AND I'LL GLADLY TAKE THE PAY CUT.

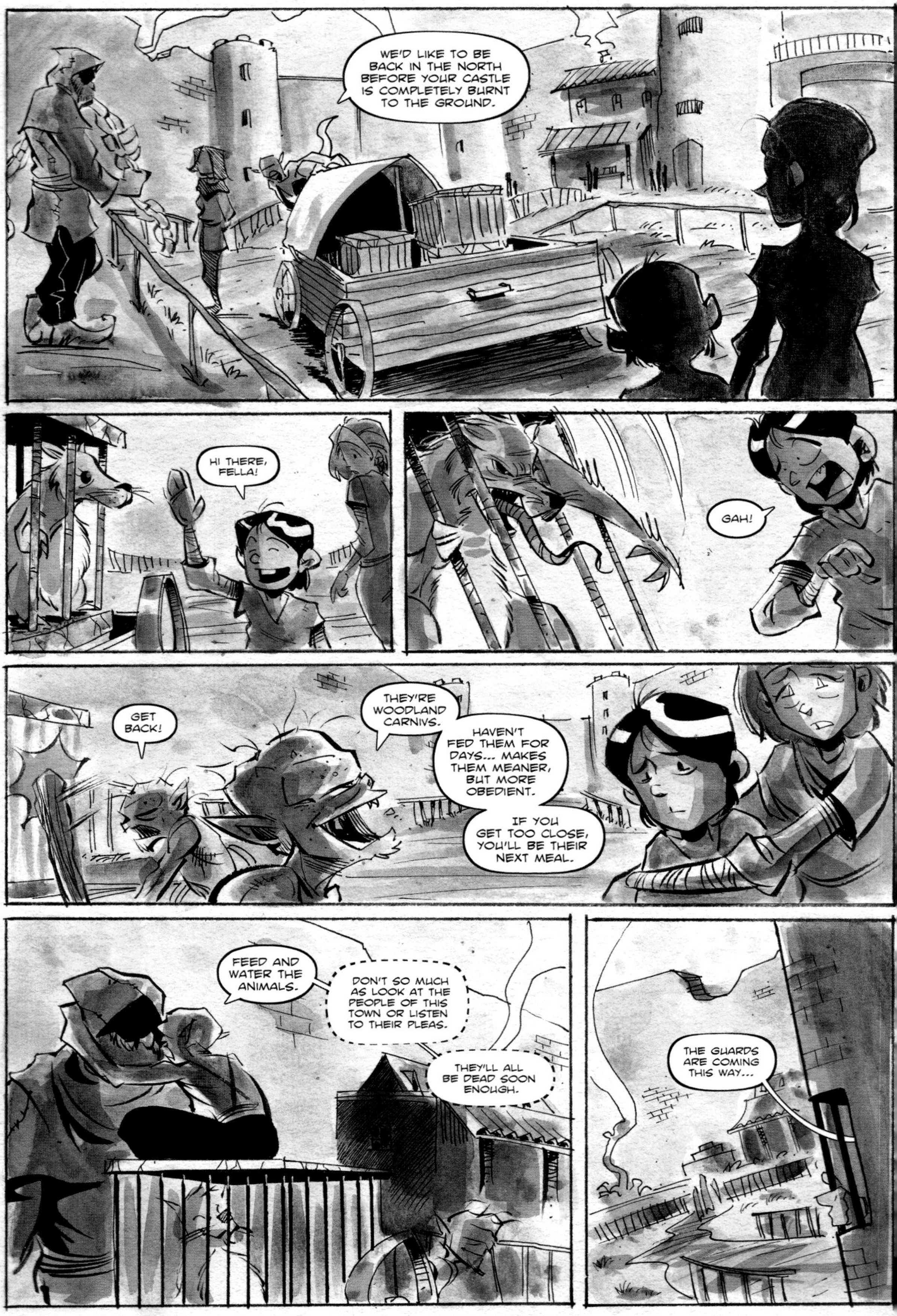
WE'D LIKE TO BE BACK IN THE NORTH BEFORE YOUR CASTLE IS COMPLETELY BURNT TO THE GROUND.
HI THERE, FELLA!
GAH!
GET BACK!
THEY'RE WOODLAND CARNIVS.
HAVEN'T FED THEM FOR DAYS... MAKES THEM MEANER, BUT MORE OBEDIENT.
IF YOU GET TOO CLOSE, YOU'LL BE THEIR NEXT MEAL.
FEED AND WATER THE ANIMALS.
DON'T SO MUCH AS LOOK AT THE PEOPLE OF THIS TOWN OR LISTEN TO THEIR PLEAS.
THEY'LL ALL BE DEAD SOON ENOUGH.
THE GUARDS ARE COMING THIS WAY...

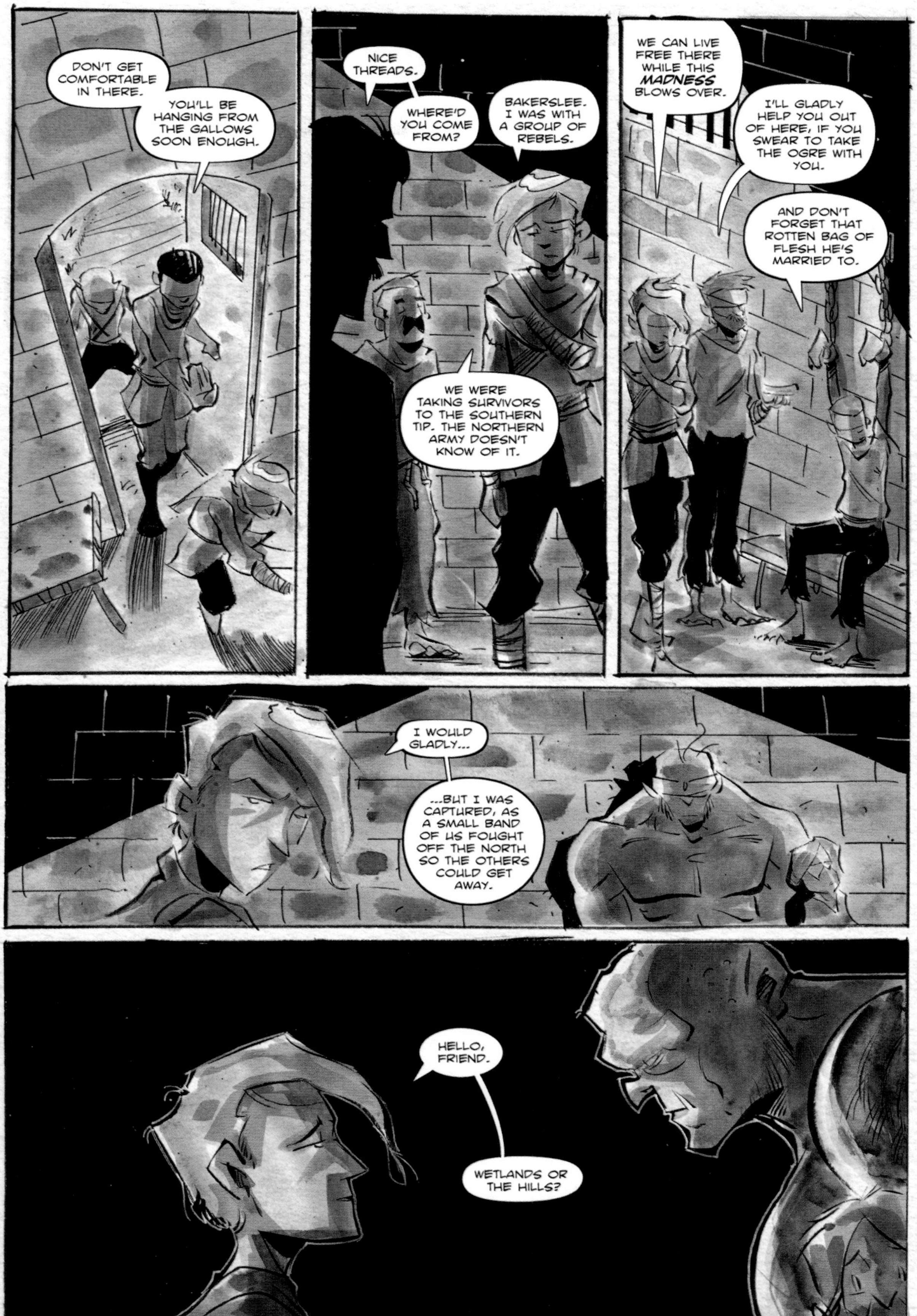
DON'T GET COMFORTABLE IN THERE.
YOU'LL BE HANGING FROM THE GALLOWS SOON ENOUGH.
NICE THREADS.
WHERE'D YOU COME FROM?
BAKERSLEE. I WAS WITH A GROUP OF REBELS.
WE WERE TAKING SURVIVORS TO THE SOUTHERN TIP. THE NORTHERN ARMY DOESN'T KNOW OF IT.
WE CAN LIVE FREE THERE WHILE THIS MADNESS BLOWS OVER.
I'LL GLADLY HELP YOU OUT OF HERE, IF YOU SWEAR TO TAKE THE OGRE WITH YOU.
AND DON'T FORGET THAT ROTTEN BAG OF FLESH HE'S MARRIED TO.
I WOULD GLADLY...
...BUT I WAS CAPTURED, AS A SMALL BAND OF US FOUGHT OFF THE NORTH SO THE OTHERS COULD GET AWAY.
HELLO, FRIEND.
WETLANDS OR THE HILLS?

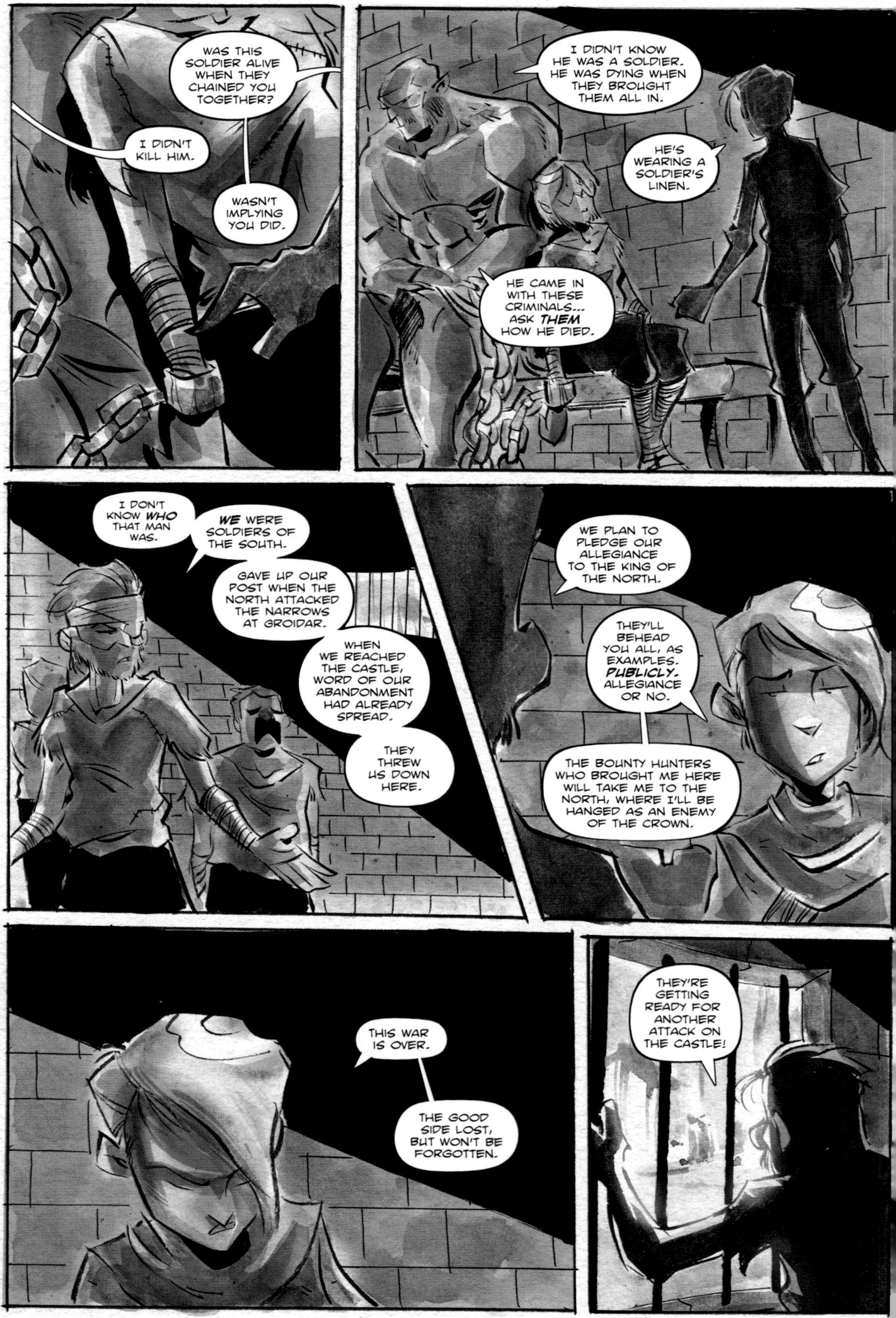
WAS THIS SOLDIER ALIVE WHEN THEY CHAINED YOU TOGETHER?
I DIDN'T KILL HIM.
WASN'T IMPLYING YOU DID.
I DIDN'T KNOW HE WAS A SOLDIER. HE WAS DYING WHEN THEY BROUGHT THEM ALL IN.
HE'S WEARING A SOLDIER'S LINEN.
HE CAME IN WITH THESE CRIMINALS... ASK THEM HOW HE DIED.
I DON'T KNOW WHO THAT MAN WAS.
WE WERE SOLDIERS OF THE SOUTH.
GAVE UP OUR POST WHEN THE NORTH ATTACKED THE NARROWS AT GROIDAR.
WHEN WE REACHED THE CASTLE, WORD OF OUR ABANDONMENT HAD ALREADY SPREAD.
THEY THREW US DOWN HERE.
WE PLAN TO PLEDGE OUR ALLEGIANCE TO THE KING OF THE NORTH.
THEY'LL BEHEAD YOU ALL, AS EXAMPLES. PUBLICLY. ALLEGIANCE OR NO.
THE BOUNTY HUNTERS WHO BROUGHT ME HERE WILL TAKE ME TO THE NORTH, WHERE I'LL BE HANGED AS AN ENEMY OF THE CROWN.
THIS WAR IS OVER.
THE GOOD SIDE LOST, BUT WON'T BE FORGOTTEN.
THEY'RE GETTING READY FOR ANOTHER ATTACK ON THE CASTLE!

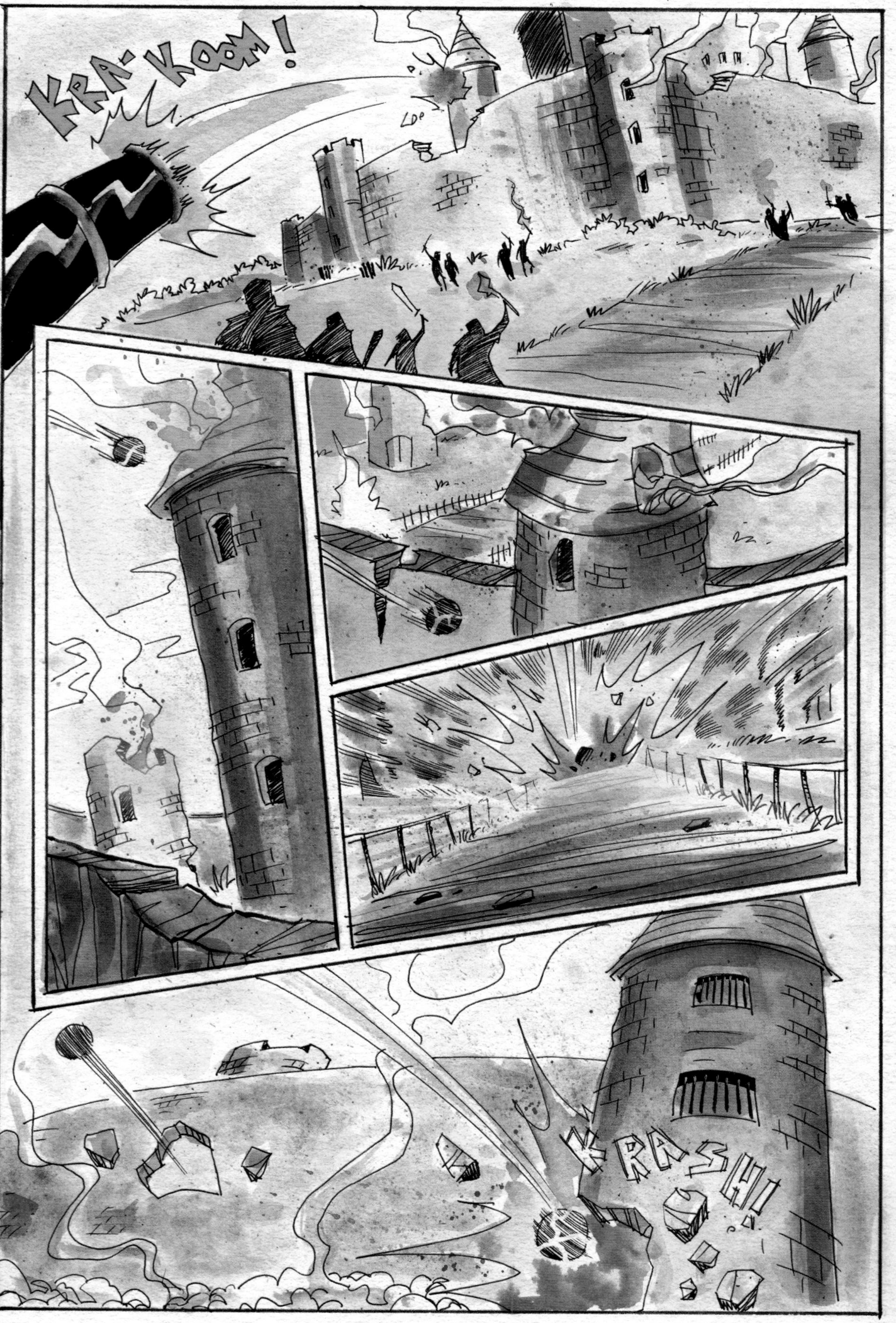
KRA-KOOM!
KRASH!

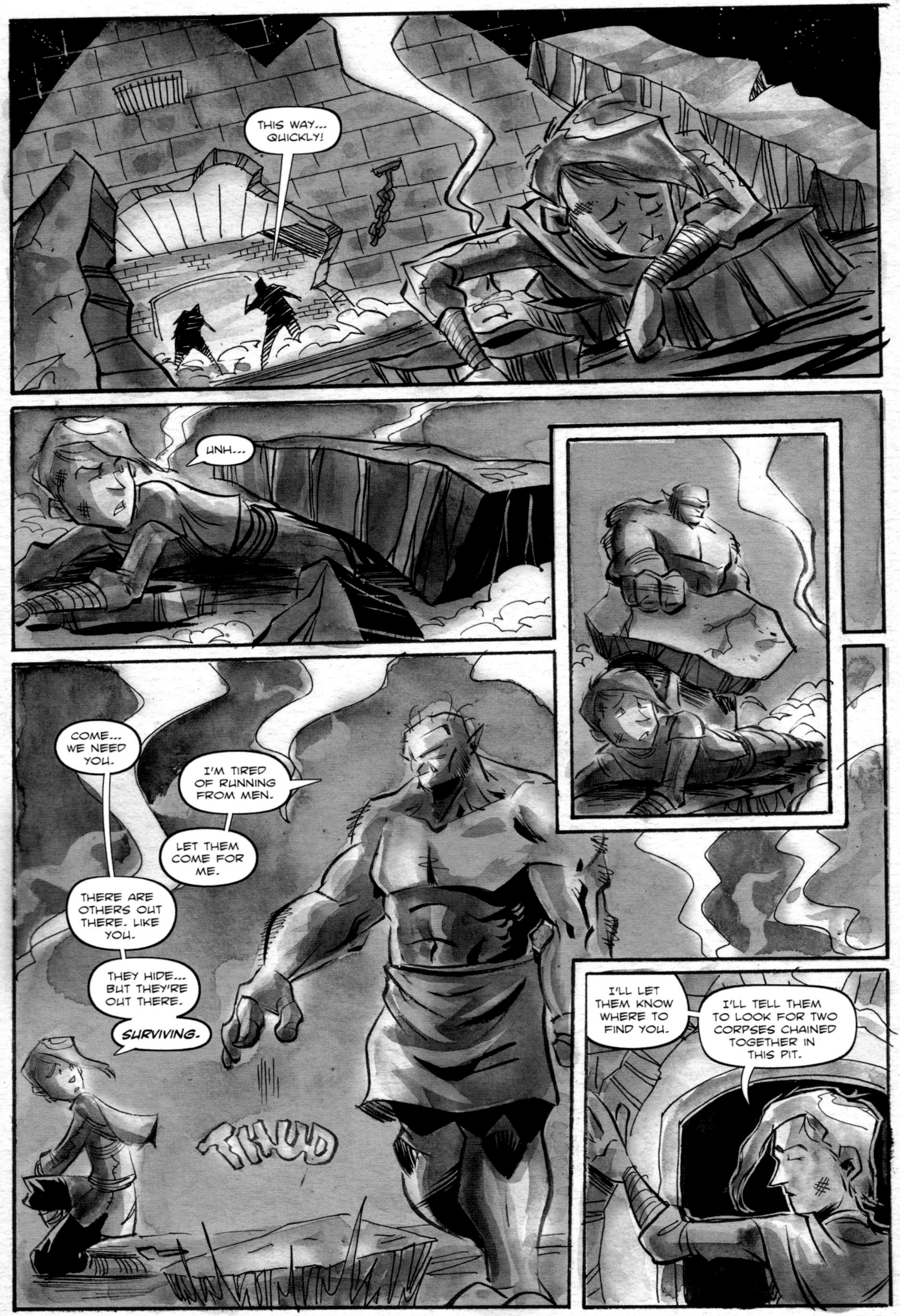
THIS WAY... QUICKLY!
UNH...
COME... WE NEED YOU.
I'M TIRED OF RUNNING FROM MEN.
LET THEM COME FOR ME.
THERE ARE OTHERS OUT THERE. LIKE YOU.
THEY HIDE... BUT THEY'RE OUT THERE.
SURVIVING.
THUD
I'LL LET THEM KNOW WHERE TO FIND YOU.
I'LL TELL THEM TO LOOK FOR TWO CORPSES CHAINED TOGETHER IN THIS PIT.

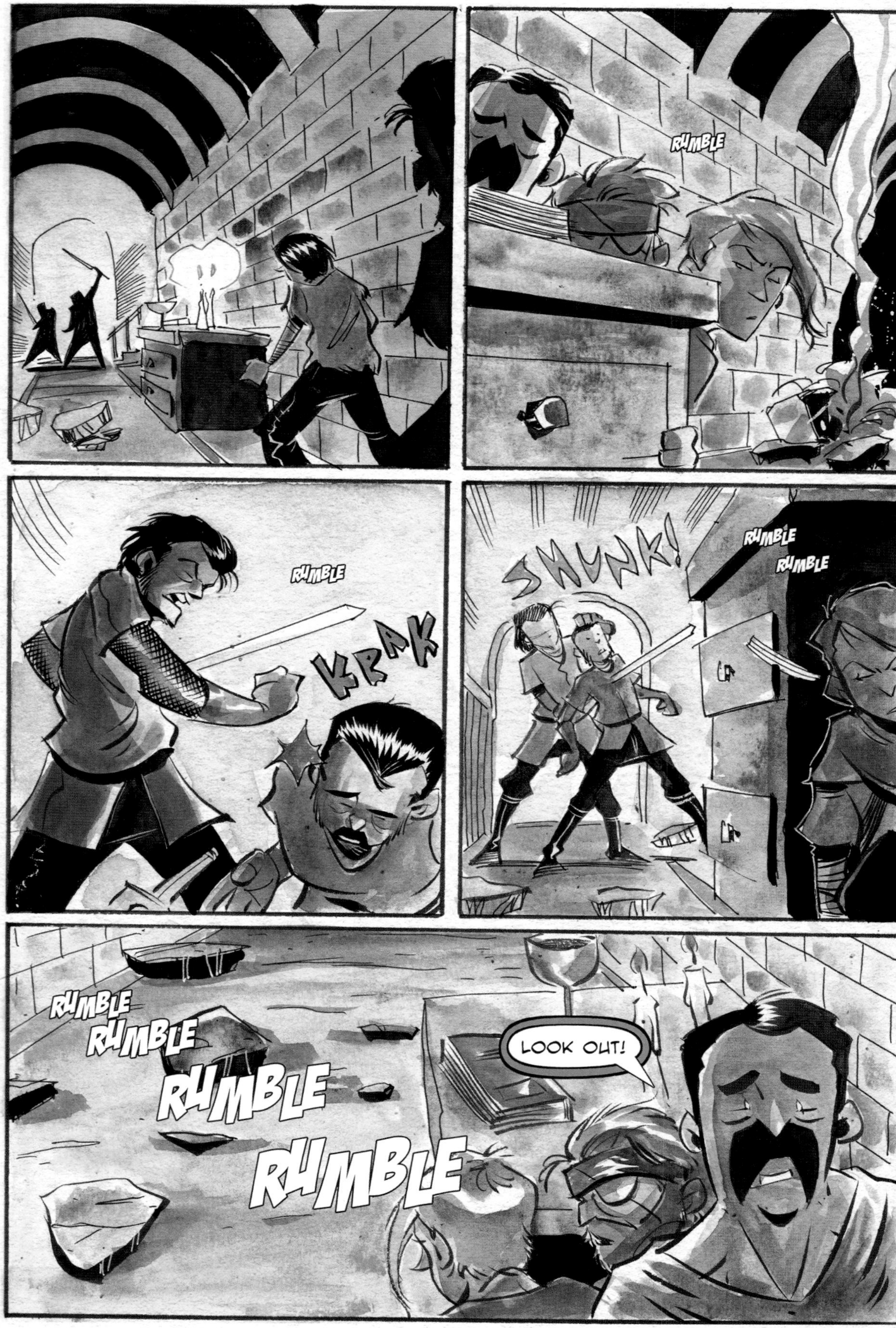
RUMBLE
RUMBLE
KRAK
SHUNK!
RUMBLE
RUMBLE
RUMBLE
RUMBLE
RUMBLE
RUMBLE
LOOK OUT!

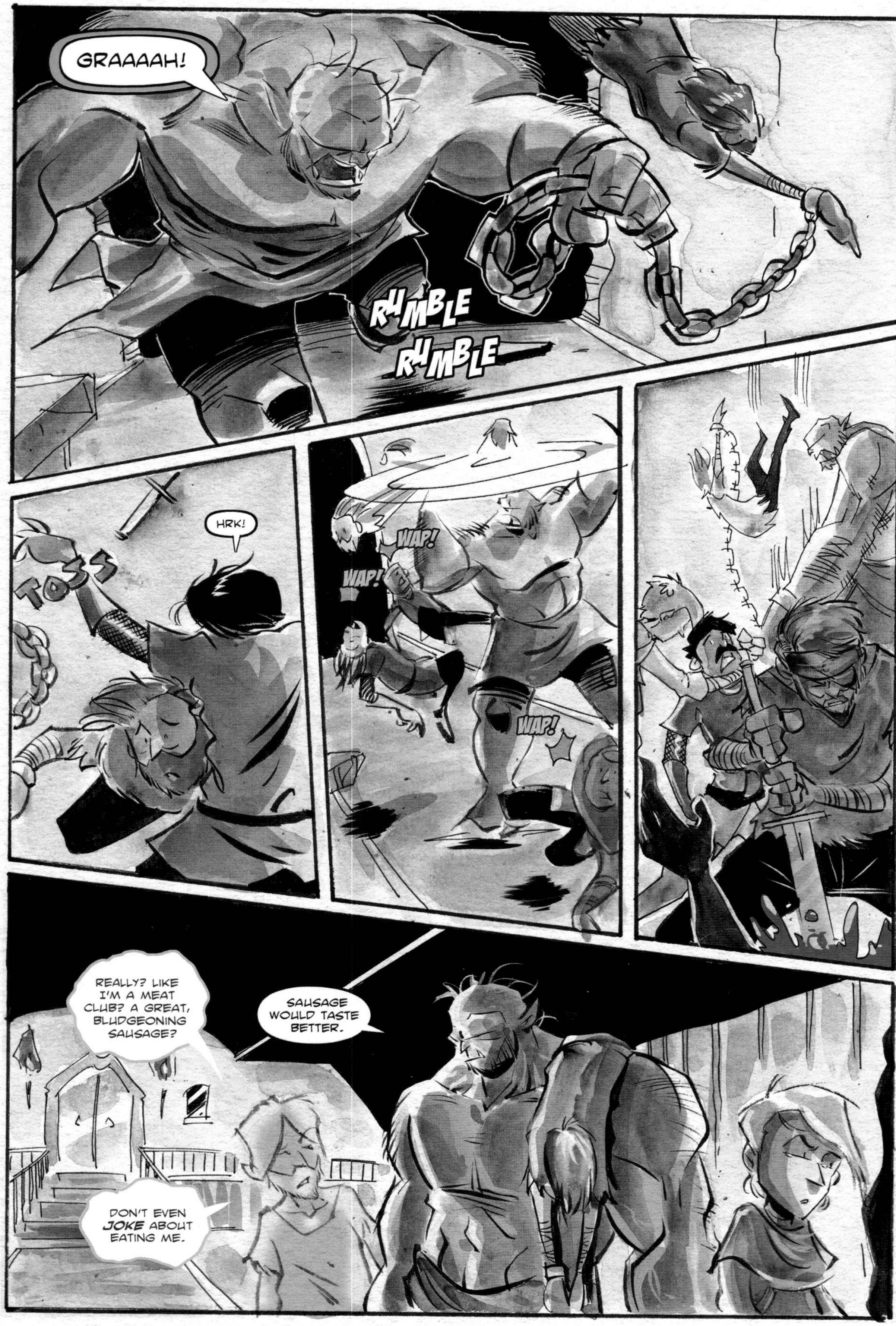
GRAAAAH!
RUMBLE
RUMBLE
TOSS
HRK!
WAP!
WAP!
WAP!
REALLY? LIKE I'M A MEAT CLUB? A GREAT, BLUDGEONING SAUSAGE?
SAUSAGE WOULD TASTE BETTER.
DON'T EVEN JOKE ABOUT EATING ME.

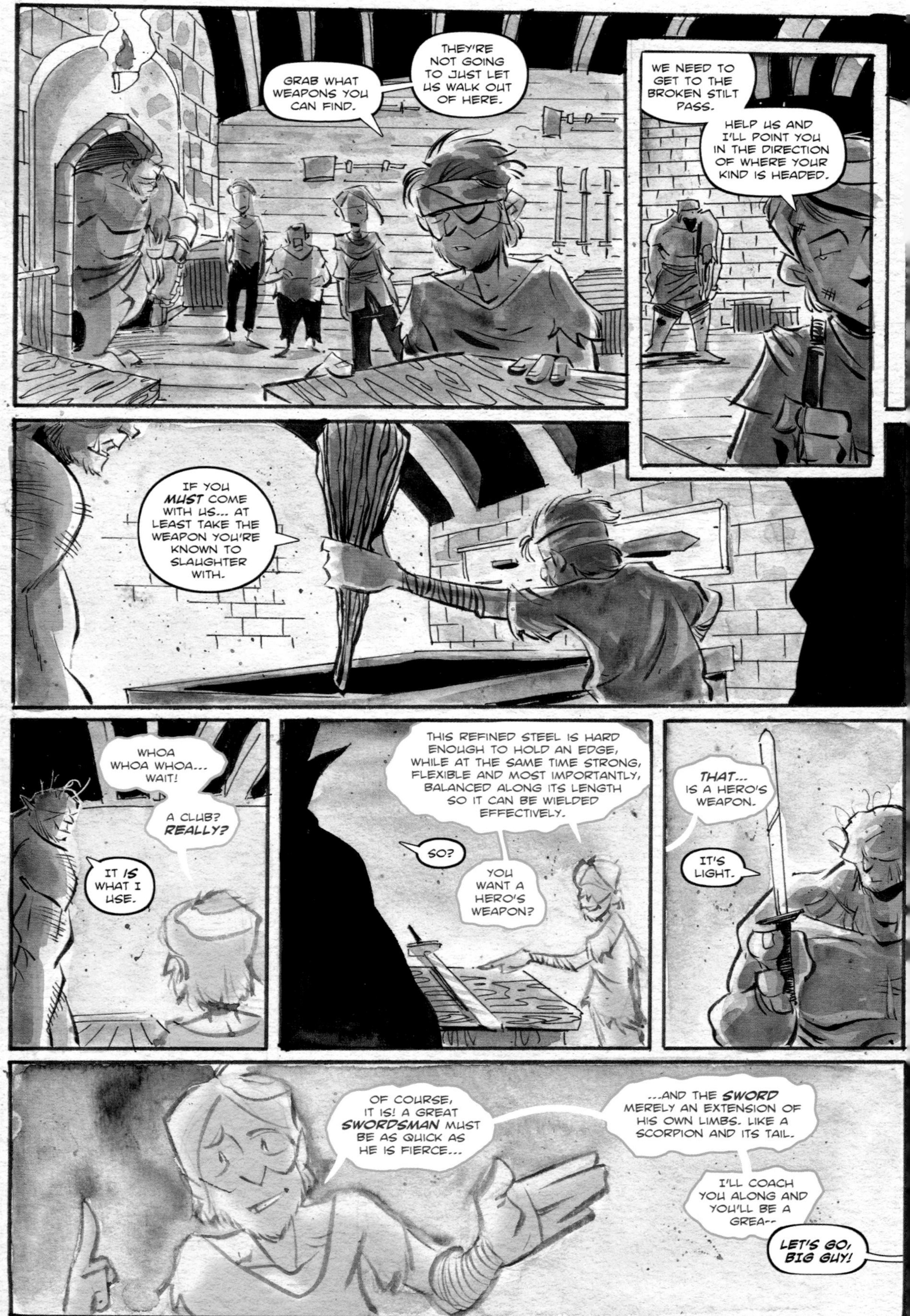
GRAB WHAT WEAPONS YOU CAN FIND.
THEY'RE NOT GOING TO JUST LET US WALK OUT OF HERE.
WE NEED TO GET TO THE BROKEN STILT PASS.
HELP US AND I'LL POINT YOU IN THE DIRECTION OF WHERE YOUR KIND IS HEADED.
IF YOU MUST COME WITH US... AT LEAST TAKE THE WEAPON YOU'RE KNOWN TO SLAUGHTER WITH.
WHOA WHOA WHOA... WAIT!
A CLUB? REALLY?
IT IS WHAT I USE.
THIS REFINED STEEL IS HARD ENOUGH TO HOLD AN EDGE, WHILE AT THE SAME TIME STRONG, FLEXIBLE AND MOST IMPORTANTLY, BALANCED ALONG ITS LENGTH SO IT CAN BE WIELDED EFFECTIVELY.
SO?
YOU WANT A HERO'S WEAPON?
THAT... IS A HERO'S WEAPON.
IT'S LIGHT.
OF COURSE, IT IS! A GREAT SWORDSMAN MUST BE AS QUICK AS HE IS FIERCE...
...AND THE SWORD MERELY AN EXTENSION OF HIS OWN LIMBS. LIKE A SCORPION AND ITS TAIL.
I'LL COACH YOU ALONG AND YOU'LL BE A GREA--
LET'S GO, BIG GUY!

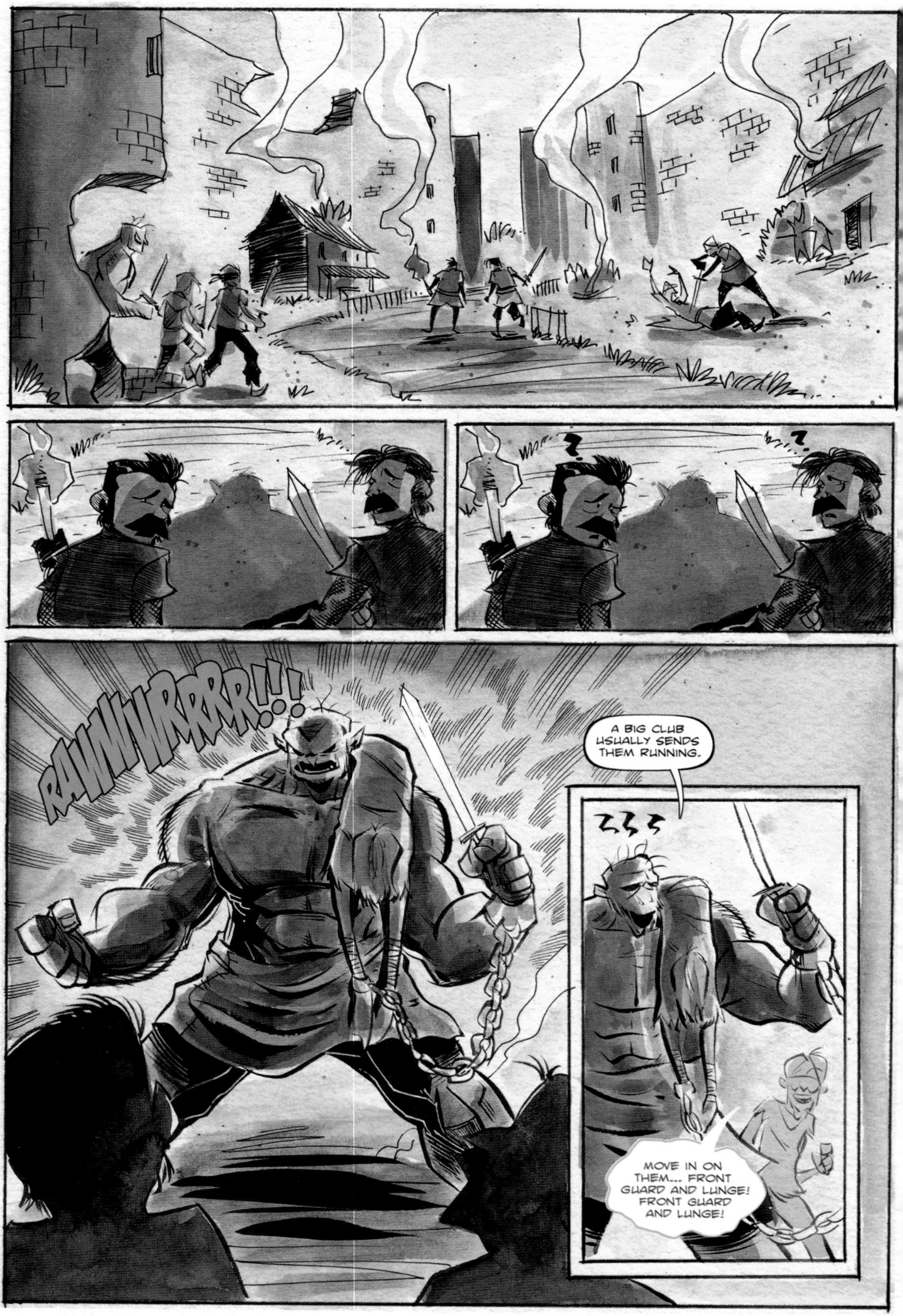
RAWWWRRRR!!!
A BIG CLUB USUALLY SENDS THEM RUNNING.
MOVE IN ON THEM... FRONT GUARD AND LUNGE! FRONT GUARD AND LUNGE!

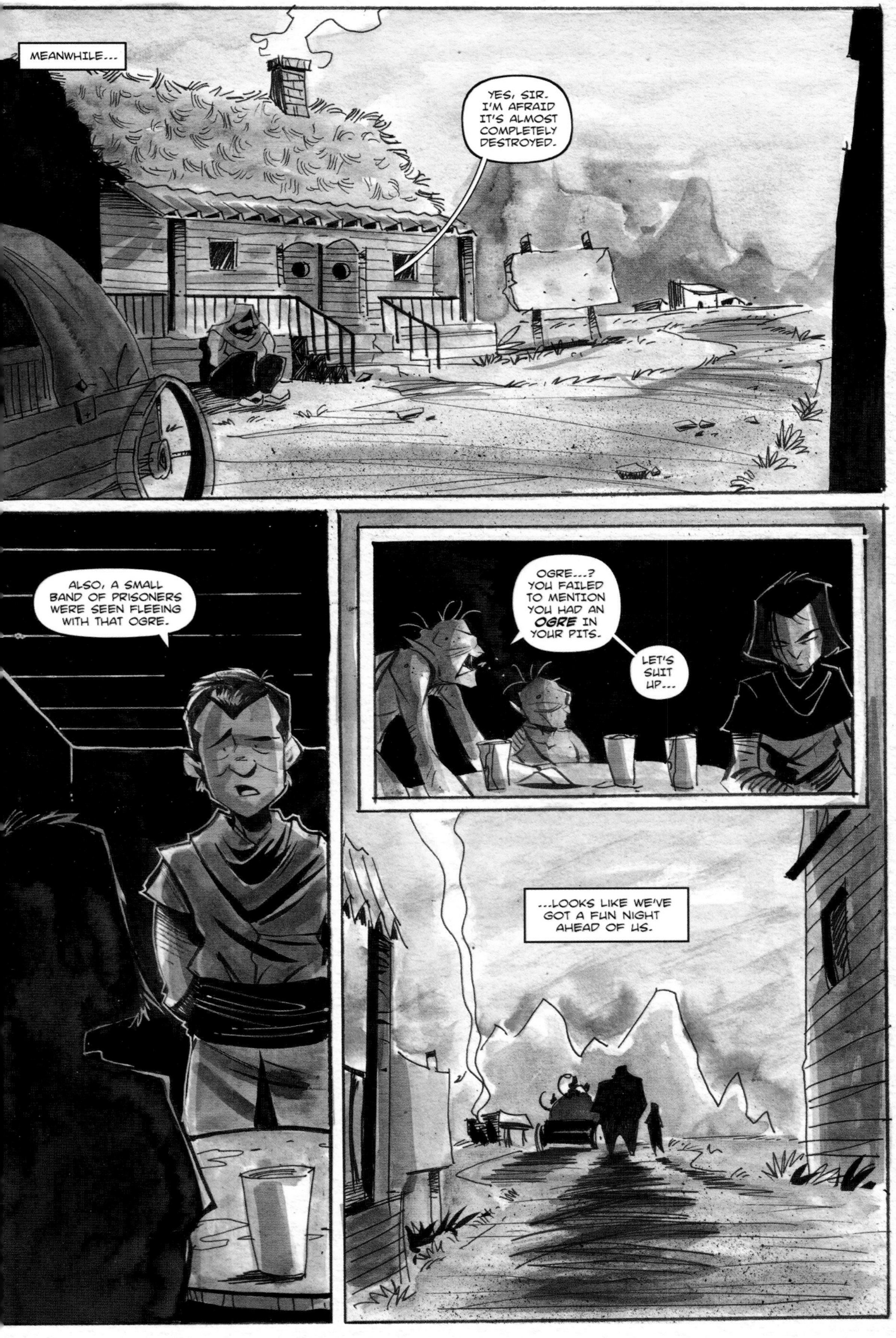
MEANWHILE...
YES, SIR. I'M AFRAID IT'S ALMOST COMPLETELY DESTROYED.
ALSO, A SMALL BAND OF PRISONERS WERE SEEN FLEEING WITH THAT OGRE.
OGRE...? YOU FAILED TO MENTION YOU HAD AN OGRE IN YOUR PITS.
LET'S SUIT UP...
...LOOKS LIKE WE'VE GOT A FUN NIGHT AHEAD OF US.

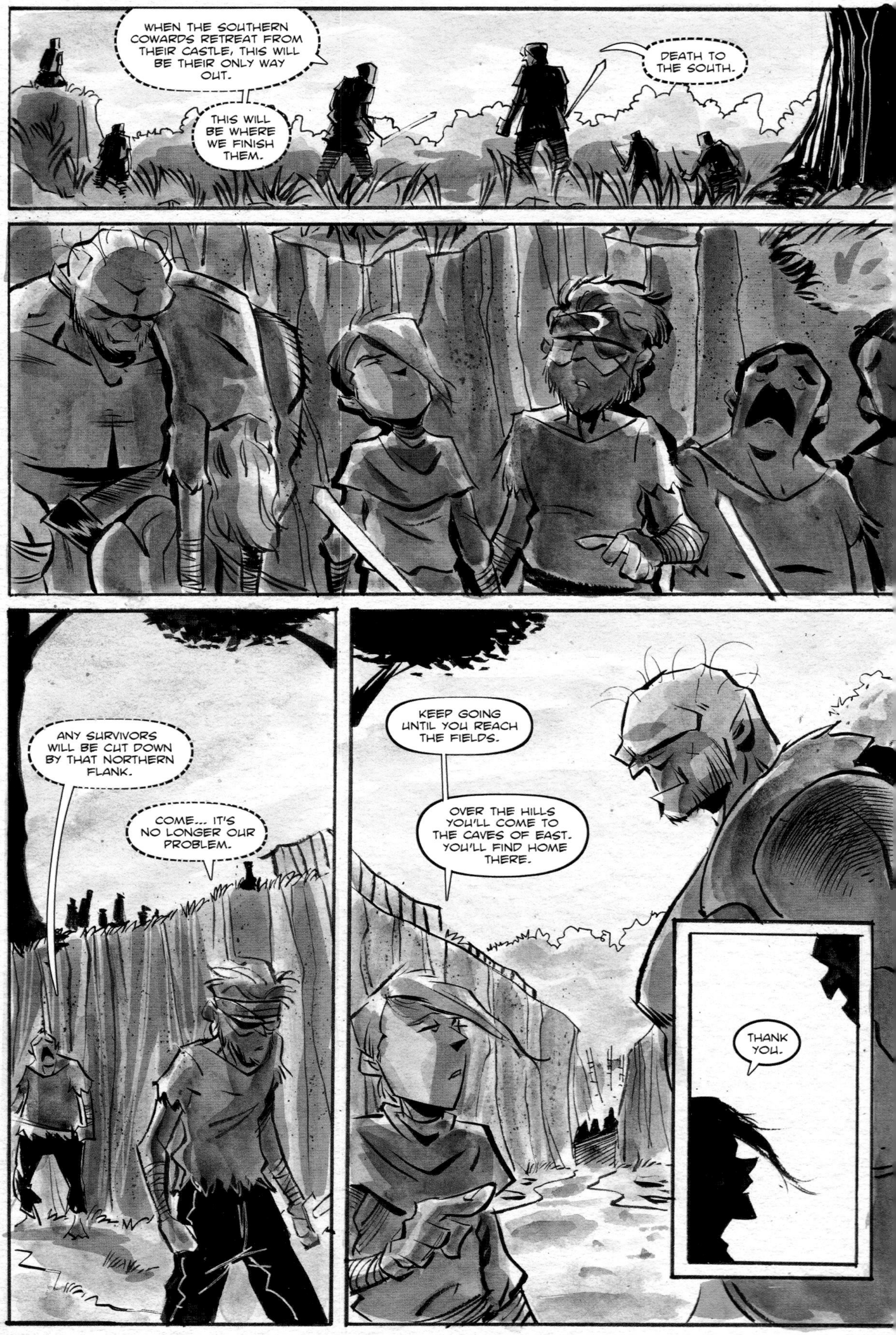

WHEN THE SOUTHERN COWARDS RETREAT FROM THEIR CASTLE, THIS WILL BE THEIR ONLY WAY OUT.
THIS WILL BE WHERE WE FINISH THEM.
DEATH TO THE SOUTH.
ANY SURVIVORS WILL BE CUT DOWN BY THAT NORTHERN FLANK.
COME... IT'S NO LONGER OUR PROBLEM.
KEEP GOING UNTIL YOU REACH THE FIELDS.
OVER THE HILLS YOU'LL COME TO THE CAVES OF EAST. YOU'LL FIND HOME THERE.
THANK YOU.

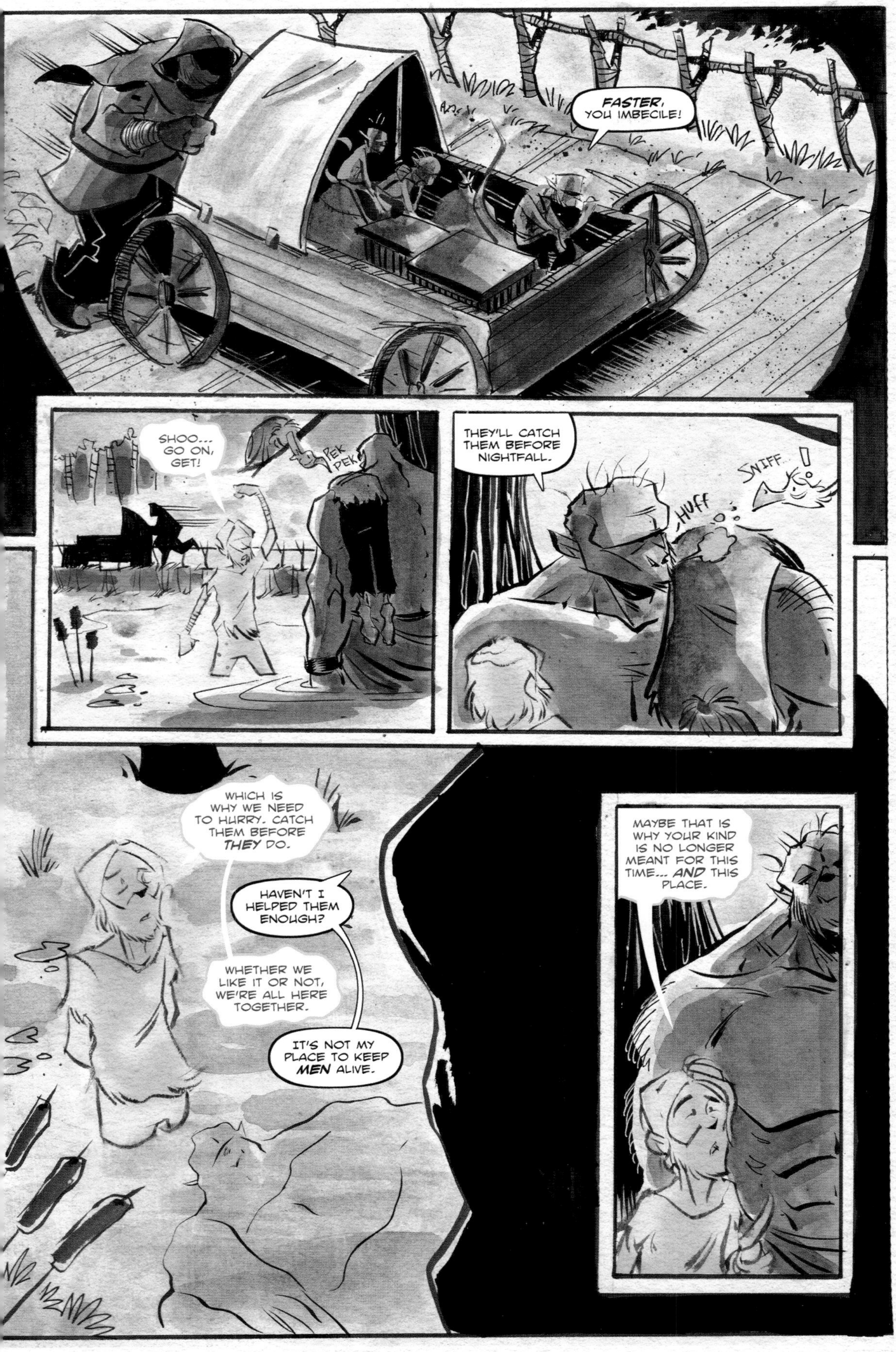

FASTER, YOU IMBECILE!
SHOO... GO ON, GET!
PEK PEK
THEY'LL CATCH THEM BEFORE NIGHTFALL.
HUFF
SNIFF... !
WHICH IS WHY WE NEED TO HURRY. CATCH THEM BEFORE THEY DO.
HAVEN'T I HELPED THEM ENOUGH?
WHETHER WE LIKE IT OR NOT, WE'RE ALL HERE TOGETHER.
IT'S NOT MY PLACE TO KEEP MEN ALIVE.
MAYBE THAT IS WHY YOUR KIND IS NO LONGER MEANT FOR THIS TIME... AND THIS PLACE.

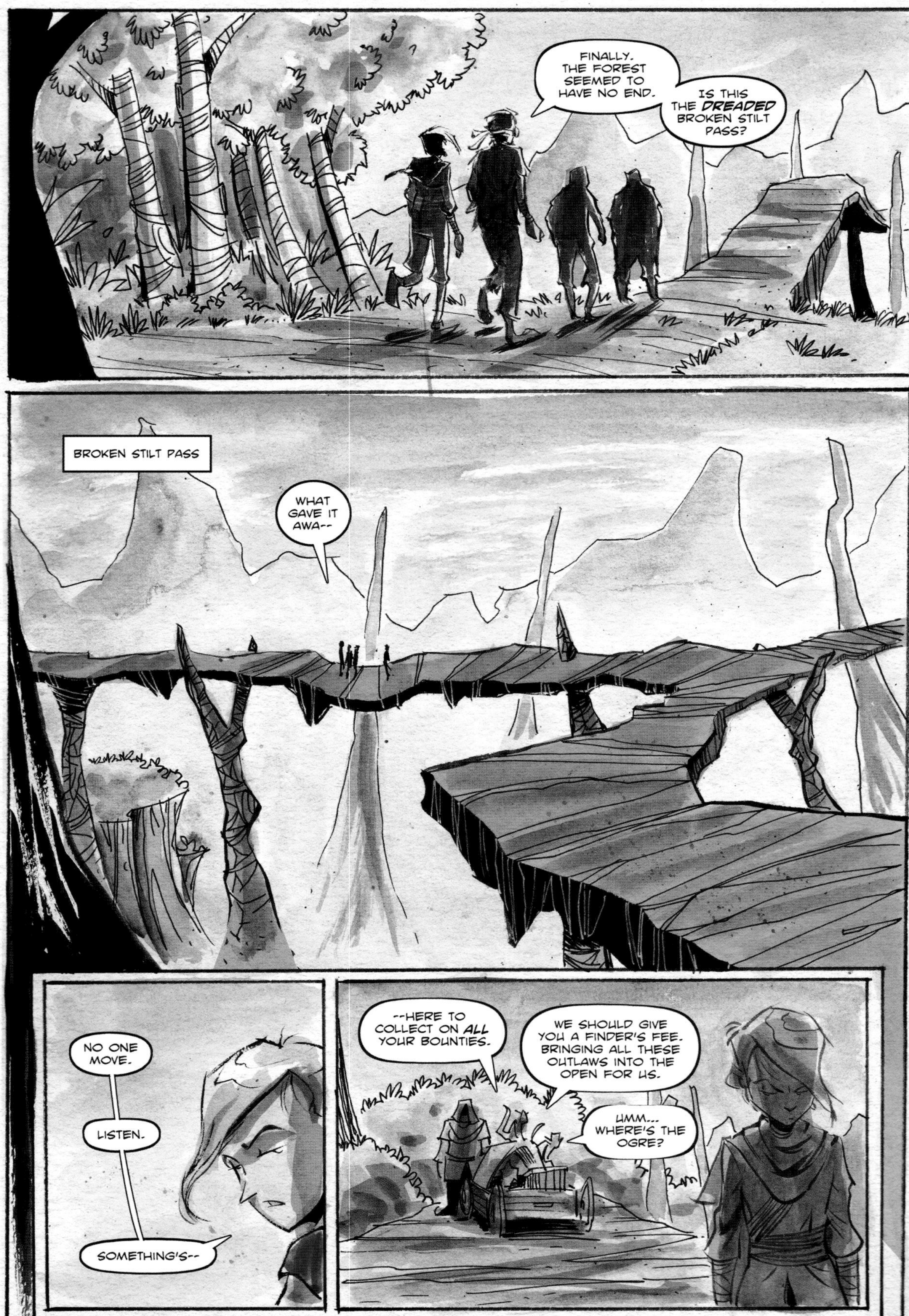
FINALLY. THE FOREST SEEMED TO HAVE NO END.
IS THIS THE DREADED BROKEN STILT PASS?
BROKEN STILT PASS
WHAT GAVE IT AWA--
NO ONE MOVE.
LISTEN.
SOMETHING'S--
--HERE TO COLLECT ON ALL YOUR BOUNTIES.
WE SHOULD GIVE YOU A FINDER'S FEE. BRINGING ALL THESE OUTLAWS INTO THE OPEN FOR US.
UMM... WHERE'S THE OGRE?

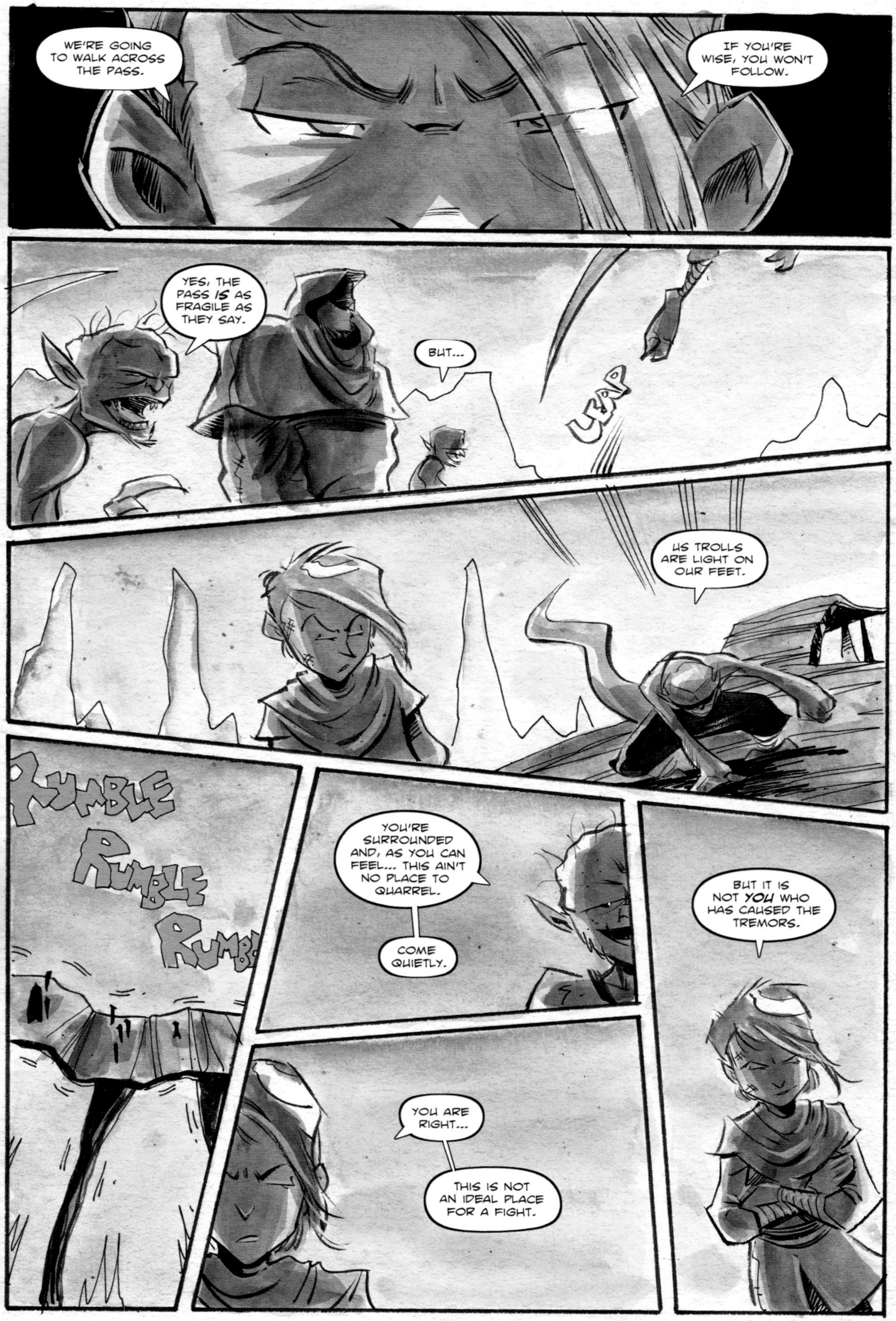
WE'RE GOING TO WALK ACROSS THE PASS.
IF YOU'RE WISE, YOU WON'T FOLLOW.
YES, THE PASS *IS* AS FRAGILE AS THEY SAY.
BUT...
LEAP
US TROLLS ARE LIGHT ON OUR FEET.
RUMBLE
RUMBLE
RUMB
YOU'RE SURROUNDED AND, AS YOU CAN FEEL... THIS AIN'T NO PLACE TO QUARREL.
COME QUIETLY.
YOU ARE RIGHT...
THIS IS NOT AN IDEAL PLACE FOR A FIGHT.
BUT IT IS NOT *YOU* WHO HAS CAUSED THE TREMORS.

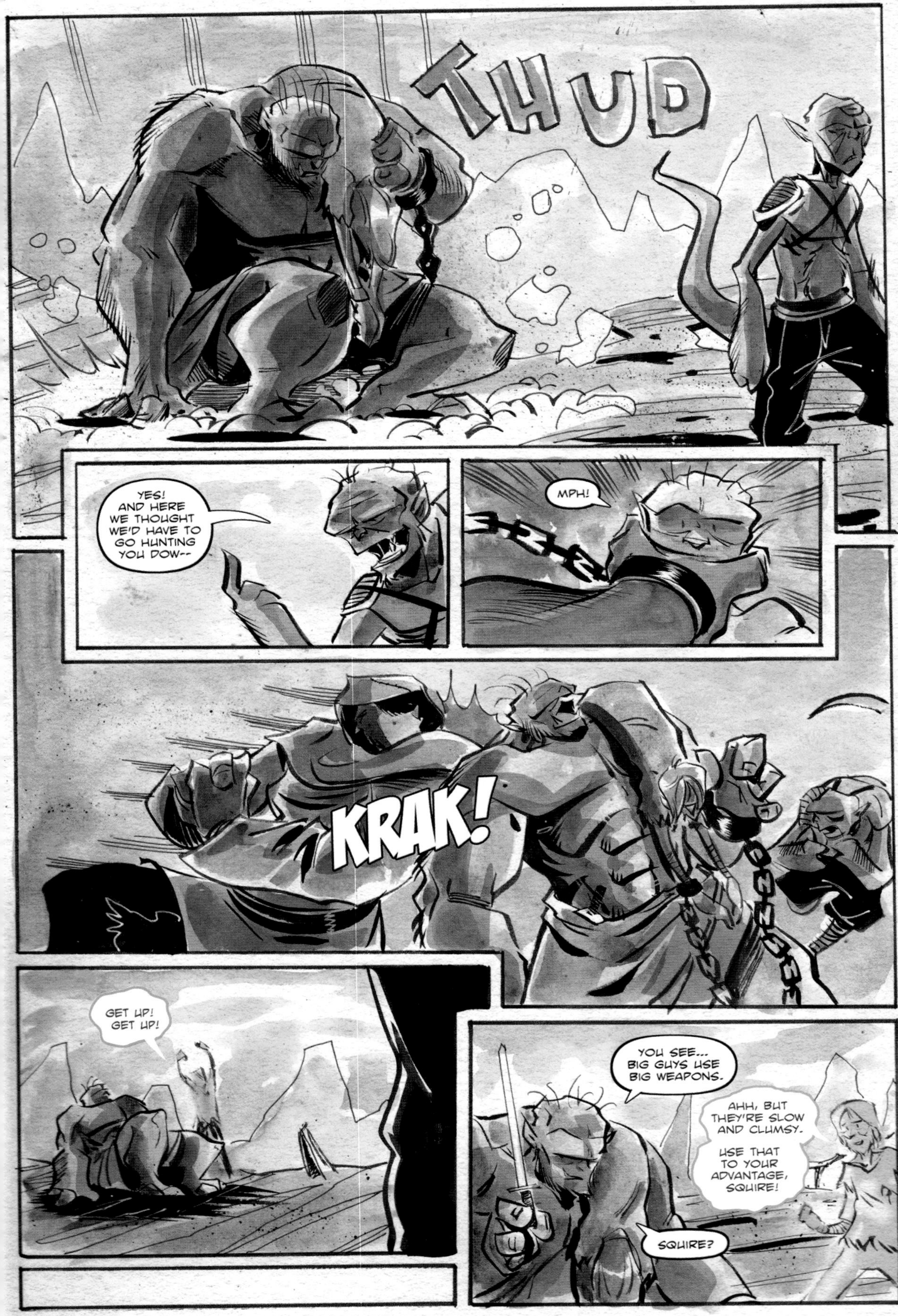
THUD
YES! AND HERE WE THOUGHT WE'D HAVE TO GO HUNTING YOU DOW--
MPH!
KRAK!
GET UP! GET UP!
YOU SEE... BIG GUYS USE BIG WEAPONS.
AHH, BUT THEY'RE SLOW AND CLUMSY.
USE THAT TO YOUR ADVANTAGE, SQUIRE!
SQUIRE?

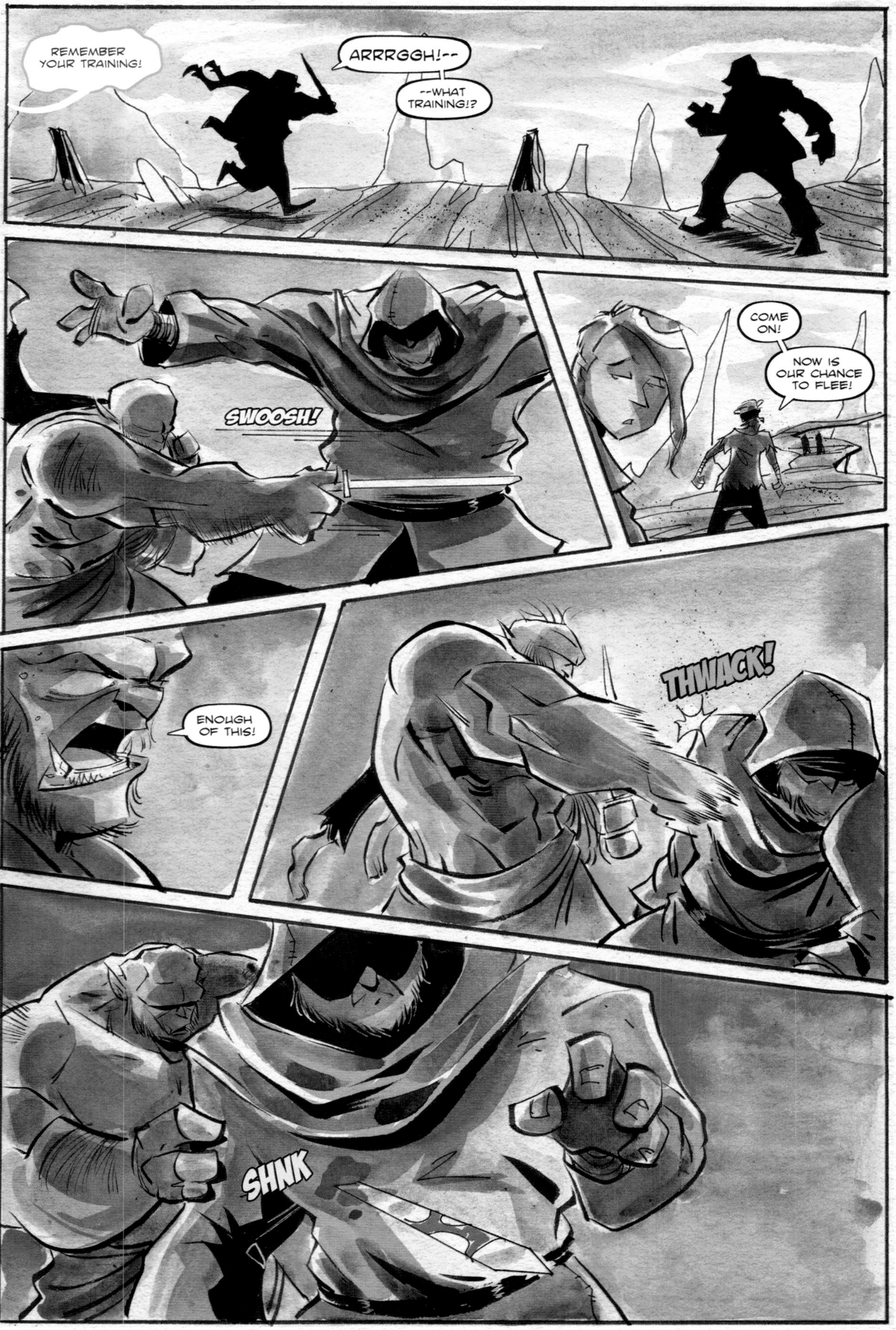
REMEMBER YOUR TRAINING!
ARRRGGH!--
--WHAT TRAINING!?
SWOOSH!
COME ON!
NOW IS OUR CHANCE TO FLEE!
ENOUGH OF THIS!
THWACK!
SHNK

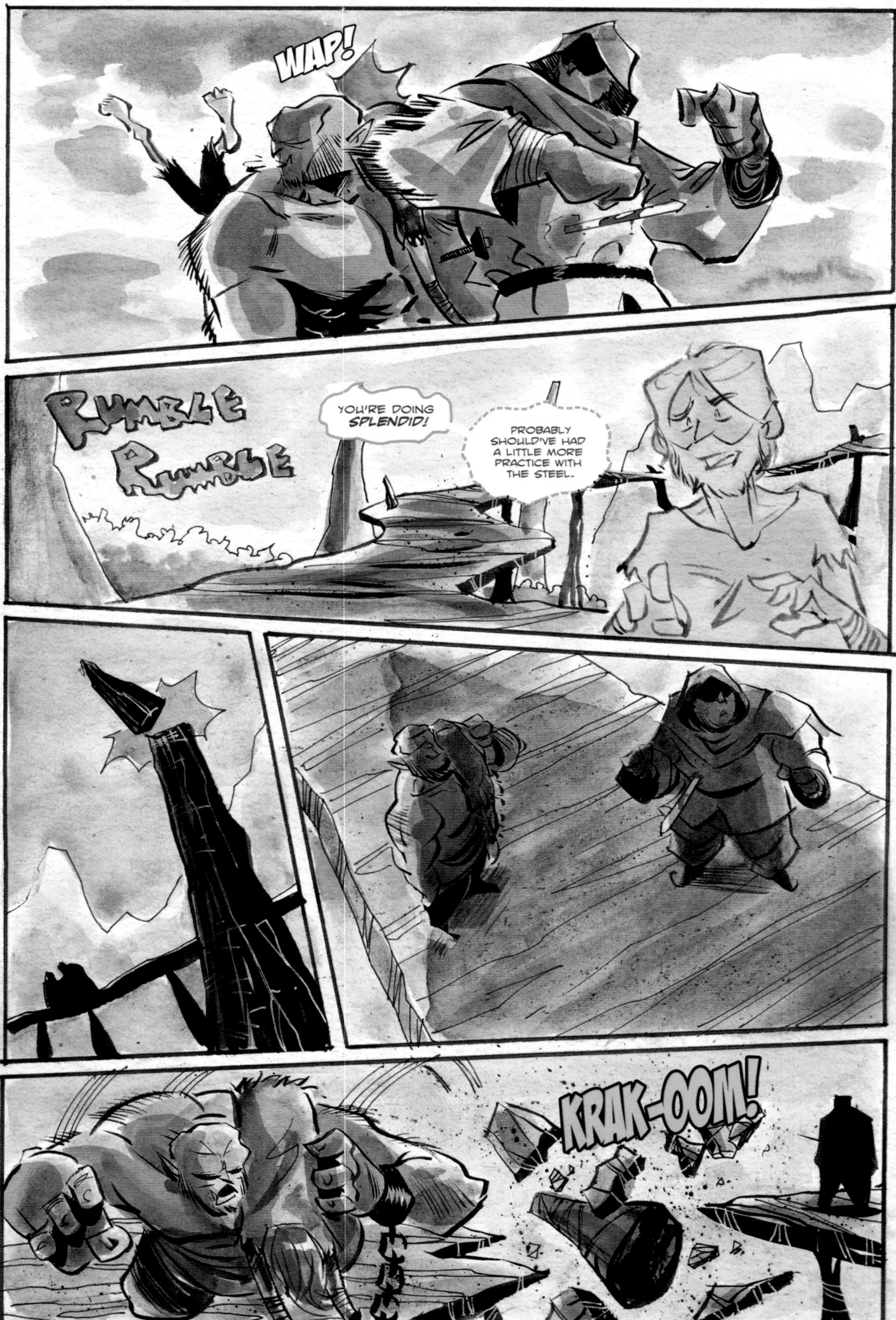
WAP!
RUMBLE
RUMBLE
YOU'RE DOING SPLENDID!
PROBABLY SHOULD'VE HAD A LITTLE MORE PRACTICE WITH THE STEEL.
KRAK-OOM!

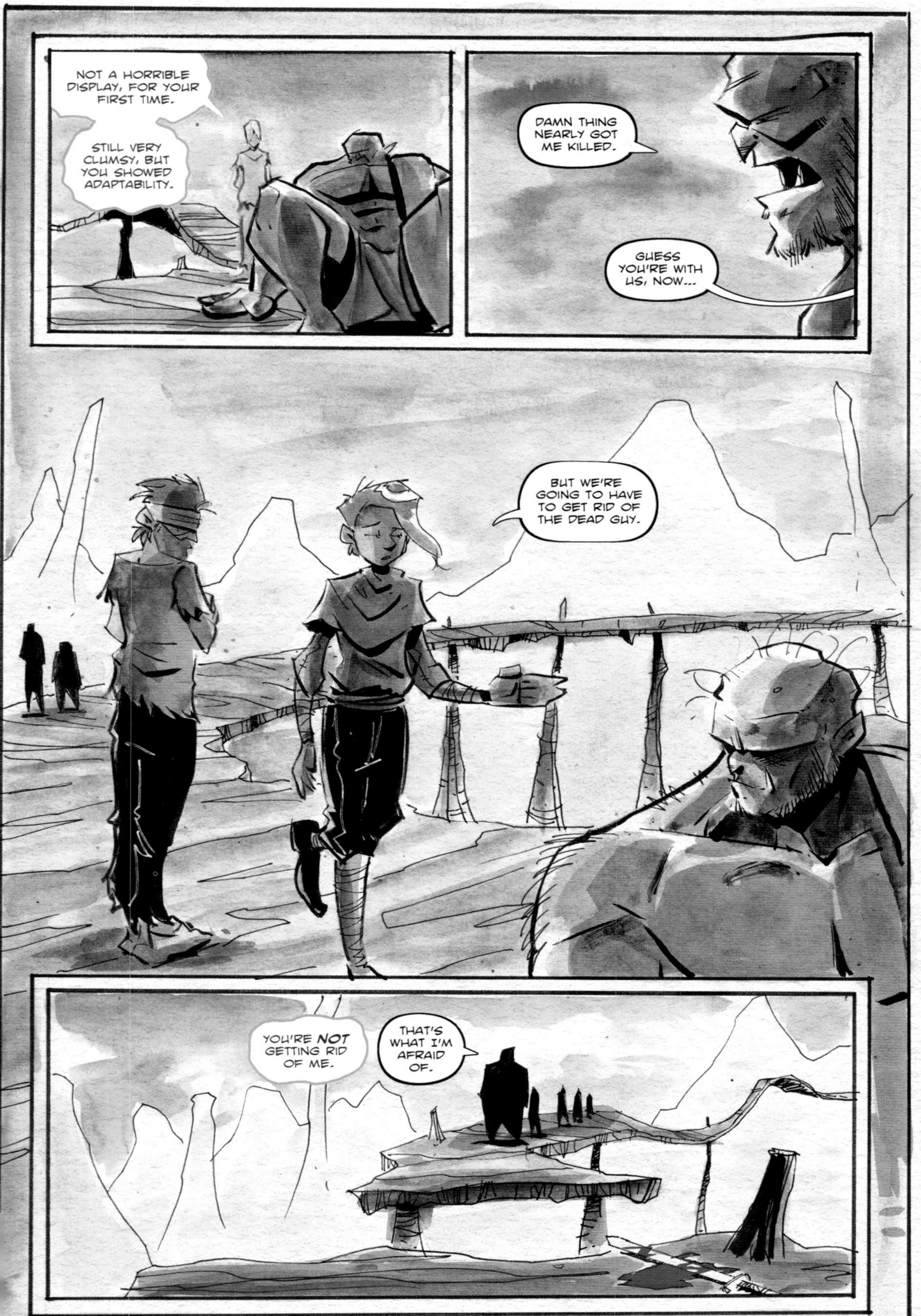
NOT A HORRIBLE DISPLAY, FOR YOUR FIRST TIME.
STILL VERY CLUMSY, BUT YOU SHOWED ADAPTABILITY.
DAMN THING NEARLY GOT ME KILLED.
GUESS YOU'RE WITH US, NOW...
BUT WE'RE GOING TO HAVE TO GET RID OF THE DEAD GUY.
YOU'RE NOT GETTING RID OF ME.
THAT'S WHAT I'M AFRAID OF.

Other versions of the 2nd issue cover by Shawn Daley

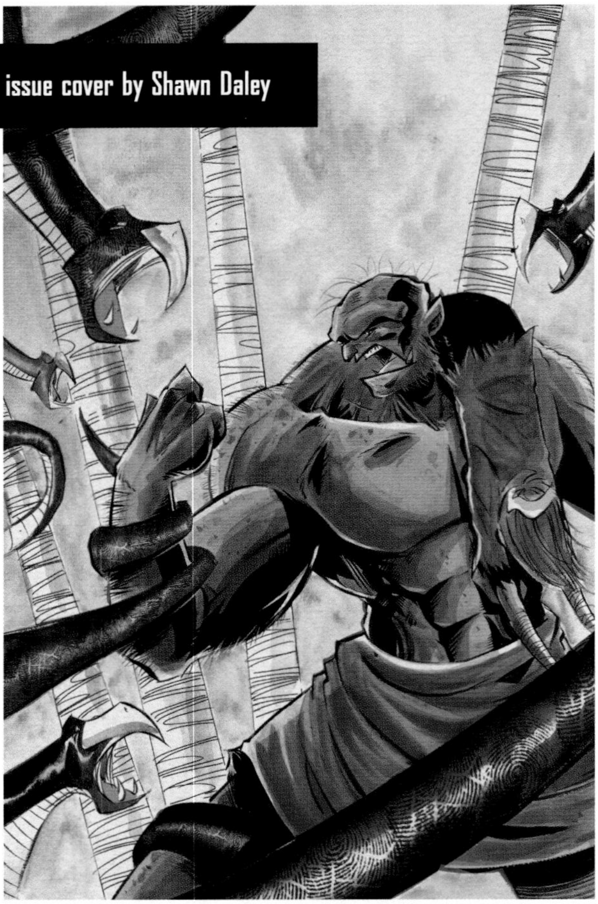

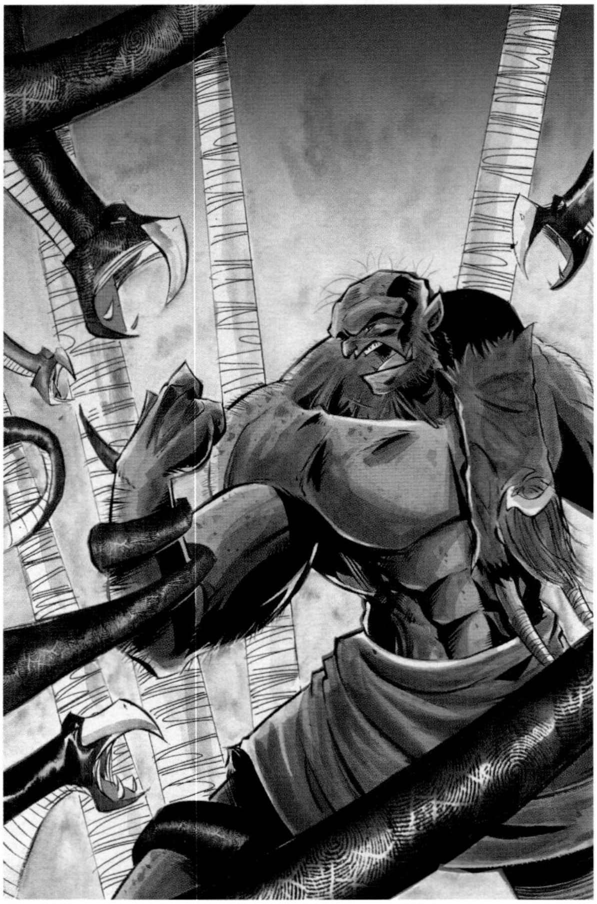

CHAPTER TWO

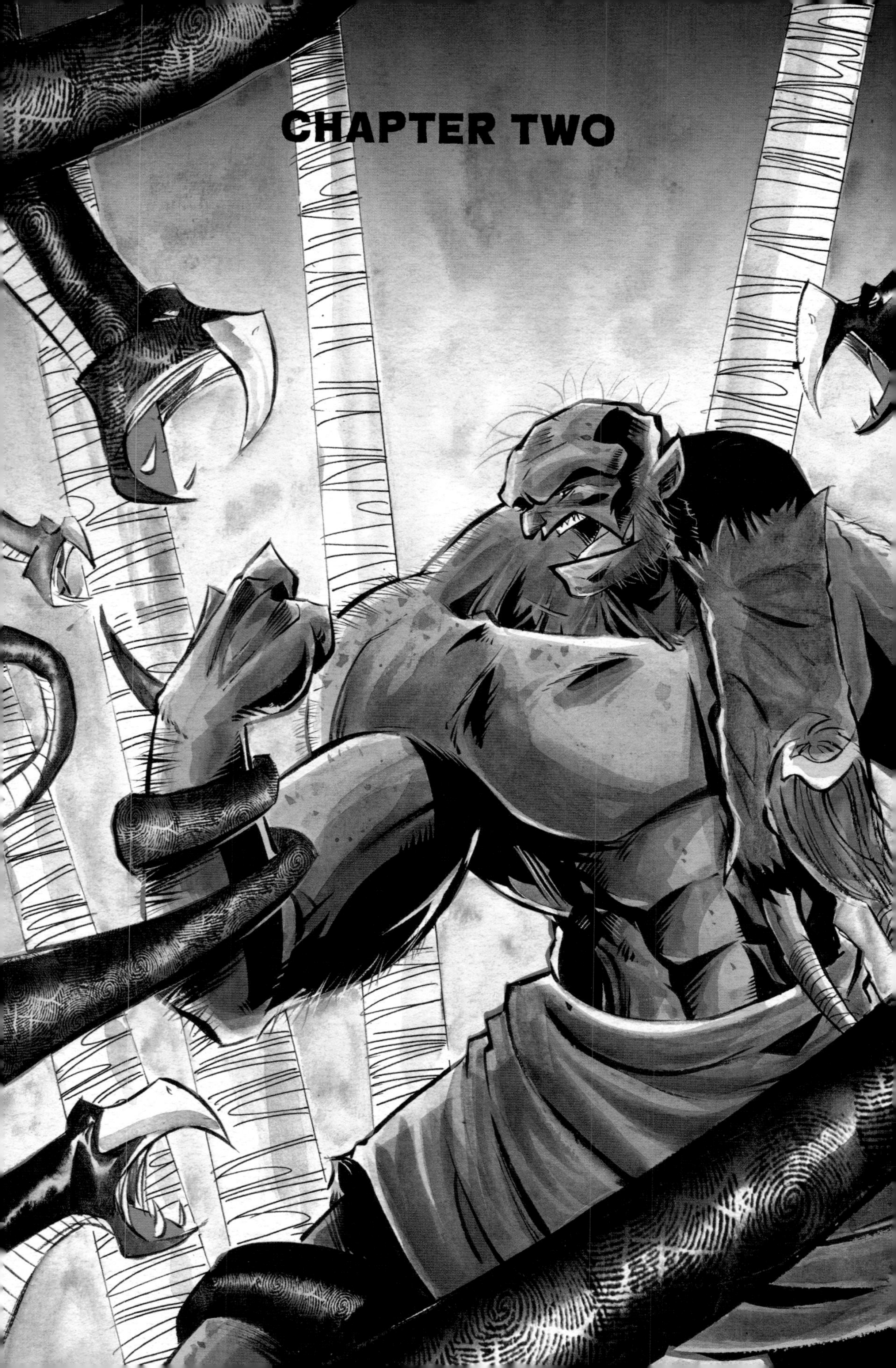

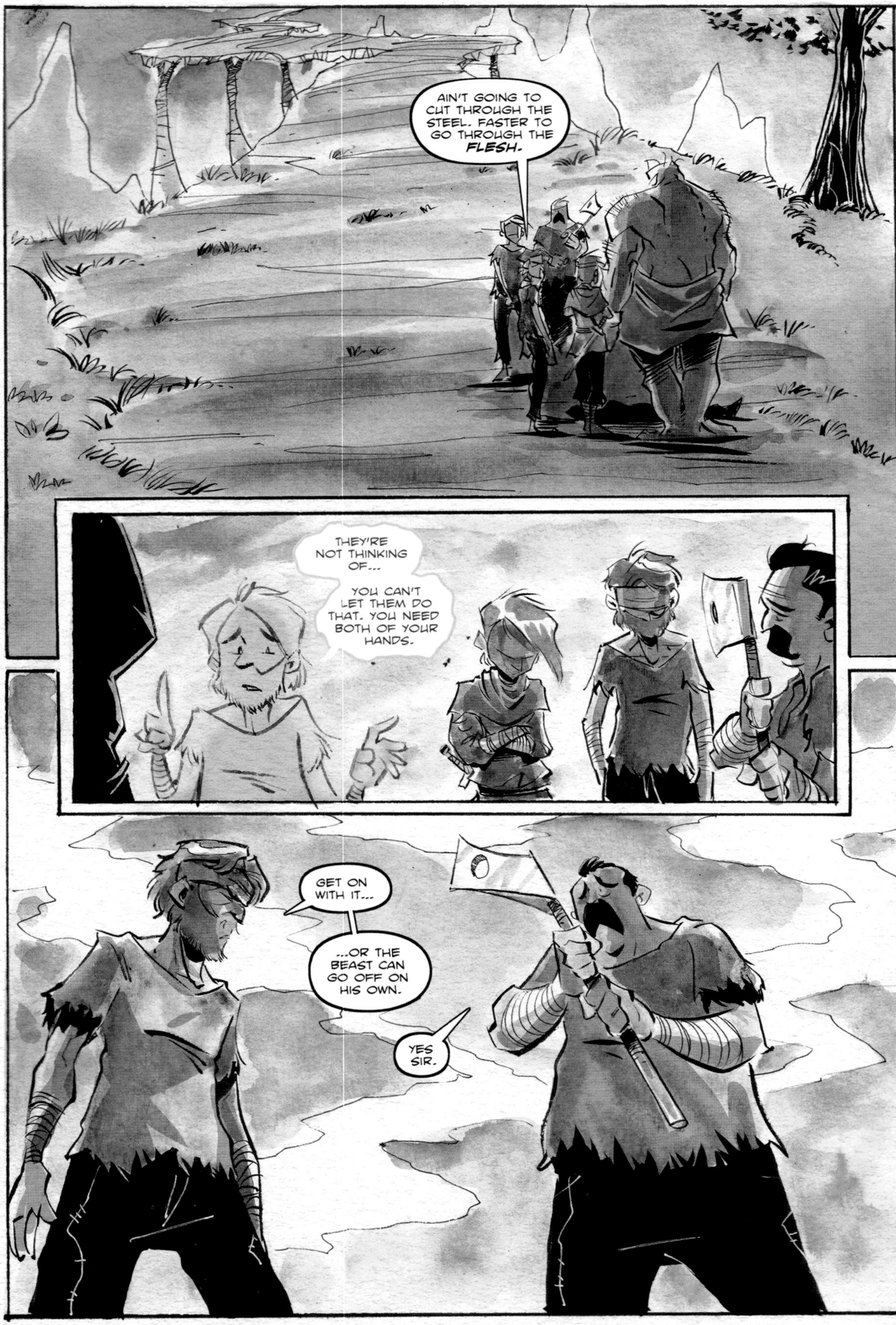
AIN'T GOING TO CUT THROUGH THE STEEL. FASTER TO GO THROUGH THE **FLESH.**
THEY'RE NOT THINKING OF...
YOU CAN'T LET THEM DO THAT. YOU NEED BOTH OF YOUR HANDS.
GET ON WITH IT...
...OR THE BEAST CAN GO OFF ON HIS OWN.
YES SIR.

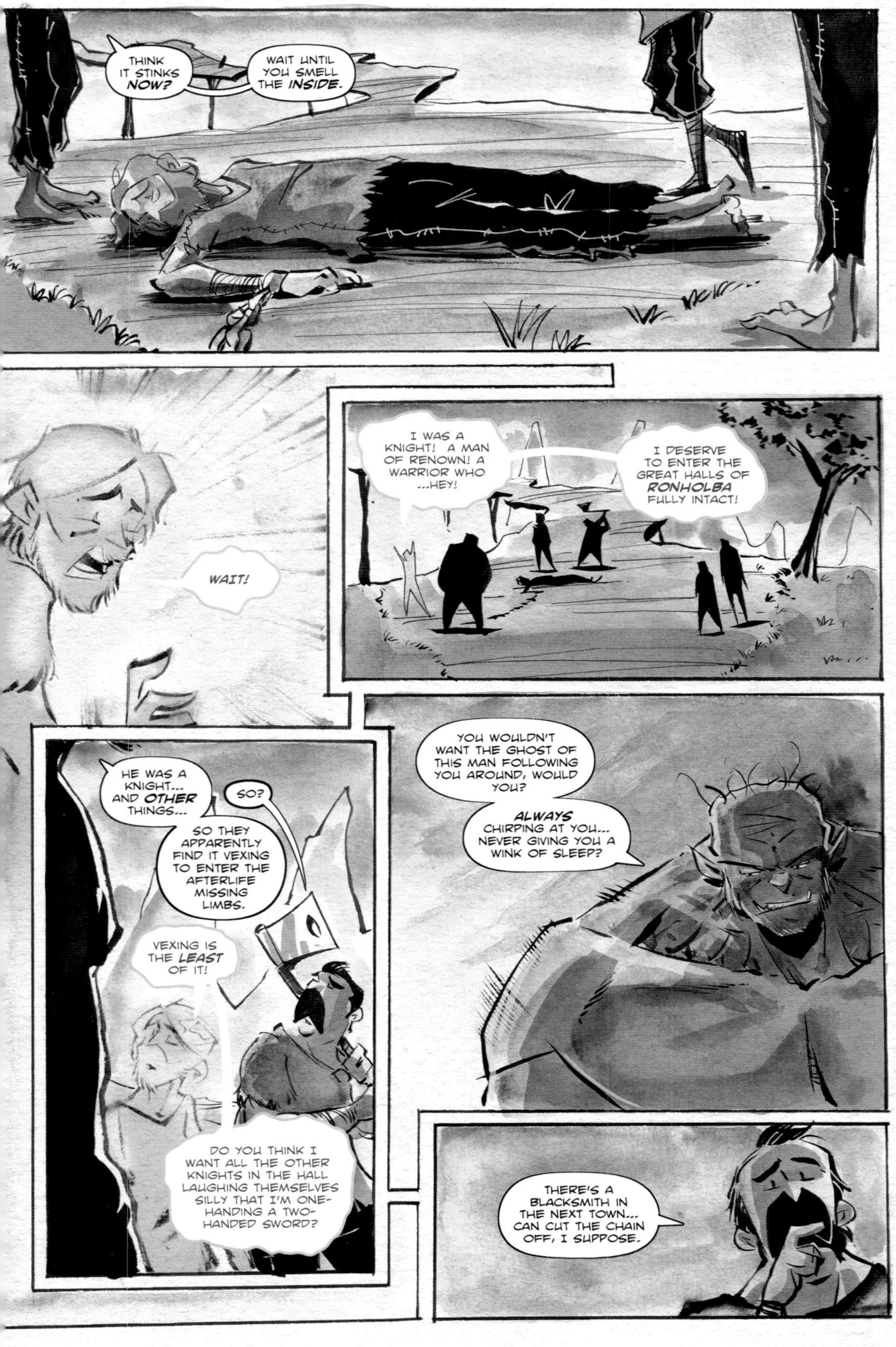
THINK IT STINKS NOW?
WAIT UNTIL YOU SMELL THE INSIDE.
WAIT!
I WAS A KNIGHT! A MAN OF RENOWN! A WARRIOR WHO ...HEY!
I DESERVE TO ENTER THE GREAT HALLS OF RONHOLBA FULLY INTACT!
HE WAS A KNIGHT... AND OTHER THINGS...
SO?
SO THEY APPARENTLY FIND IT VEXING TO ENTER THE AFTERLIFE MISSING LIMBS.
VEXING IS THE LEAST OF IT!
DO YOU THINK I WANT ALL THE OTHER KNIGHTS IN THE HALL LAUGHING THEMSELVES SILLY THAT I'M ONE-HANDING A TWO-HANDED SWORD?
YOU WOULDN'T WANT THE GHOST OF THIS MAN FOLLOWING YOU AROUND, WOULD YOU?
ALWAYS CHIRPING AT YOU... NEVER GIVING YOU A WINK OF SLEEP?
THERE'S A BLACKSMITH IN THE NEXT TOWN... CAN CUT THE CHAIN OFF, I SUPPOSE.

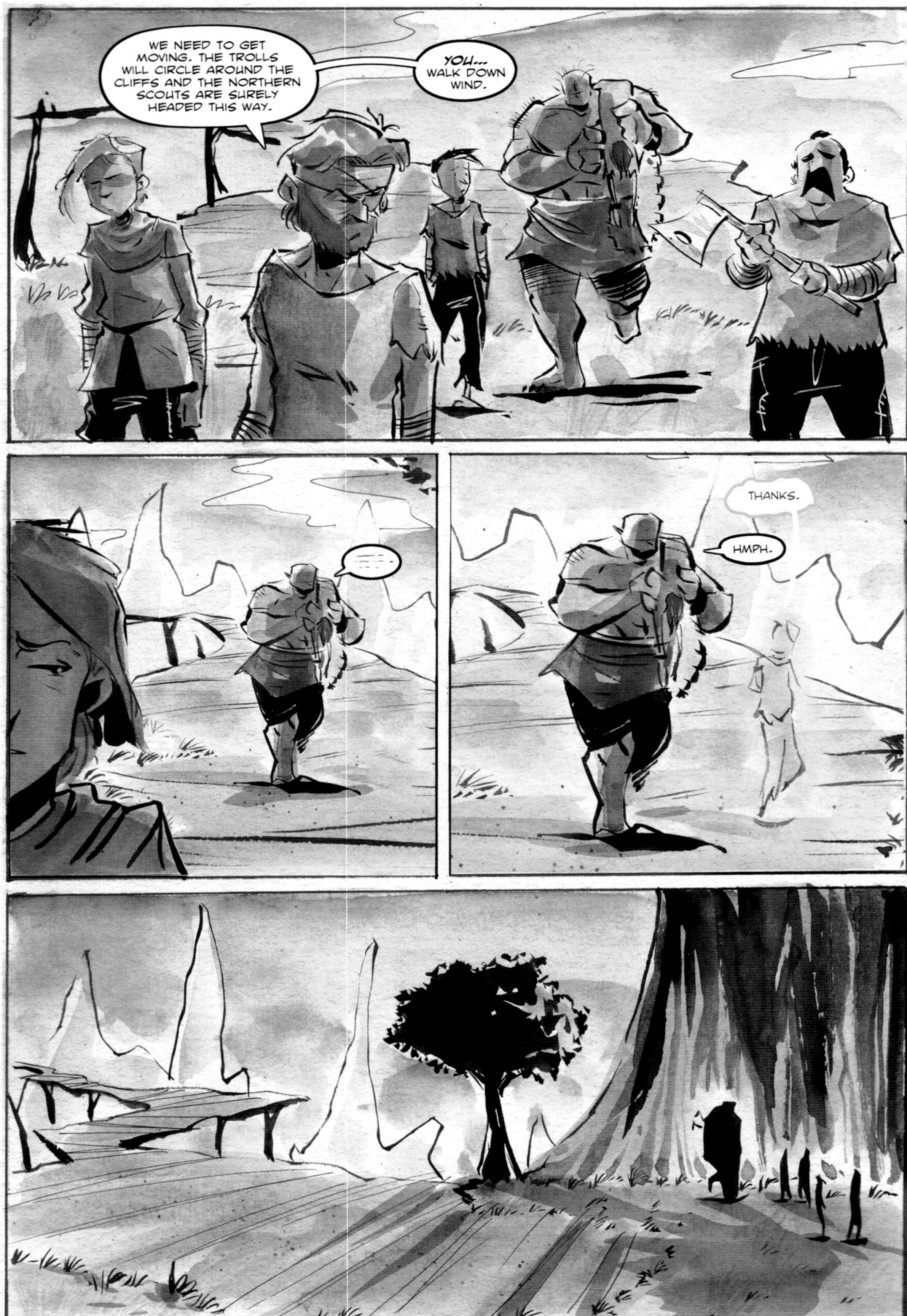
WE NEED TO GET MOVING. THE TROLLS WILL CIRCLE AROUND THE CLIFFS AND THE NORTHERN SCOUTS ARE SURELY HEADED THIS WAY.
YOU... WALK DOWN WIND.
THANKS.
HMPH.

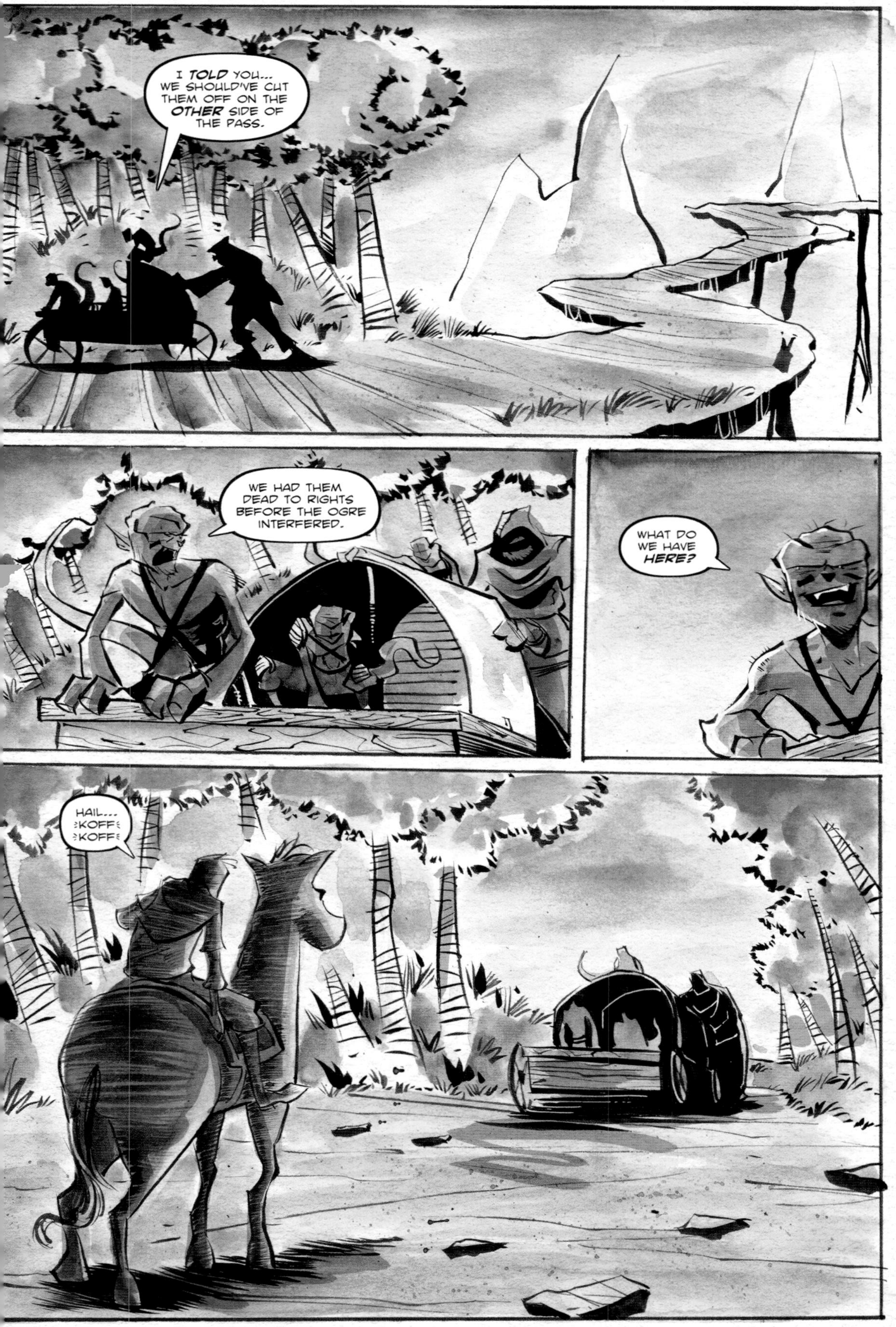
I *TOLD* YOU... WE SHOULD'VE CUT THEM OFF ON THE *OTHER* SIDE OF THE PASS.
WE HAD THEM DEAD TO RIGHTS BEFORE THE OGRE INTERFERED.
WHAT DO WE HAVE *HERE?*
HAIL... KOFF KOFF

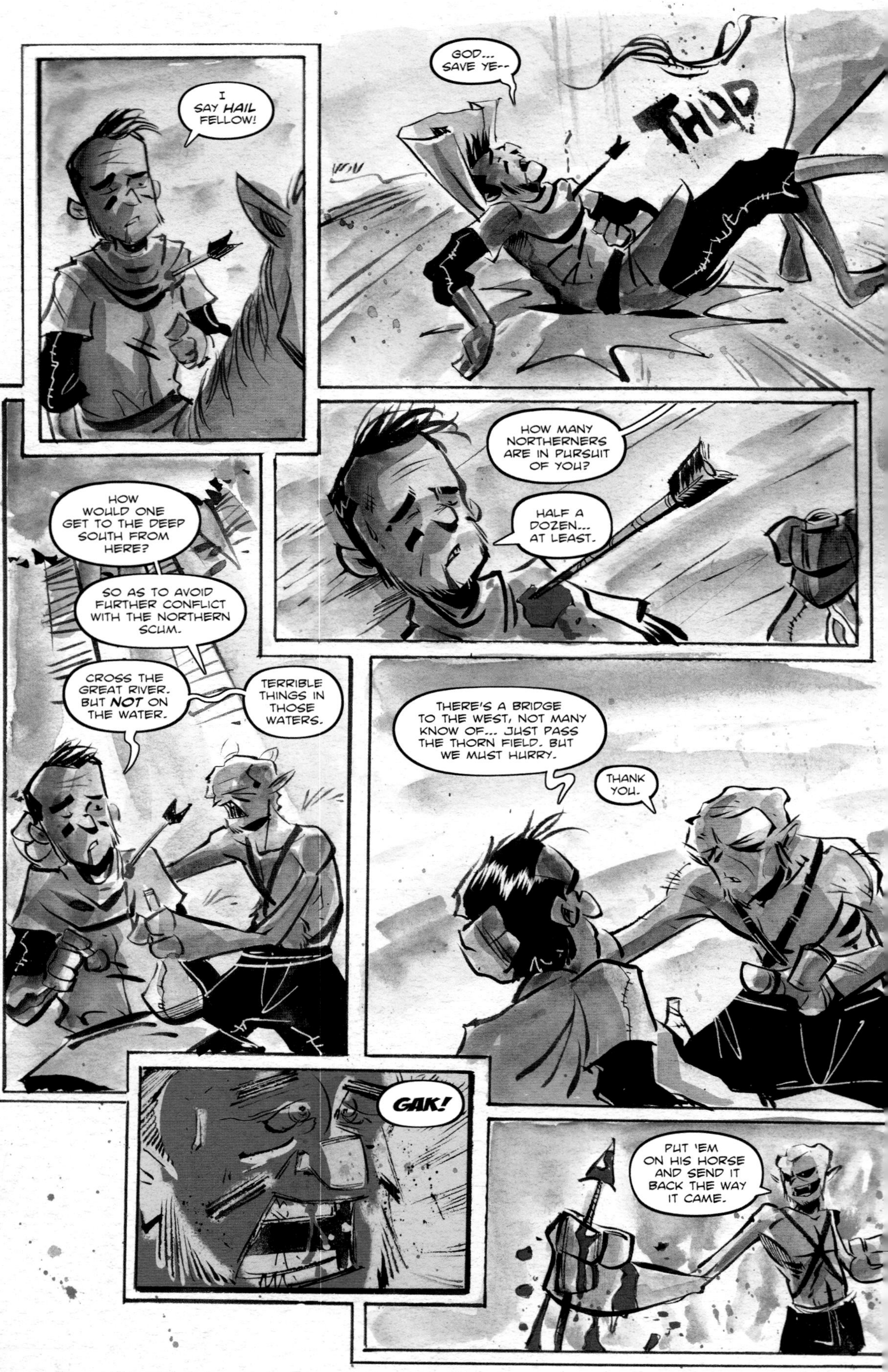

I SAY HAIL FELLOW!
GOD... SAVE YE--
THUD
HOW MANY NORTHERNERS ARE IN PURSUIT OF YOU?
HALF A DOZEN... AT LEAST.
HOW WOULD ONE GET TO THE DEEP SOUTH FROM HERE?
SO AS TO AVOID FURTHER CONFLICT WITH THE NORTHERN SCUM.
CROSS THE GREAT RIVER. BUT NOT ON THE WATER.
TERRIBLE THINGS IN THOSE WATERS.
THERE'S A BRIDGE TO THE WEST, NOT MANY KNOW OF... JUST PASS THE THORN FIELD. BUT WE MUST HURRY.
THANK YOU.
GAK!
PUT 'EM ON HIS HORSE AND SEND IT BACK THE WAY IT CAME.

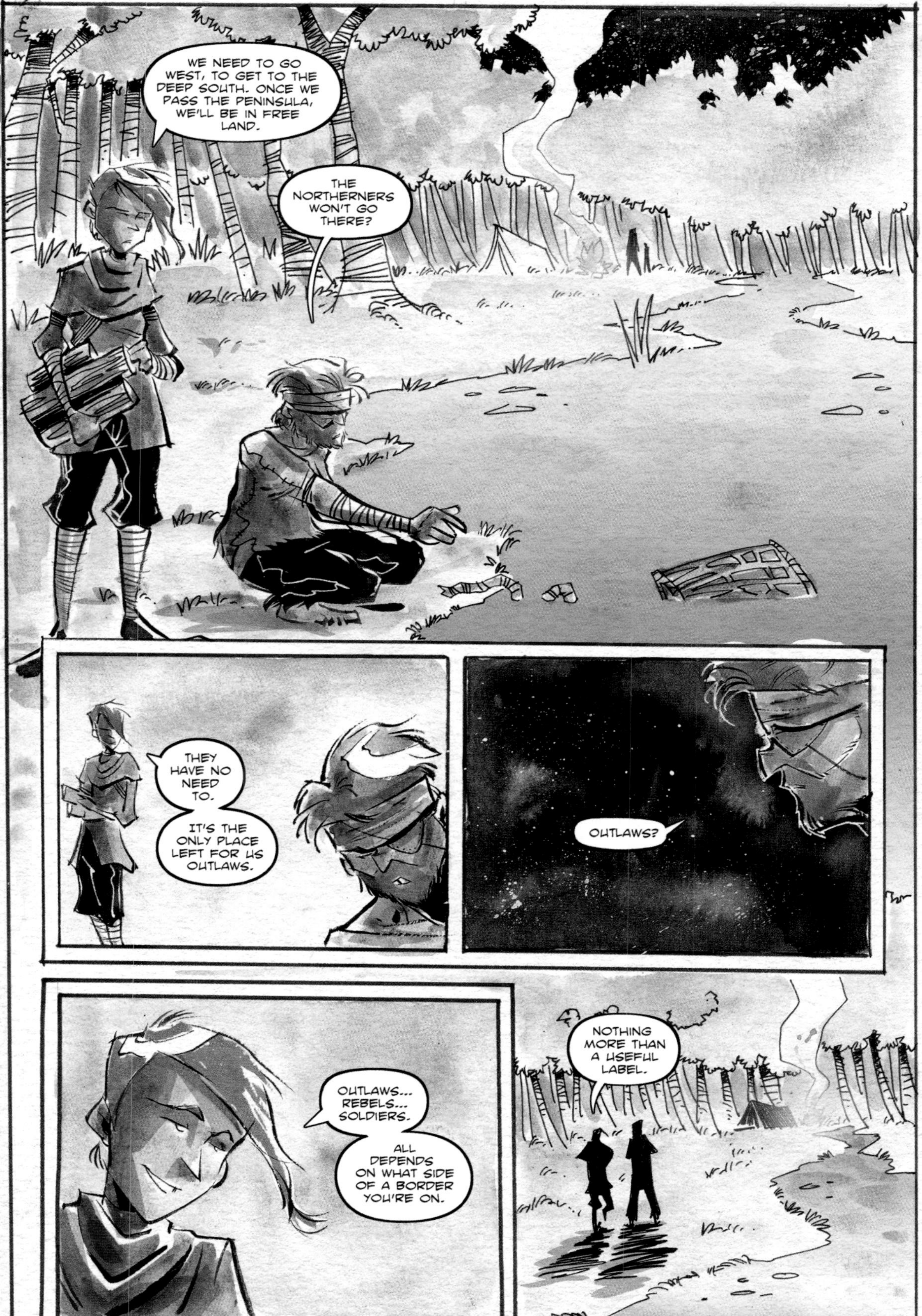
WE NEED TO GO WEST, TO GET TO THE DEEP SOUTH. ONCE WE PASS THE PENINSULA, WE'LL BE IN FREE LAND.
THE NORTHERNERS WON'T GO THERE?
THEY HAVE NO NEED TO.
IT'S THE ONLY PLACE LEFT FOR US OUTLAWS.
OUTLAWS?
OUTLAWS... REBELS... SOLDIERS.
ALL DEPENDS ON WHAT SIDE OF A BORDER YOU'RE ON.
NOTHING MORE THAN A USEFUL LABEL.

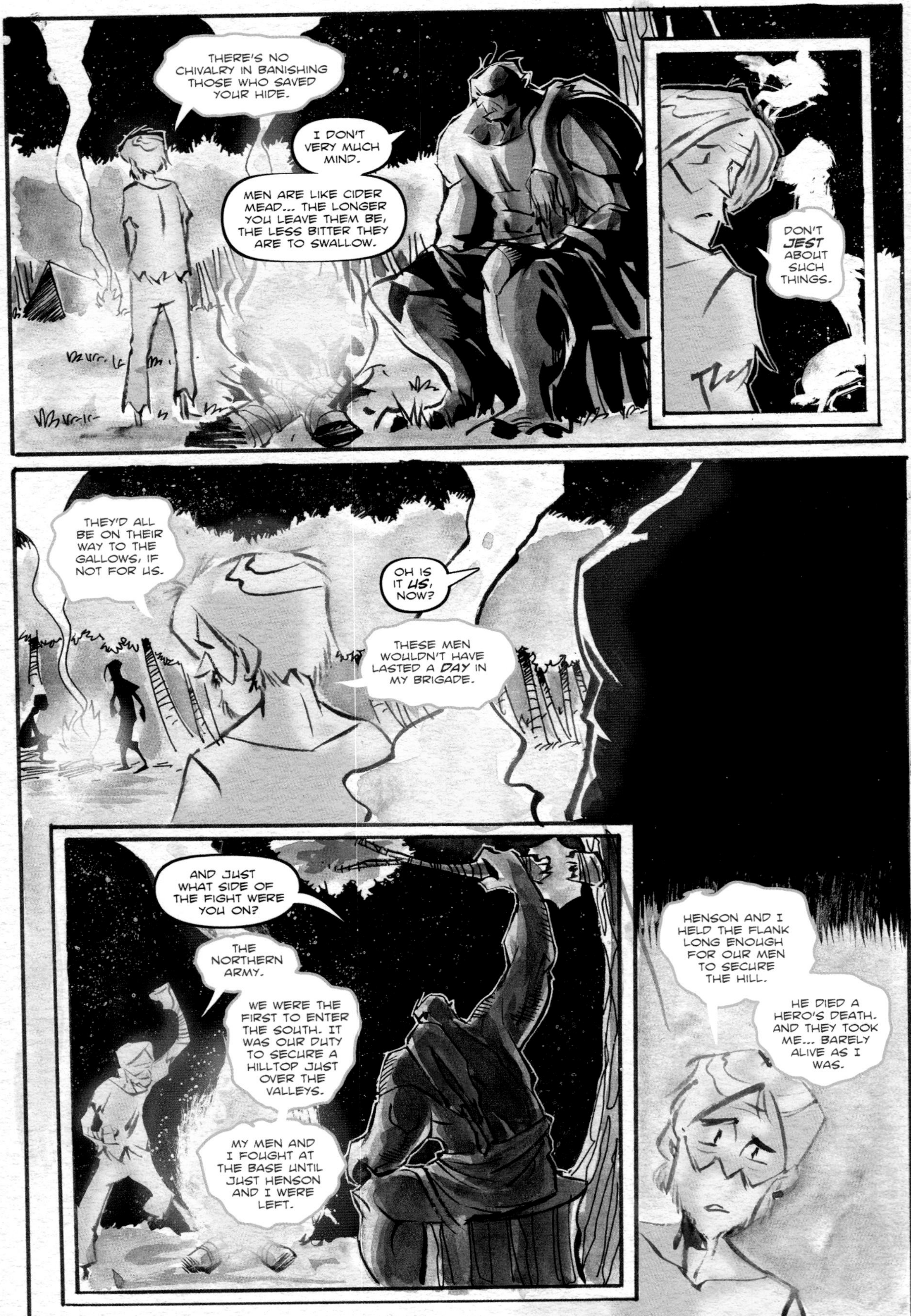
THERE'S NO CHIVALRY IN BANISHING THOSE WHO SAVED YOUR HIDE.
I DON'T VERY MUCH MIND.
MEN ARE LIKE CIDER MEAD... THE LONGER YOU LEAVE THEM BE, THE LESS BITTER THEY ARE TO SWALLOW.
DON'T JEST ABOUT SUCH THINGS.
THEY'D ALL BE ON THEIR WAY TO THE GALLOWS, IF NOT FOR US.
OH IS IT US, NOW?
THESE MEN WOULDN'T HAVE LASTED A DAY IN MY BRIGADE.
AND JUST WHAT SIDE OF THE FIGHT WERE YOU ON?
THE NORTHERN ARMY.
WE WERE THE FIRST TO ENTER THE SOUTH. IT WAS OUR DUTY TO SECURE A HILLTOP JUST OVER THE VALLEYS.
MY MEN AND I FOUGHT AT THE BASE UNTIL JUST HENSON AND I WERE LEFT.
HENSON AND I HELD THE FLANK LONG ENOUGH FOR OUR MEN TO SECURE THE HILL.
HE DIED A HERO'S DEATH. AND THEY TOOK ME... BARELY ALIVE AS I WAS.

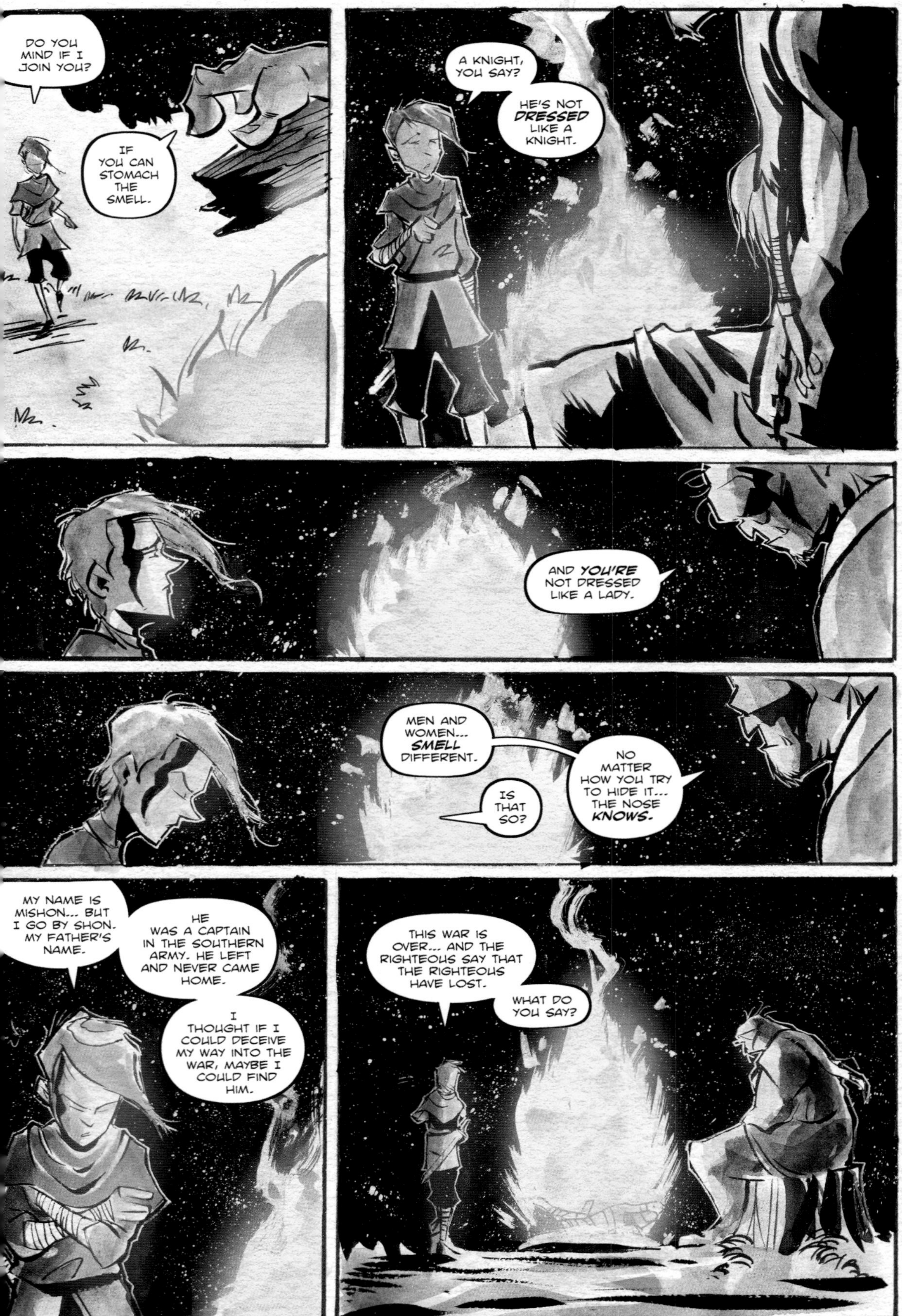
DO YOU MIND IF I JOIN YOU?
IF YOU CAN STOMACH THE SMELL.
A KNIGHT, YOU SAY?
HE'S NOT DRESSED LIKE A KNIGHT.
AND YOU'RE NOT DRESSED LIKE A LADY.
MEN AND WOMEN... SMELL DIFFERENT.
NO MATTER HOW YOU TRY TO HIDE IT... THE NOSE KNOWS.
IS THAT SO?
MY NAME IS MISHON... BUT I GO BY SHON. MY FATHER'S NAME.
HE WAS A CAPTAIN IN THE SOUTHERN ARMY. HE LEFT AND NEVER CAME HOME.
I THOUGHT IF I COULD DECEIVE MY WAY INTO THE WAR, MAYBE I COULD FIND HIM.
THIS WAR IS OVER... AND THE RIGHTEOUS SAY THAT THE RIGHTEOUS HAVE LOST.
WHAT DO YOU SAY?

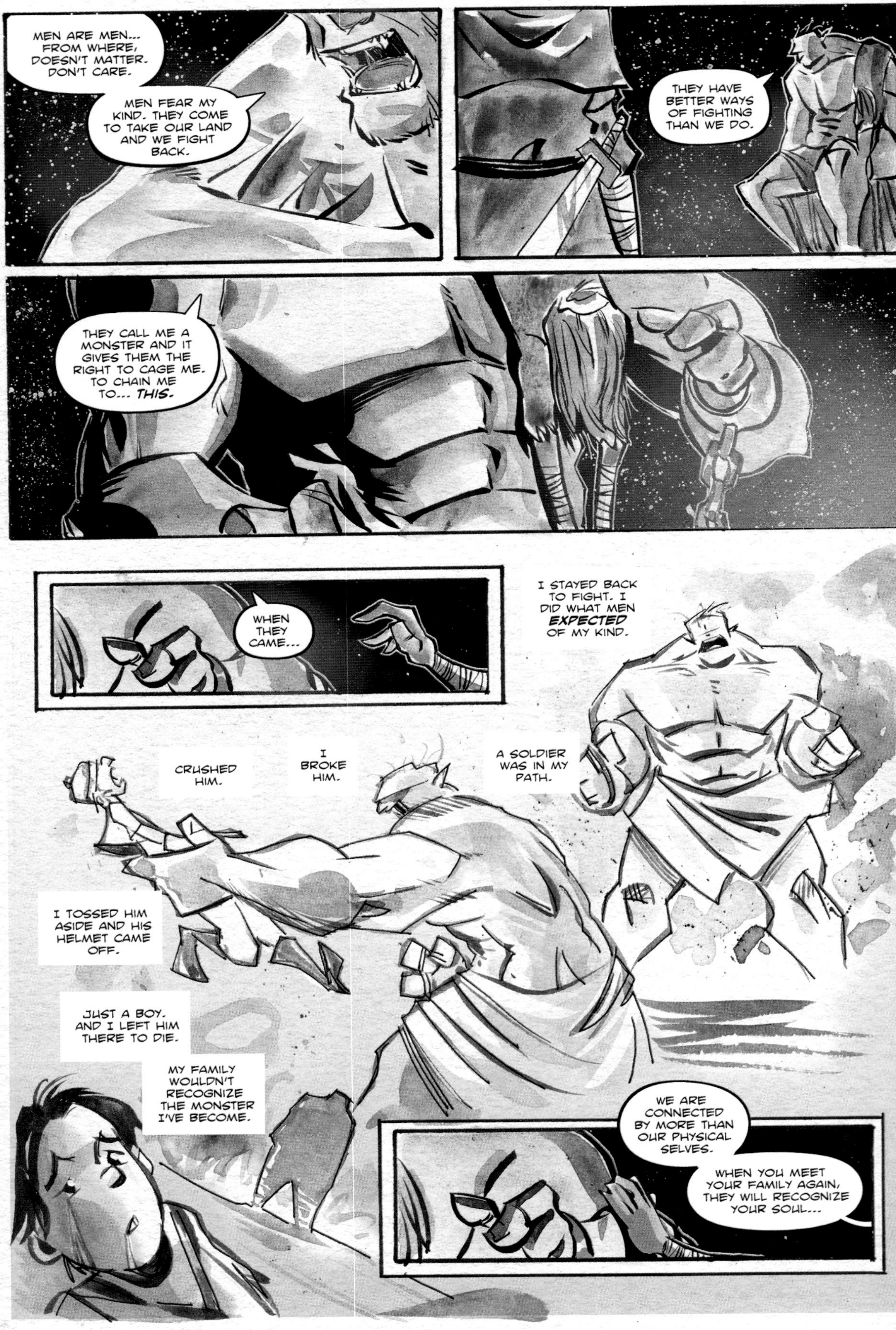

MEN ARE MEN... FROM WHERE, DOESN'T MATTER. DON'T CARE.
MEN FEAR MY KIND. THEY COME TO TAKE OUR LAND AND WE FIGHT BACK.
THEY HAVE BETTER WAYS OF FIGHTING THAN WE DO.
THEY CALL ME A MONSTER AND IT GIVES THEM THE RIGHT TO CAGE ME. TO CHAIN ME TO... THIS.
WHEN THEY CAME...
I STAYED BACK TO FIGHT. I DID WHAT MEN EXPECTED OF MY KIND.
A SOLDIER WAS IN MY PATH.
I BROKE HIM.
CRUSHED HIM.
I TOSSED HIM ASIDE AND HIS HELMET CAME OFF.
JUST A BOY. AND I LEFT HIM THERE TO DIE.
MY FAMILY WOULDN'T RECOGNIZE THE MONSTER I'VE BECOME.
WE ARE CONNECTED BY MORE THAN OUR PHYSICAL SELVES.
WHEN YOU MEET YOUR FAMILY AGAIN, THEY WILL RECOGNIZE YOUR SOUL...

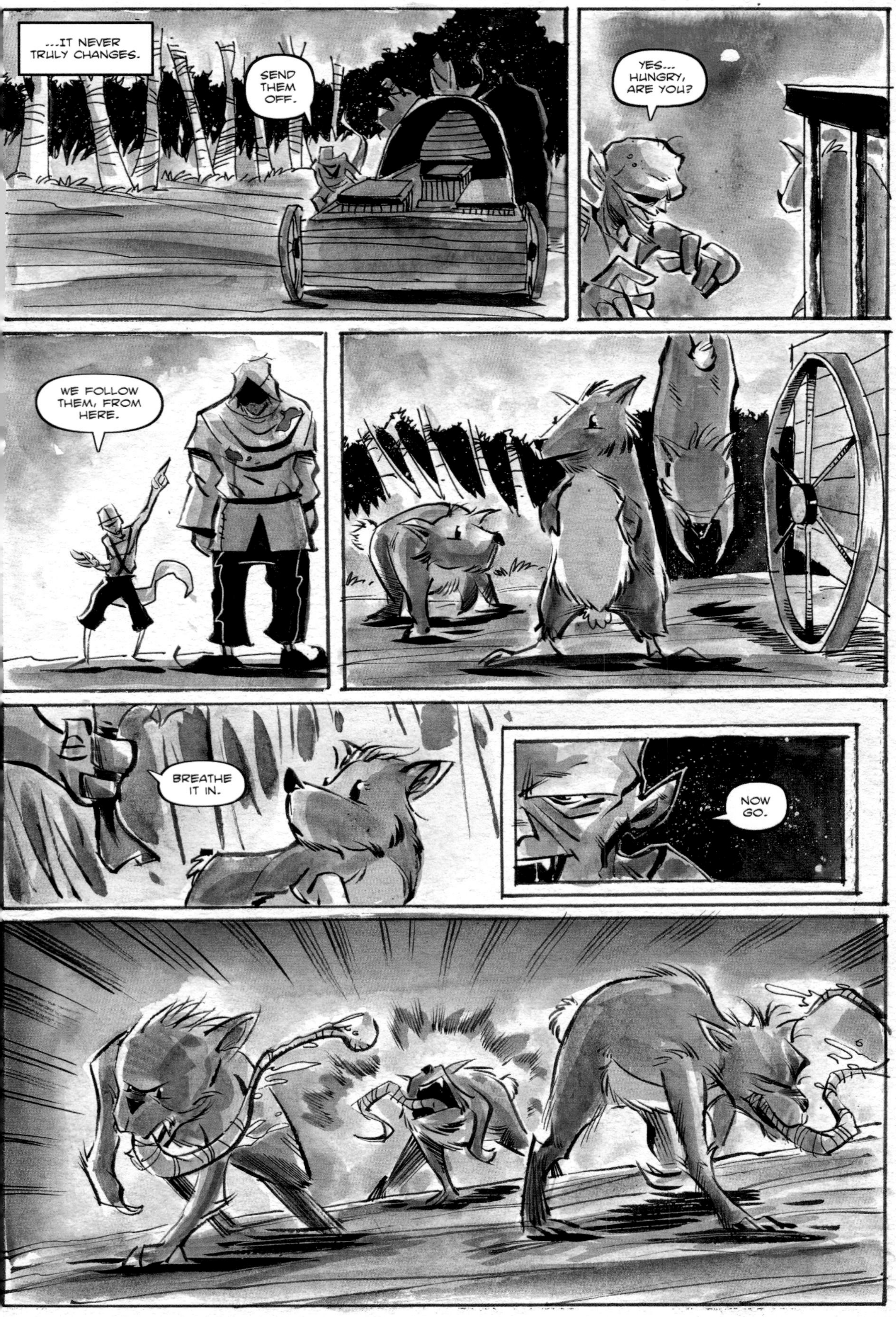
...IT NEVER TRULY CHANGES.
SEND THEM OFF.
YES... HUNGRY, ARE YOU?
WE FOLLOW THEM, FROM HERE.
BREATHE IT IN.
NOW GO.

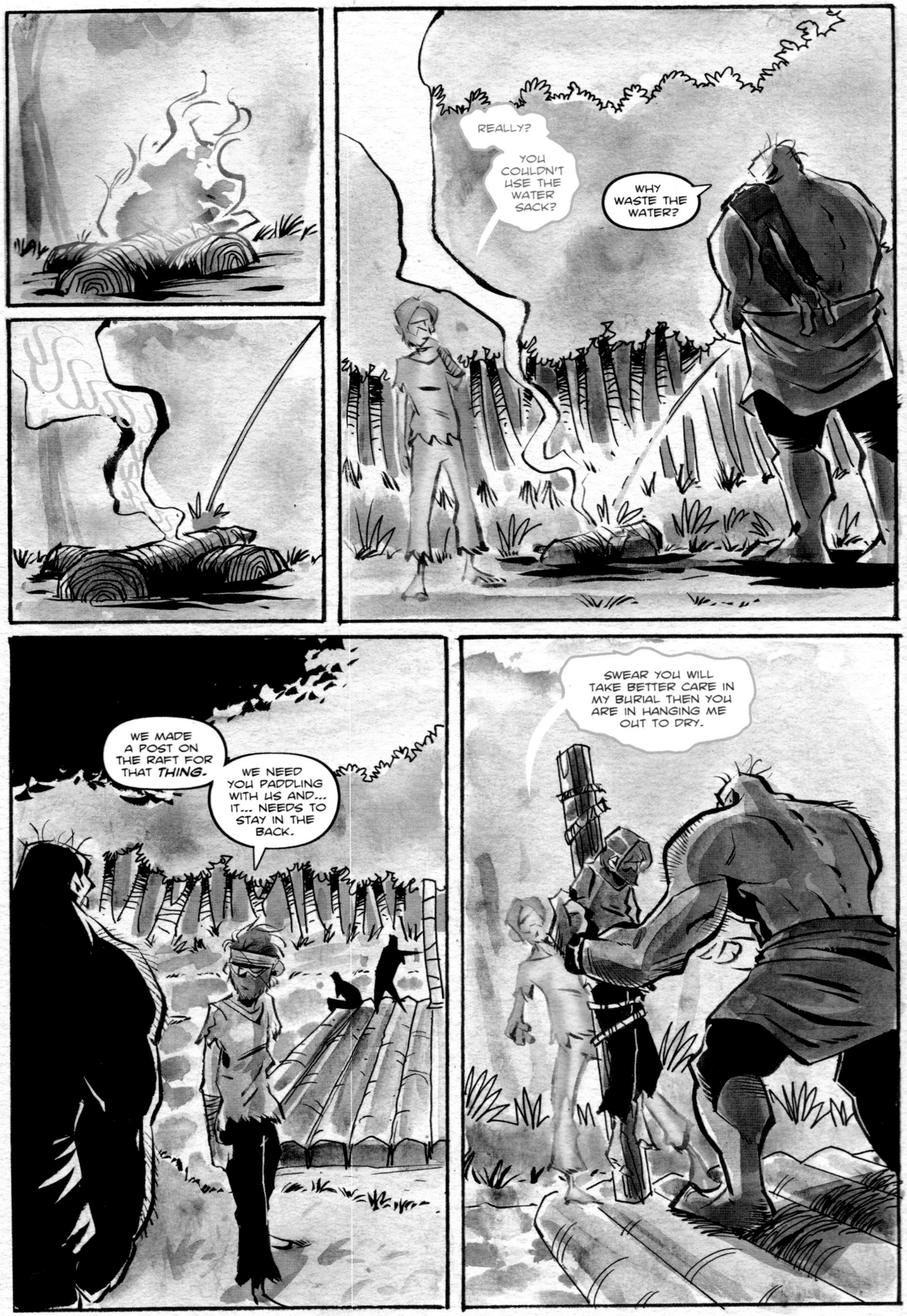
REALLY?
YOU COULDN'T USE THE WATER SACK?
WHY WASTE THE WATER?
WE MADE A POST ON THE RAFT FOR THAT THING.
WE NEED YOU PADDLING WITH US AND... IT... NEEDS TO STAY IN THE BACK.
SWEAR YOU WILL TAKE BETTER CARE IN MY BURIAL THEN YOU ARE IN HANGING ME OUT TO DRY.

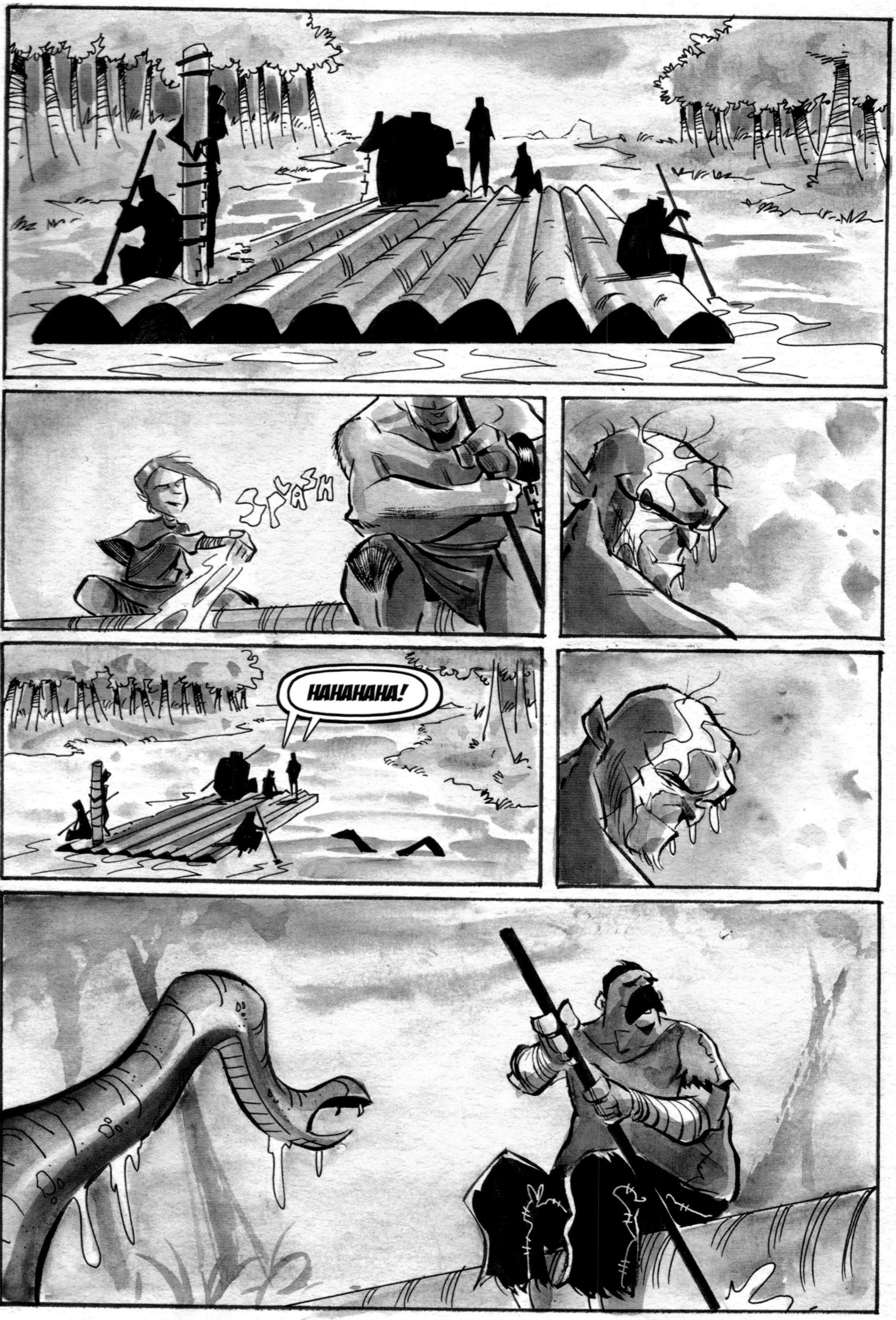
SPLASH
HAHAHAHA!

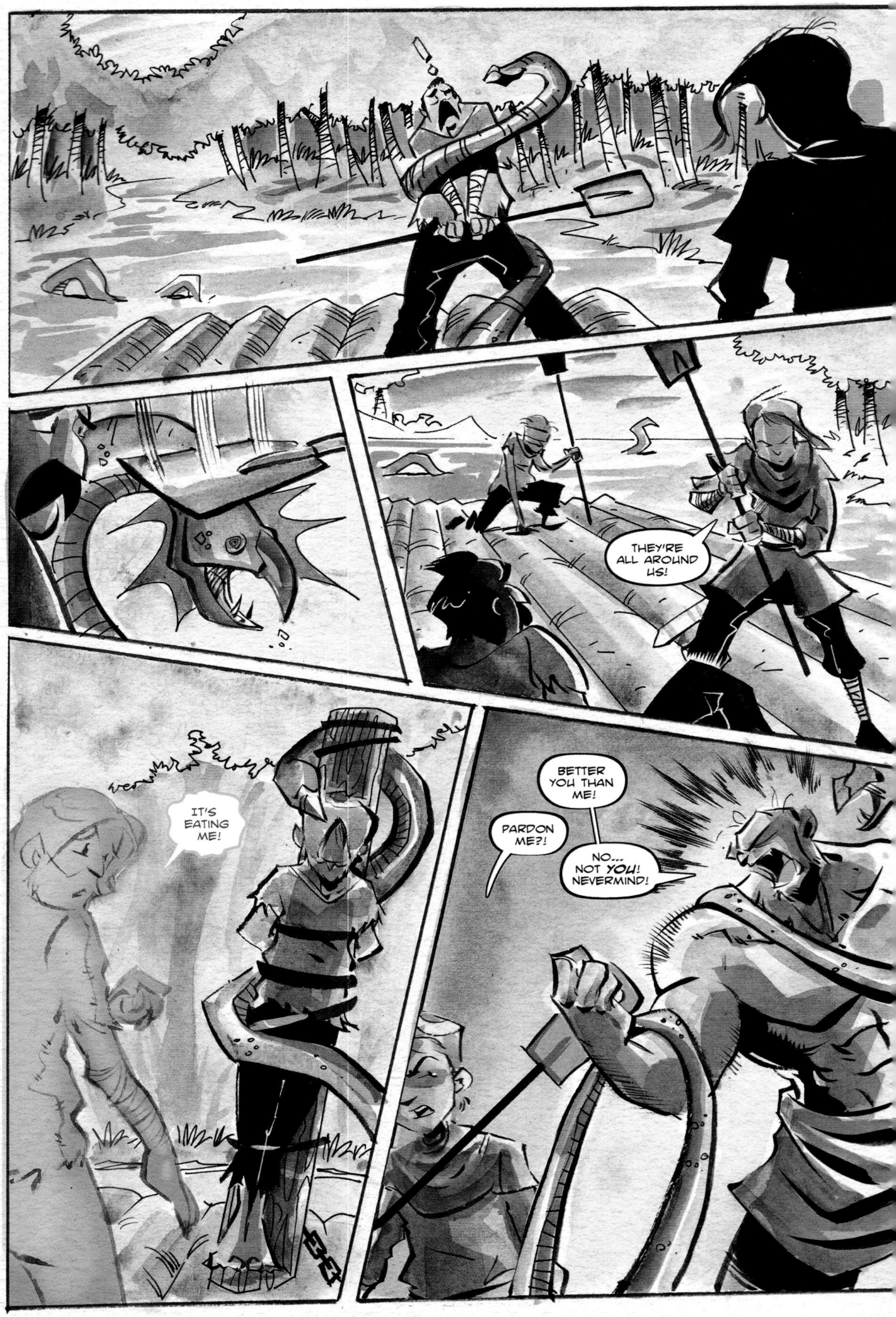
THEY'RE ALL AROUND US!
IT'S EATING ME!
BETTER YOU THAN ME!
PARDON ME?!
NO... NOT YOU! NEVERMIND!

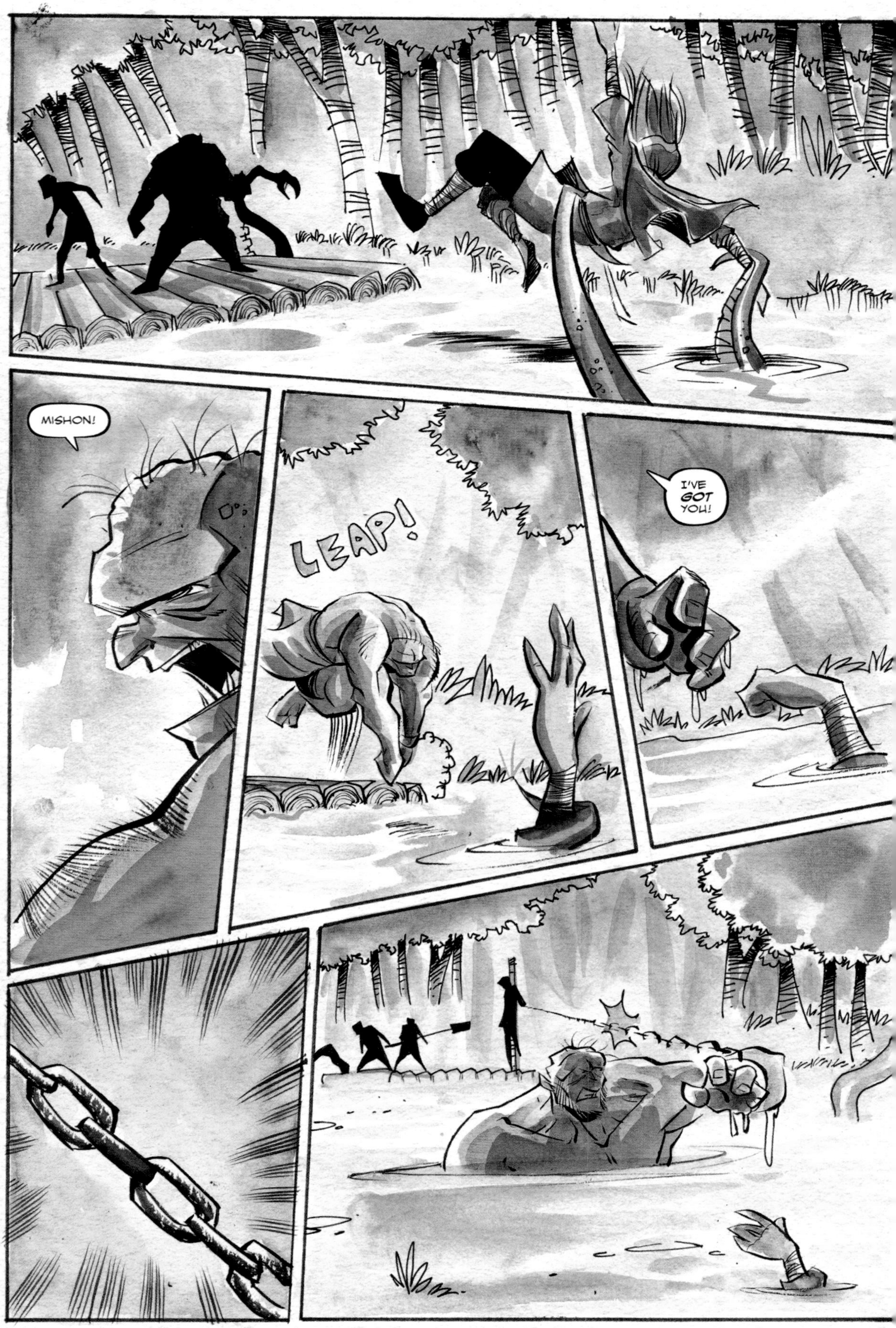
MISHON!
LEAP!
I'VE GOT YOU!

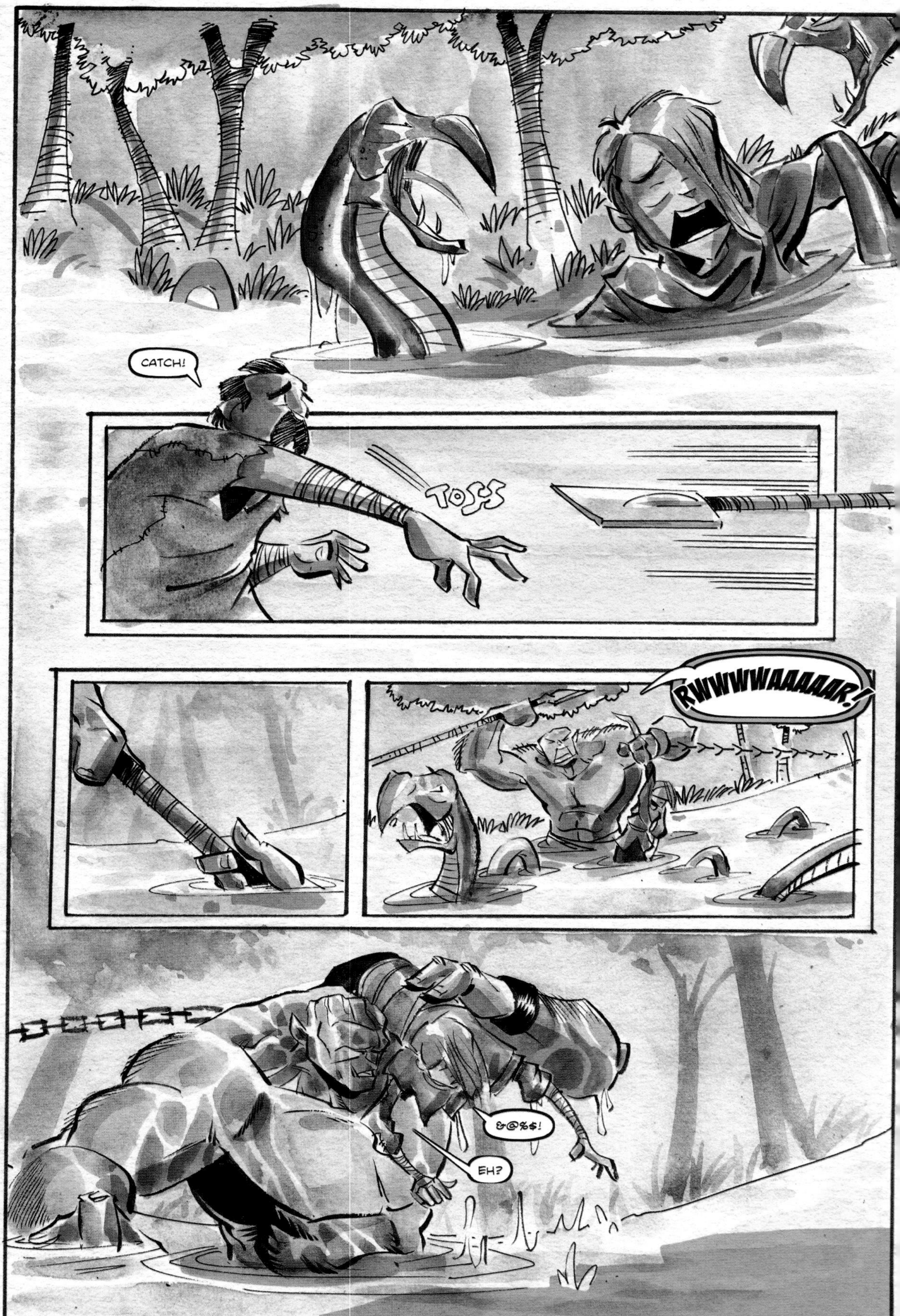
CATCH!
TOSS
RWWWWAAAAAR!
&@%$!
EH?

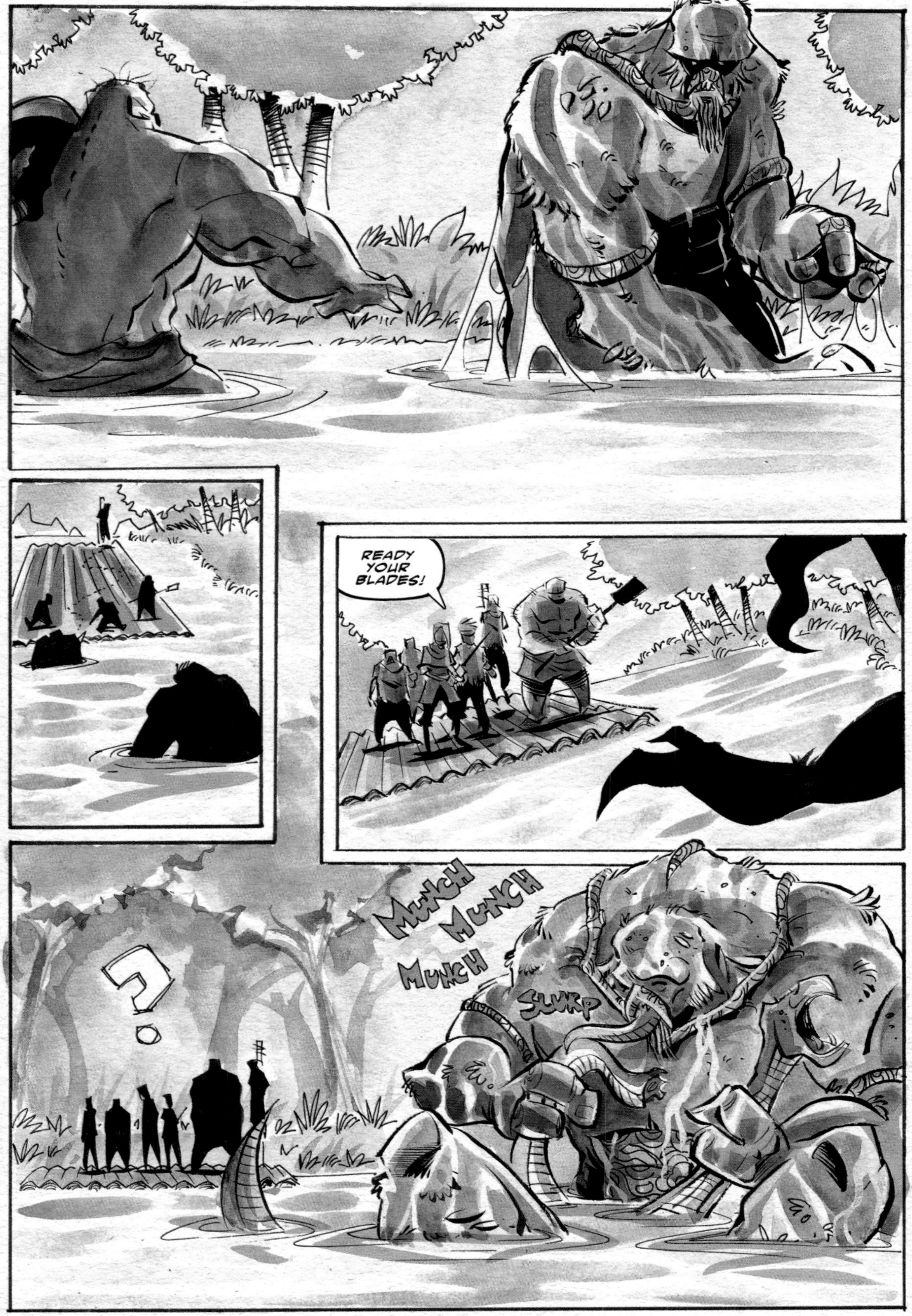
READY YOUR BLADES!
MUNCH
MUNCH
MUNCH
SLURP
?

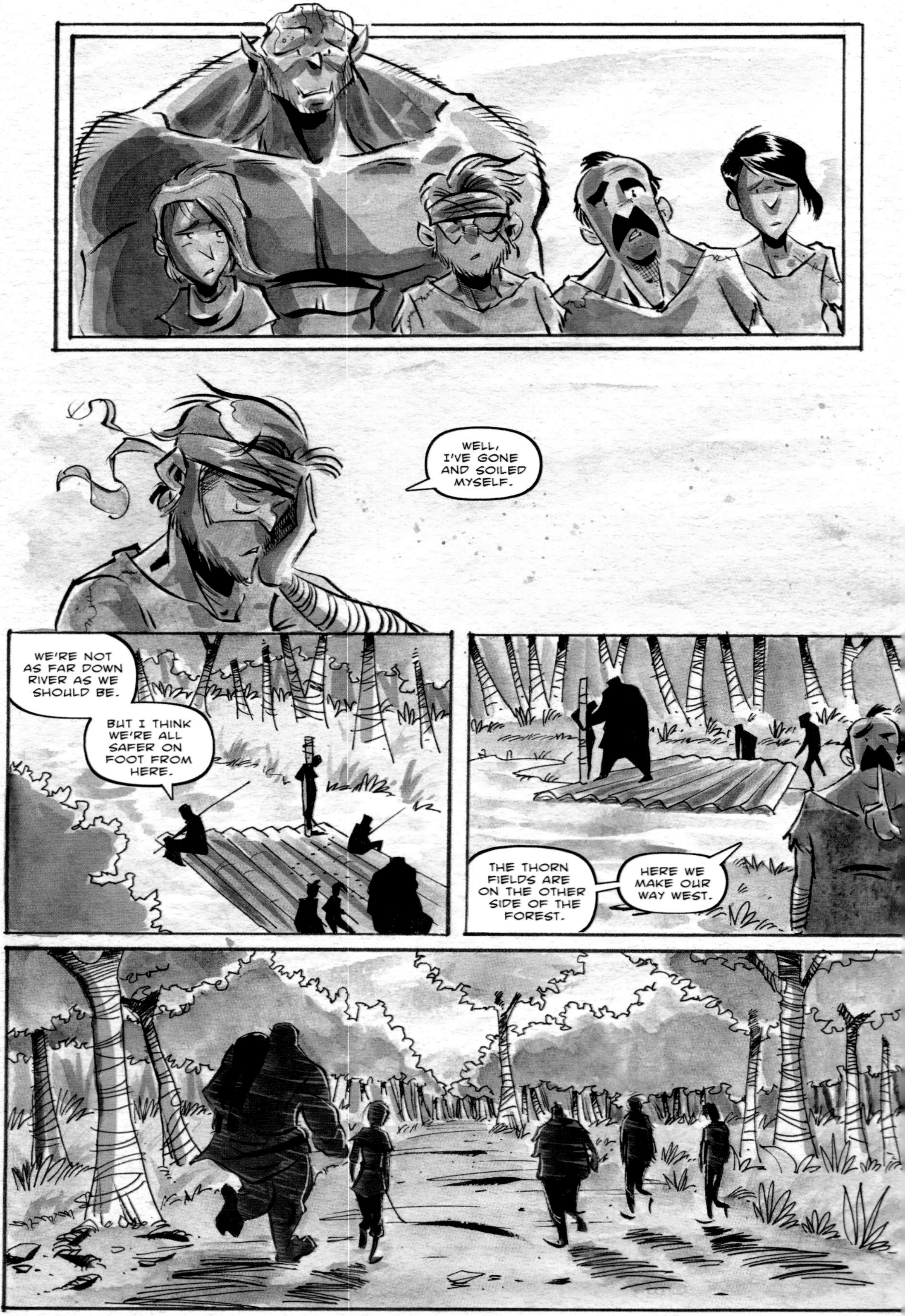

WELL, I'VE GONE AND SOILED MYSELF.
WE'RE NOT AS FAR DOWN RIVER AS WE SHOULD BE.
BUT I THINK WE'RE ALL SAFER ON FOOT FROM HERE.
HERE WE MAKE OUR WAY WEST.
THE THORN FIELDS ARE ON THE OTHER SIDE OF THE FOREST.

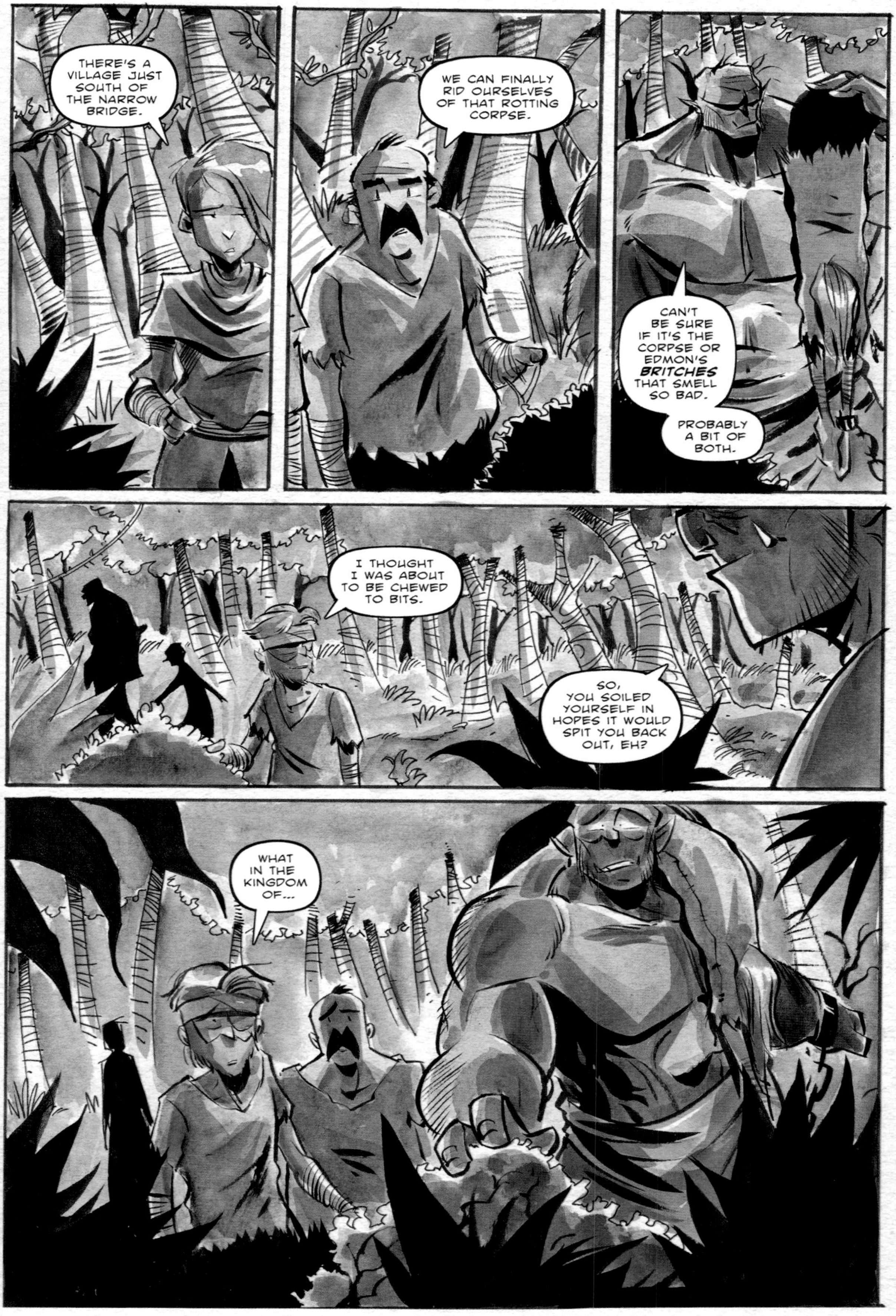
THERE'S A VILLAGE JUST SOUTH OF THE NARROW BRIDGE.
WE CAN FINALLY RID OURSELVES OF THAT ROTTING CORPSE.
CAN'T BE SURE IF IT'S THE CORPSE OR EDMON'S BRITCHES THAT SMELL SO BAD.
PROBABLY A BIT OF BOTH.
I THOUGHT I WAS ABOUT TO BE CHEWED TO BITS.
SO, YOU SOILED YOURSELF IN HOPES IT WOULD SPIT YOU BACK OUT, EH?
WHAT IN THE KINGDOM OF...

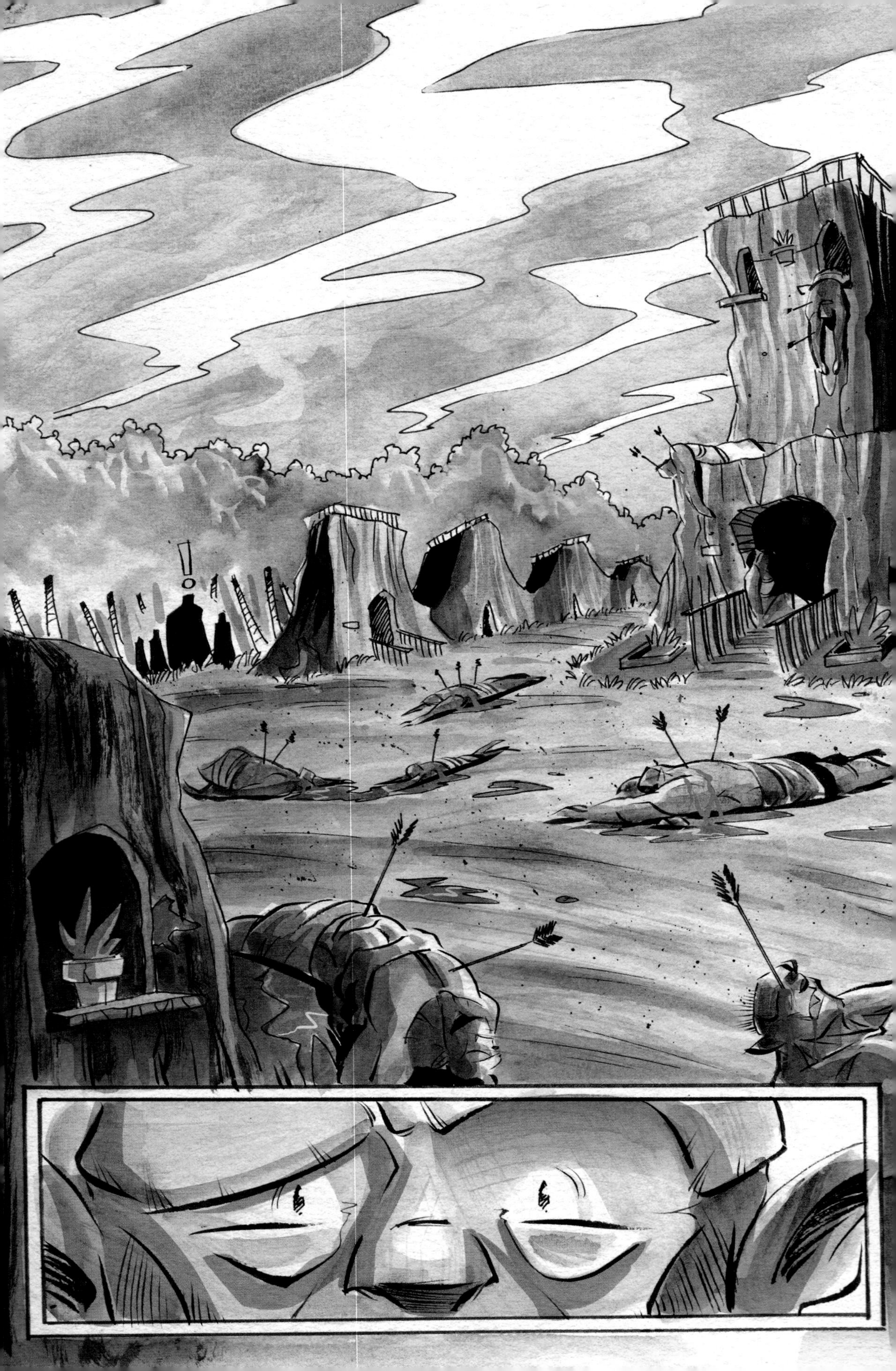
!

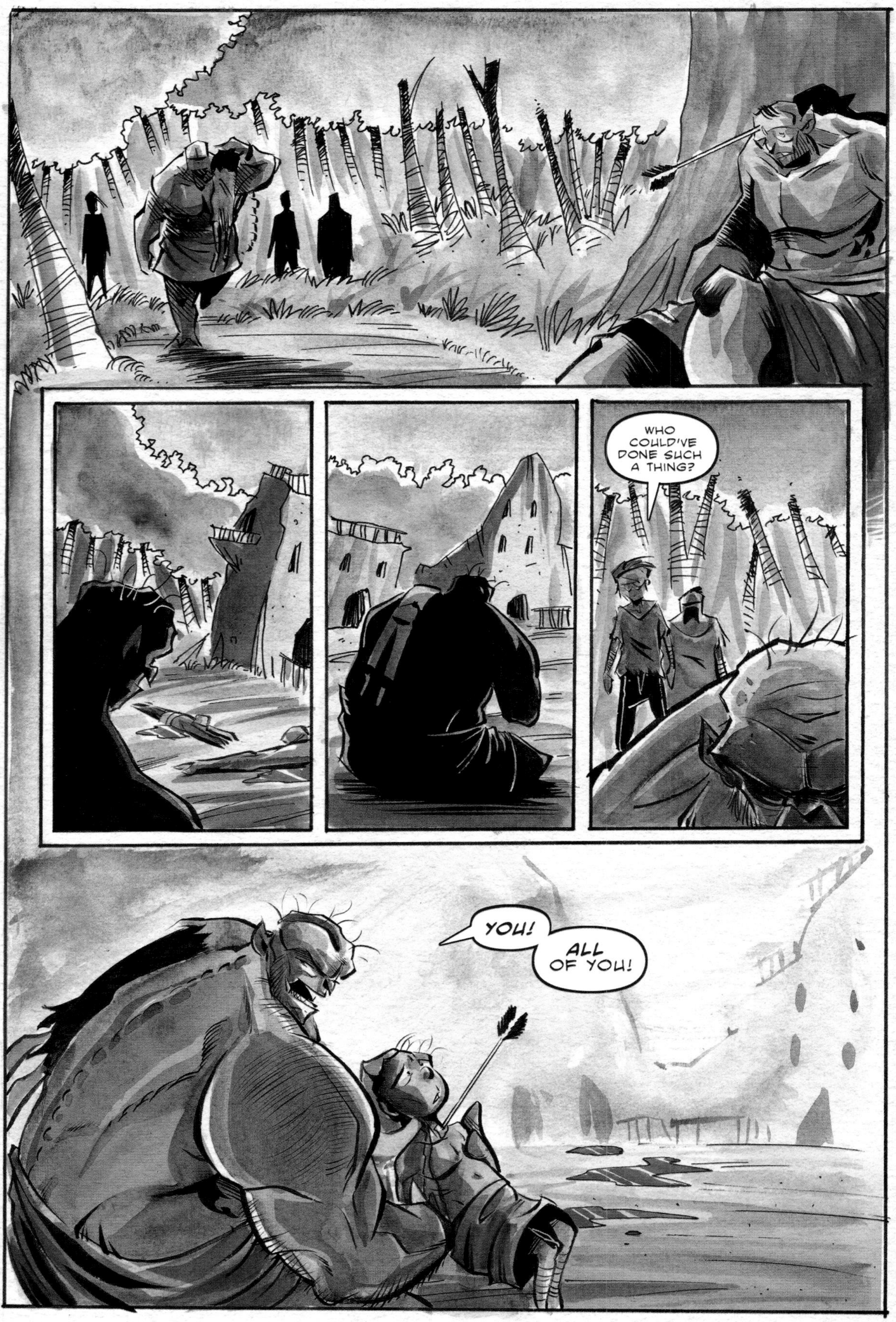
WHO COULD'VE DONE SUCH A THING?
YOU!
ALL OF YOU!

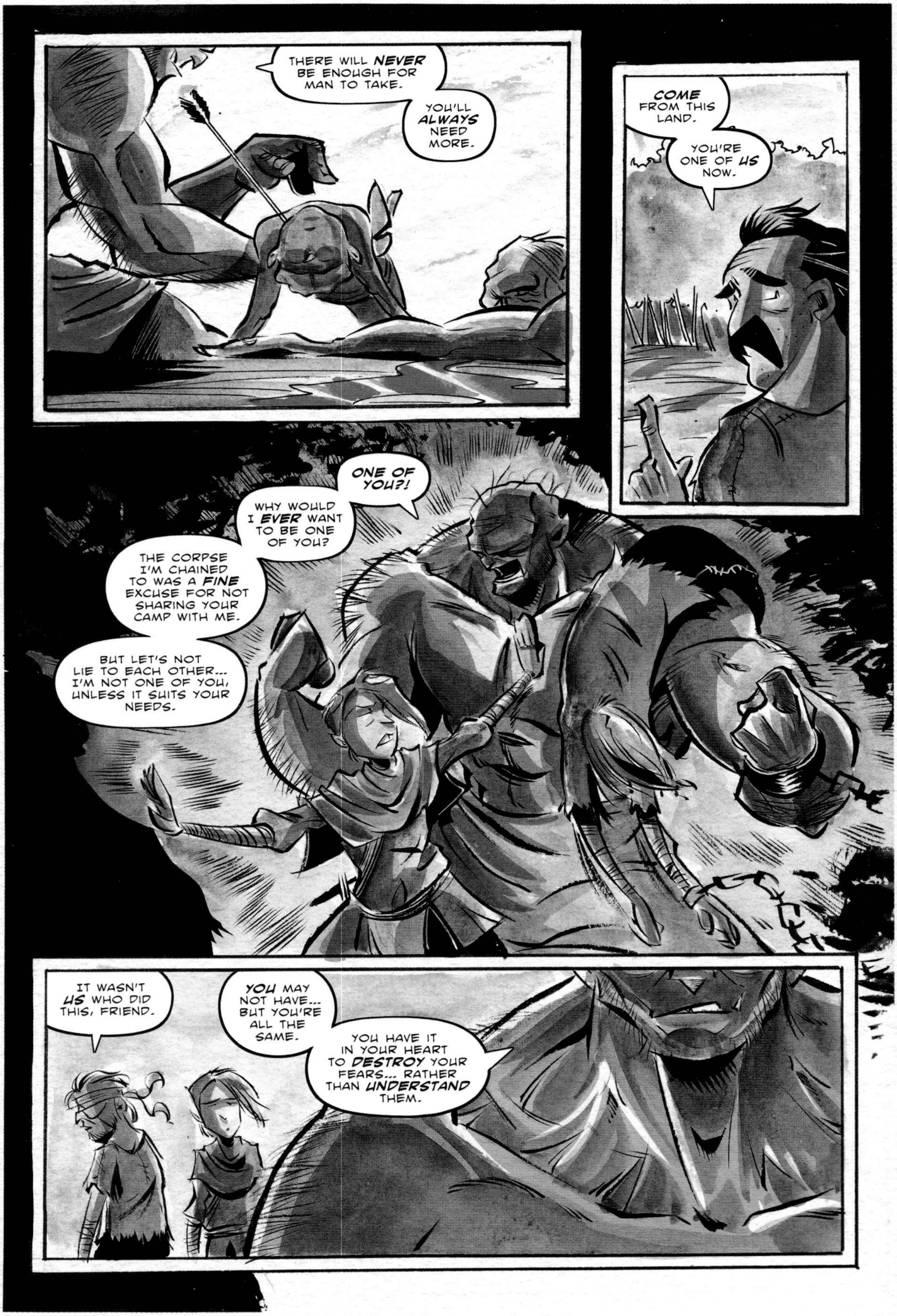
THERE WILL NEVER BE ENOUGH FOR MAN TO TAKE.
YOU'LL ALWAYS NEED MORE.
COME FROM THIS LAND.
YOU'RE ONE OF US NOW.
ONE OF YOU?!
WHY WOULD I EVER WANT TO BE ONE OF YOU?
THE CORPSE I'M CHAINED TO WAS A FINE EXCUSE FOR NOT SHARING YOUR CAMP WITH ME.
BUT LET'S NOT LIE TO EACH OTHER... I'M NOT ONE OF YOU, UNLESS IT SUITS YOUR NEEDS.
IT WASN'T US WHO DID THIS, FRIEND.
YOU MAY NOT HAVE... BUT YOU'RE ALL THE SAME.
YOU HAVE IT IN YOUR HEART TO DESTROY YOUR FEARS... RATHER THAN UNDERSTAND THEM.

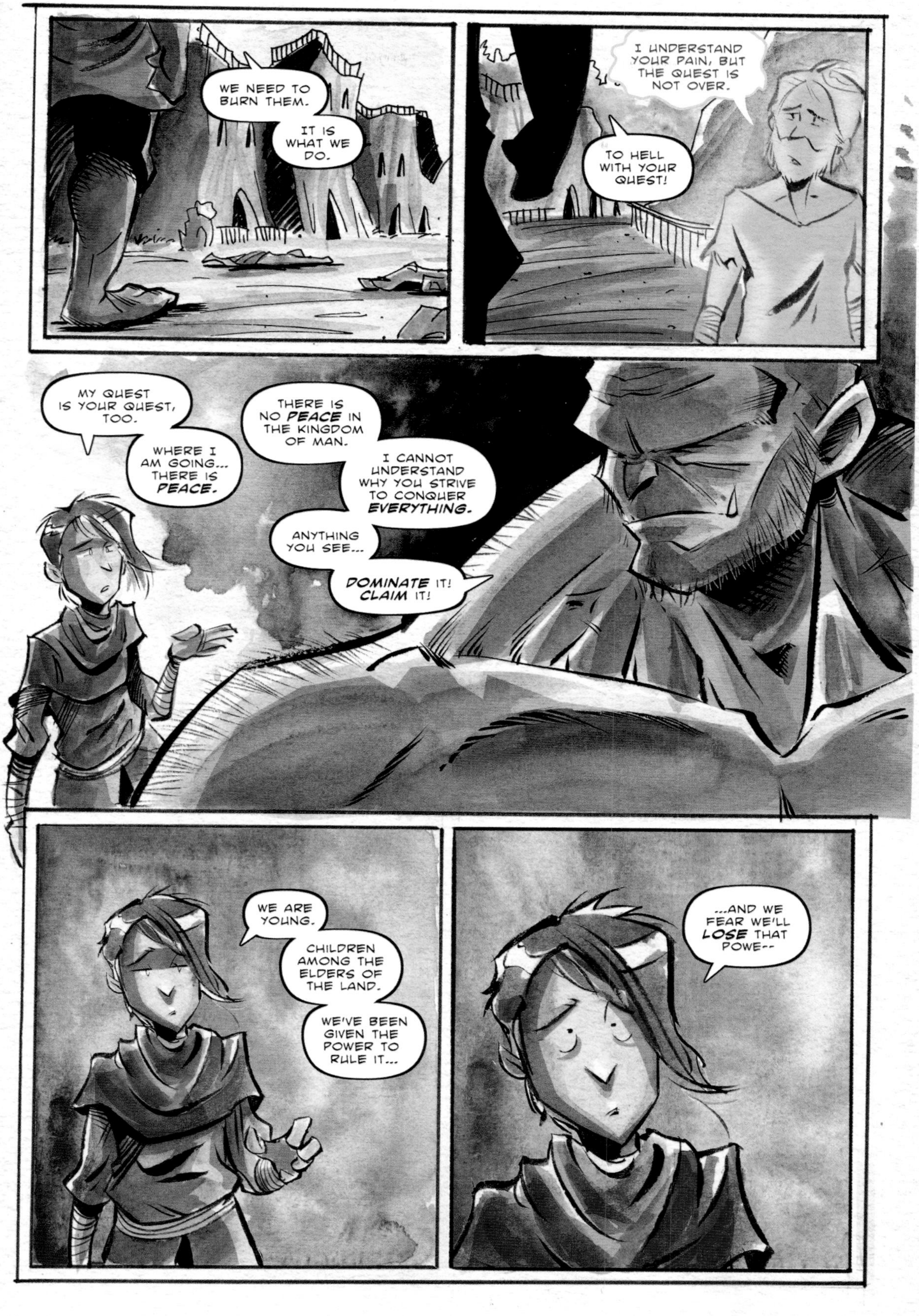
WE NEED TO BURN THEM.
IT IS WHAT WE DO.
I UNDERSTAND YOUR PAIN, BUT THE QUEST IS NOT OVER.
TO HELL WITH YOUR QUEST!
MY QUEST IS YOUR QUEST, TOO.
WHERE I AM GOING... THERE IS PEACE.
THERE IS NO PEACE IN THE KINGDOM OF MAN.
I CANNOT UNDERSTAND WHY YOU STRIVE TO CONQUER EVERYTHING.
ANYTHING YOU SEE...
DOMINATE IT! CLAIM IT!
WE ARE YOUNG.
CHILDREN AMONG THE ELDERS OF THE LAND.
WE'VE BEEN GIVEN THE POWER TO RULE IT...
...AND WE FEAR WE'LL LOSE THAT POWE--

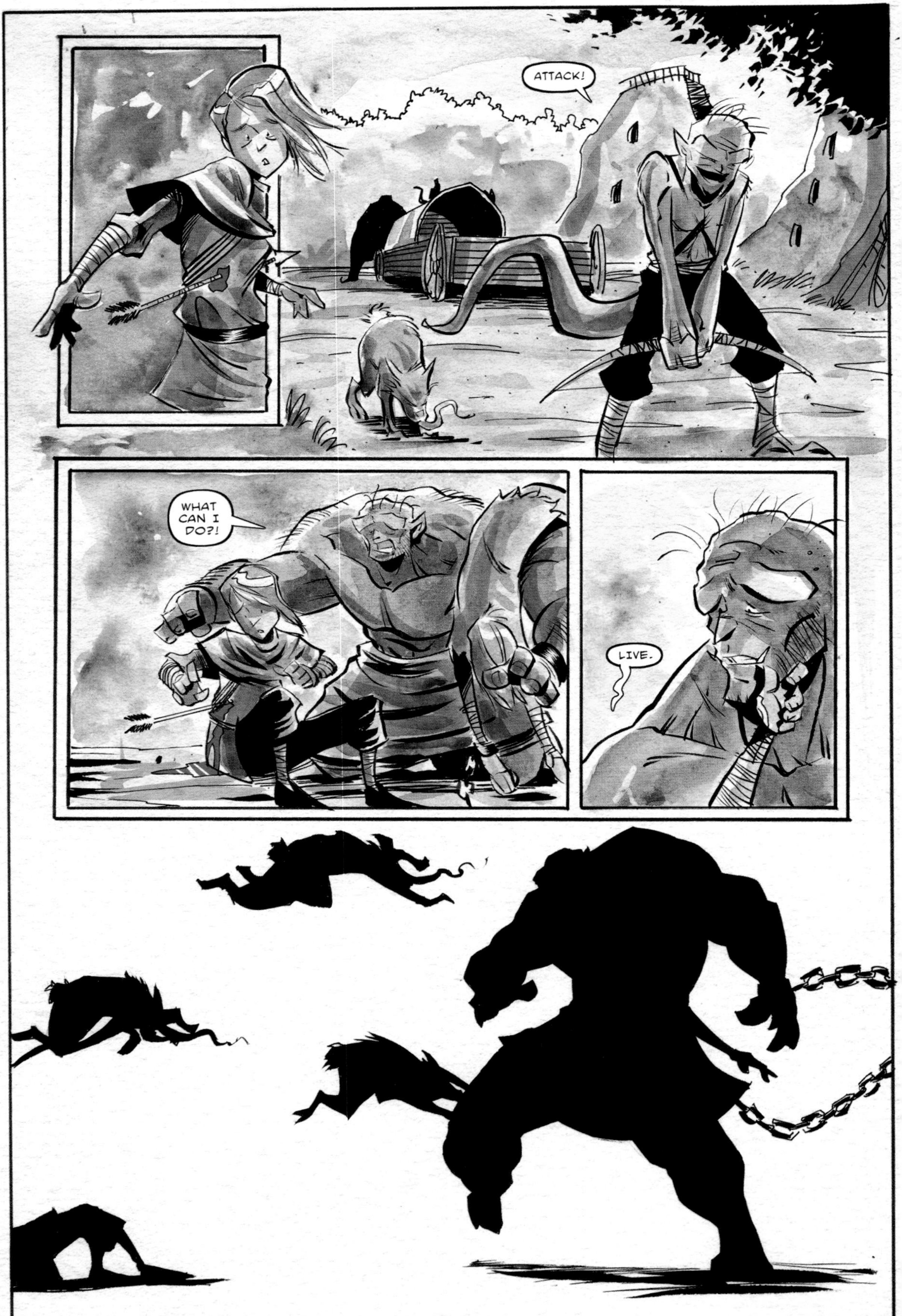
ATTACK!
WHAT CAN I DO?!
LIVE.

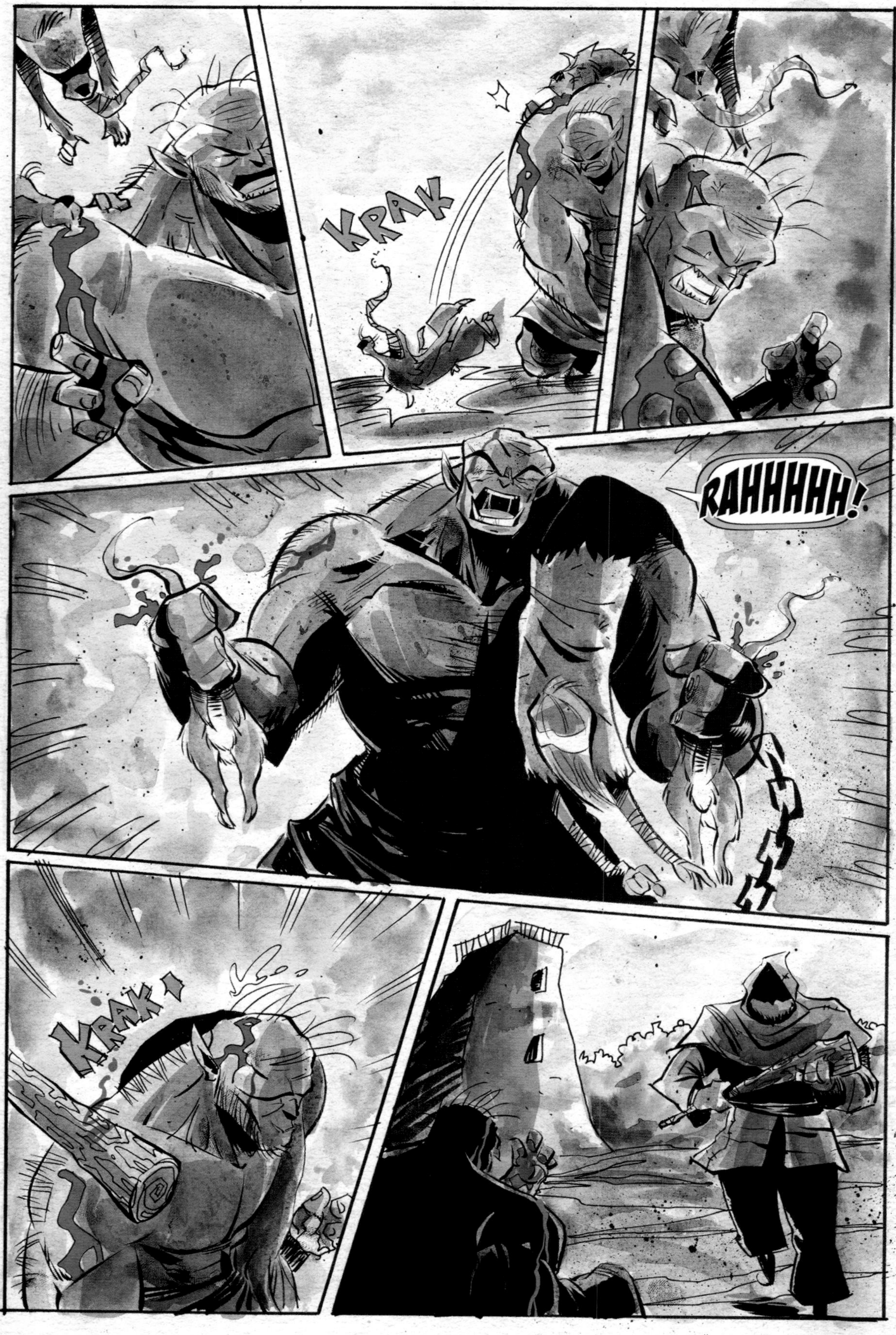
KRAK
RAHHHHH!
KRAK!

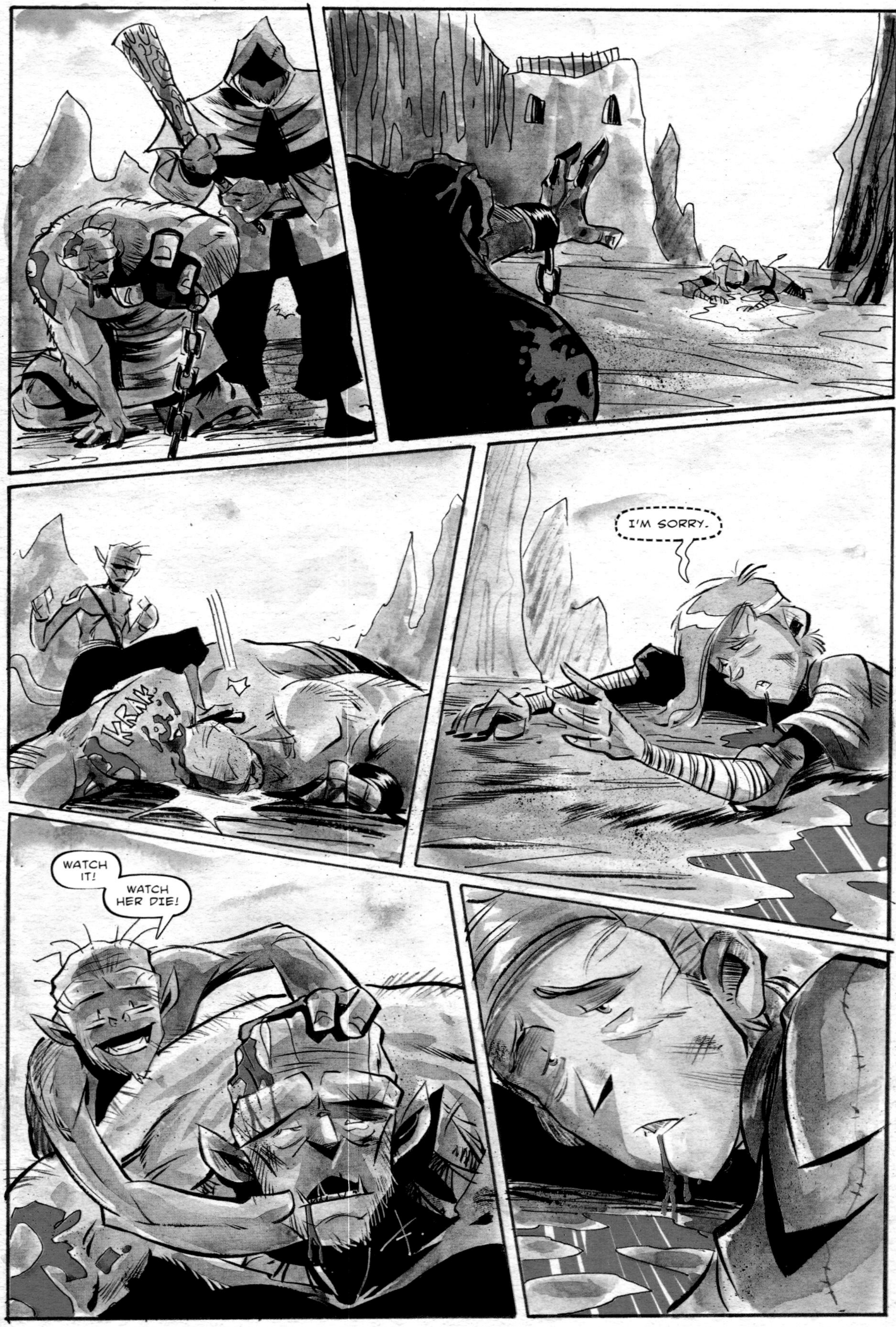
I'M SORRY.
WATCH IT!
WATCH HER DIE!

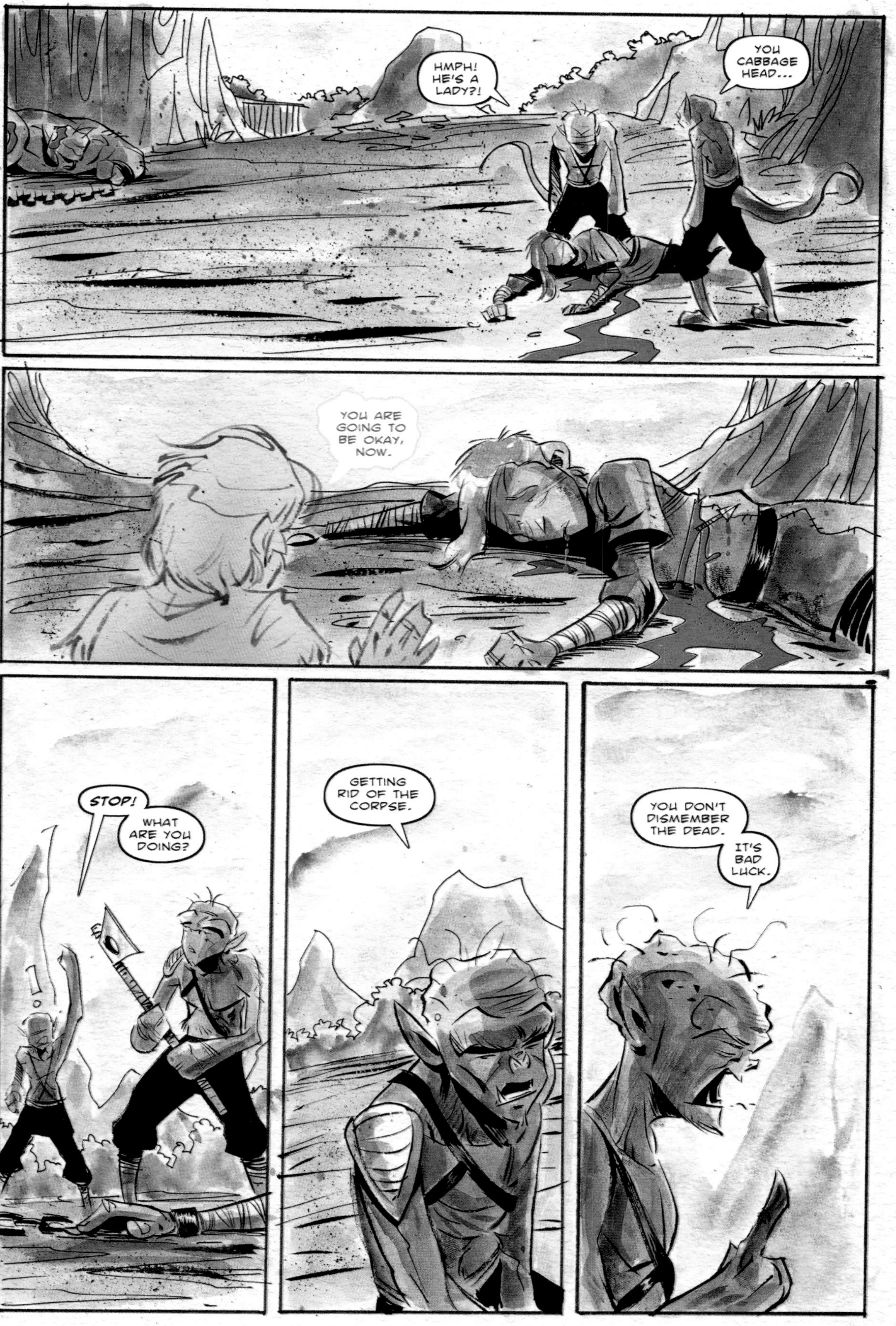
HMPH! HE'S A LADY?!
YOU CABBAGE HEAD...
YOU ARE GOING TO BE OKAY, NOW.
STOP!
WHAT ARE YOU DOING?
GETTING RID OF THE CORPSE.
YOU DON'T DISMEMBER THE DEAD.
IT'S BAD LUCK.

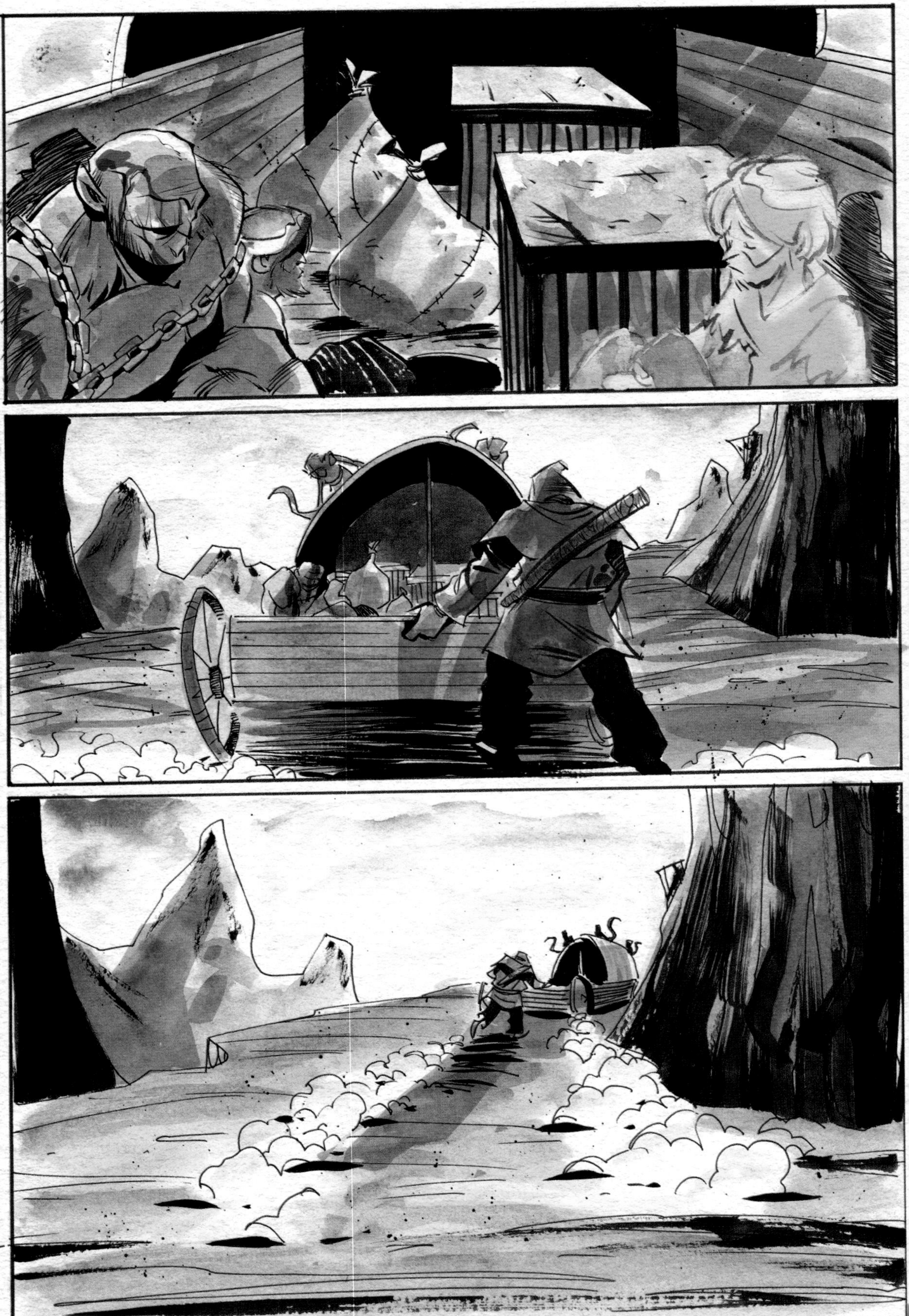

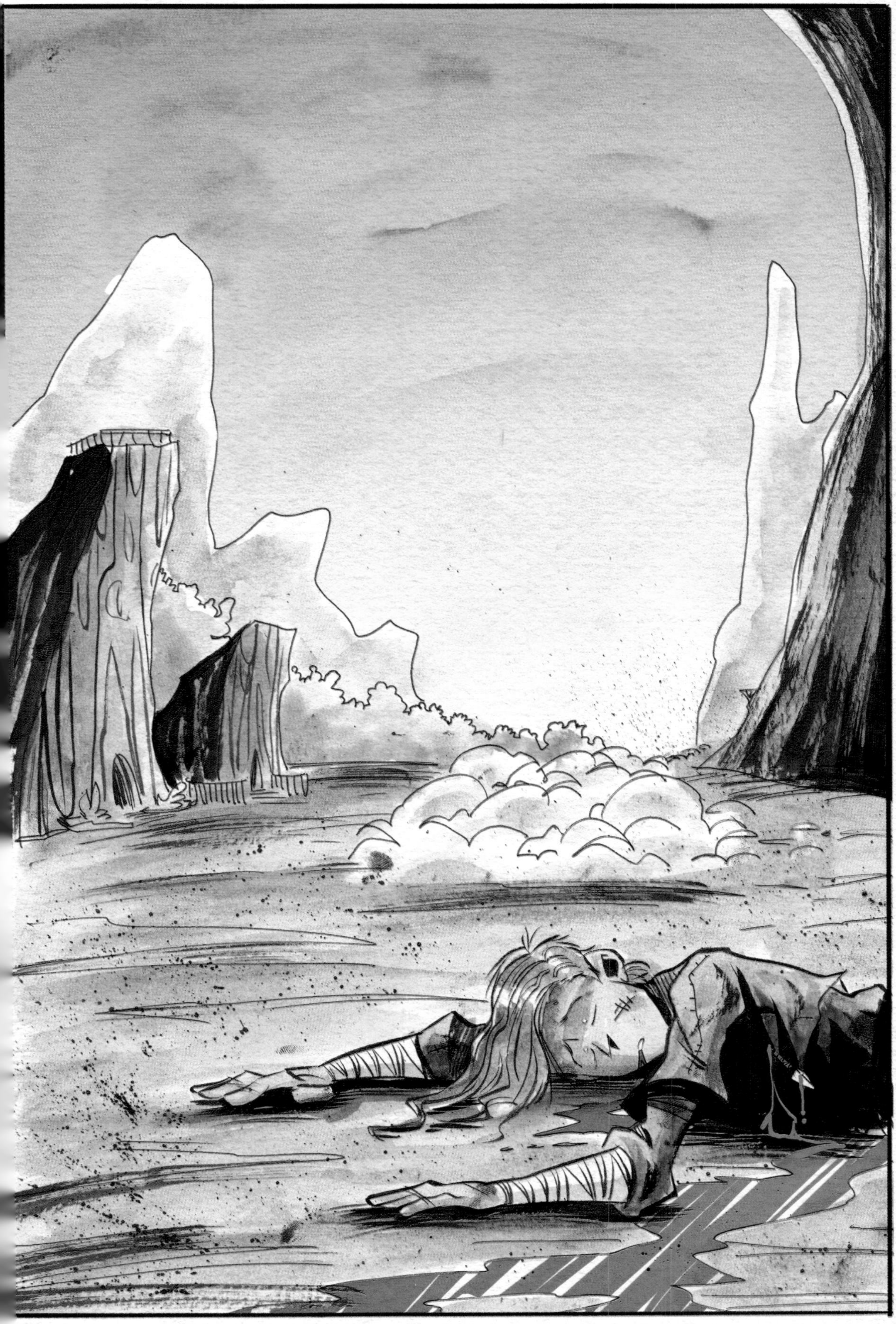

Other versions of the 3rd issue cover by Shawn Daley.

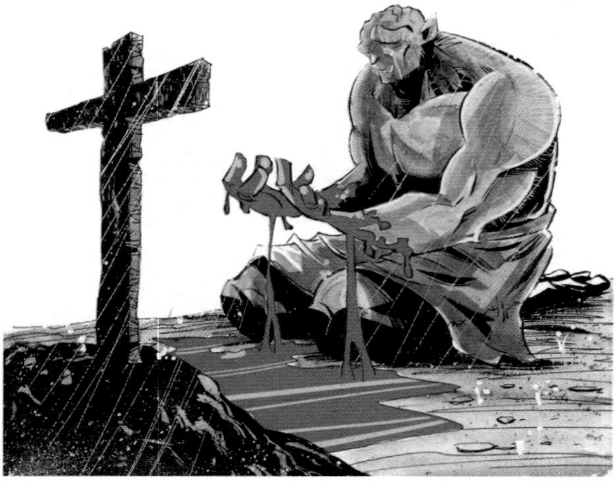

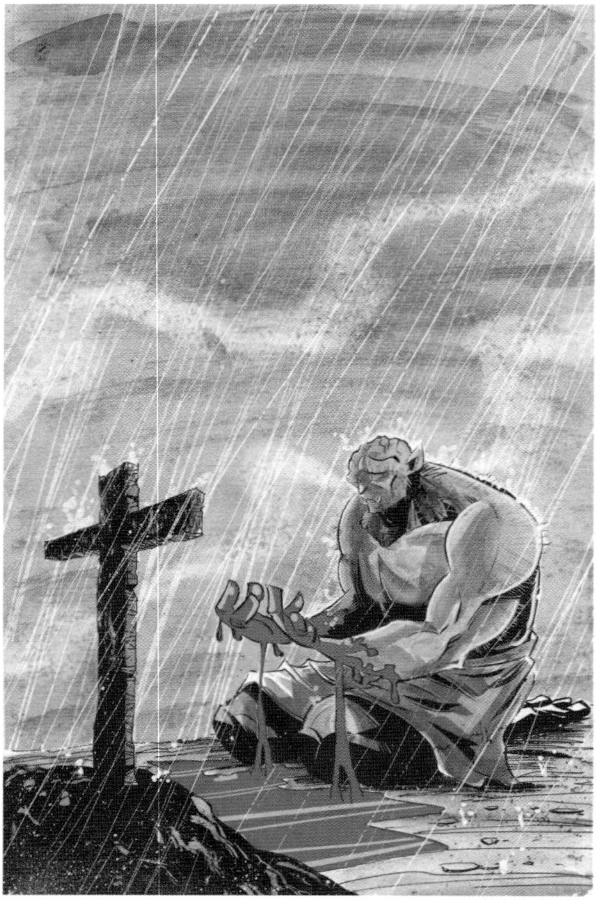

CHAPTER THREE

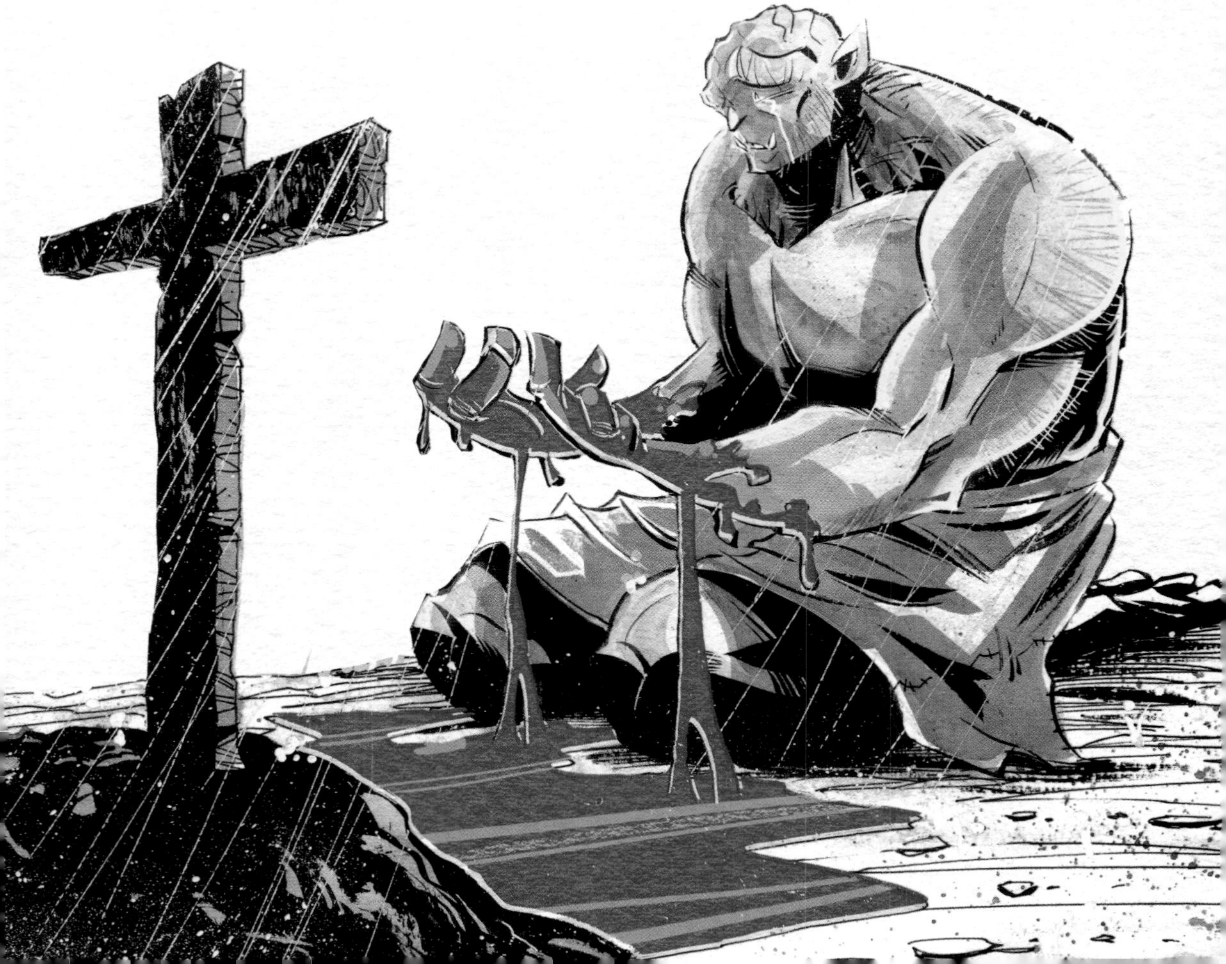

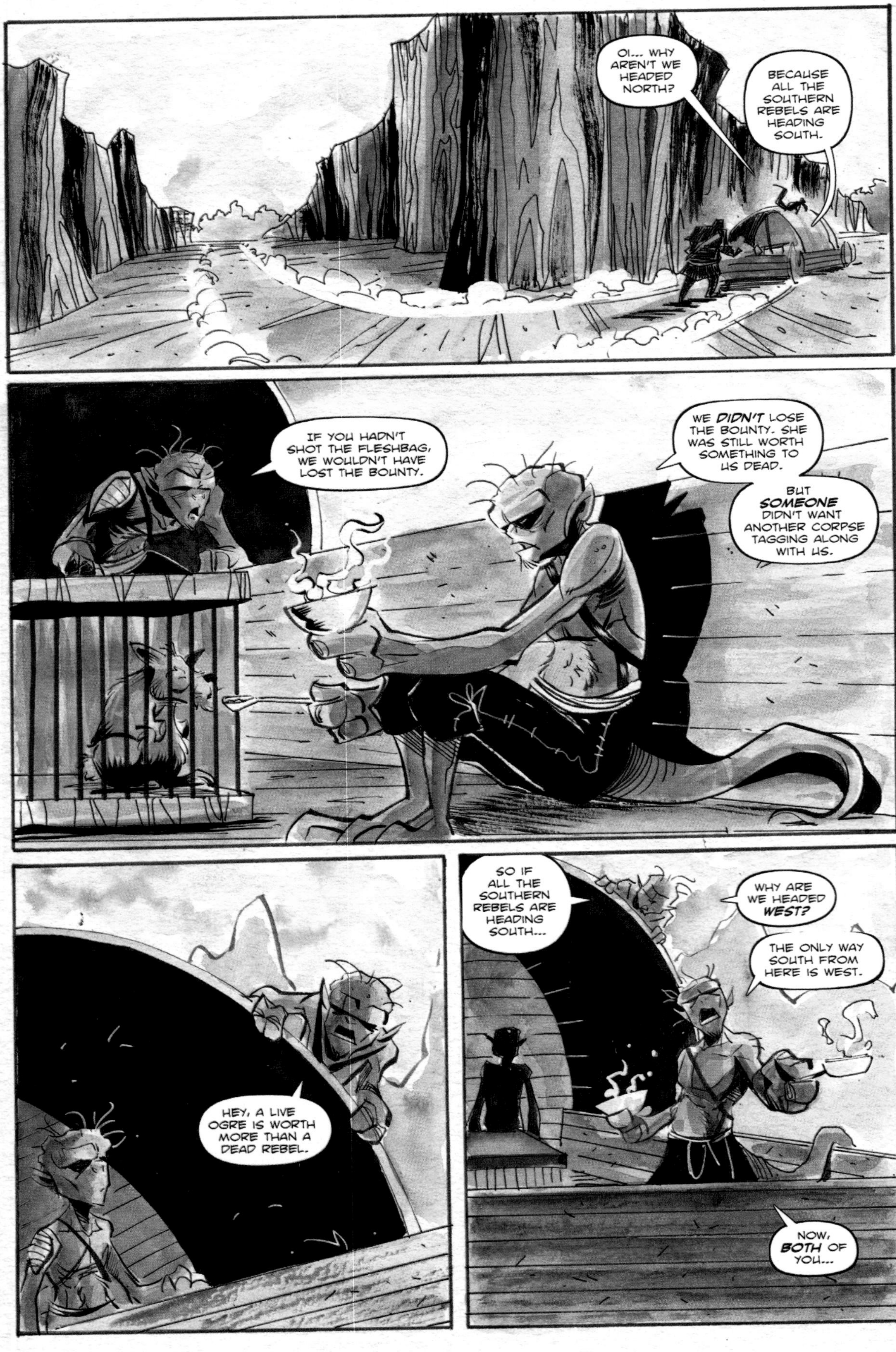
OI... WHY AREN'T WE HEADED NORTH?
BECAUSE ALL THE SOUTHERN REBELS ARE HEADING SOUTH.
IF YOU HADN'T SHOT THE FLESHBAG, WE WOULDN'T HAVE LOST THE BOUNTY.
WE DIDN'T LOSE THE BOUNTY. SHE WAS STILL WORTH SOMETHING TO US DEAD.
BUT SOMEONE DIDN'T WANT ANOTHER CORPSE TAGGING ALONG WITH US.
HEY, A LIVE OGRE IS WORTH MORE THAN A DEAD REBEL.
SO IF ALL THE SOUTHERN REBELS ARE HEADING SOUTH...
WHY ARE WE HEADED WEST?
THE ONLY WAY SOUTH FROM HERE IS WEST.
NOW, BOTH OF YOU...

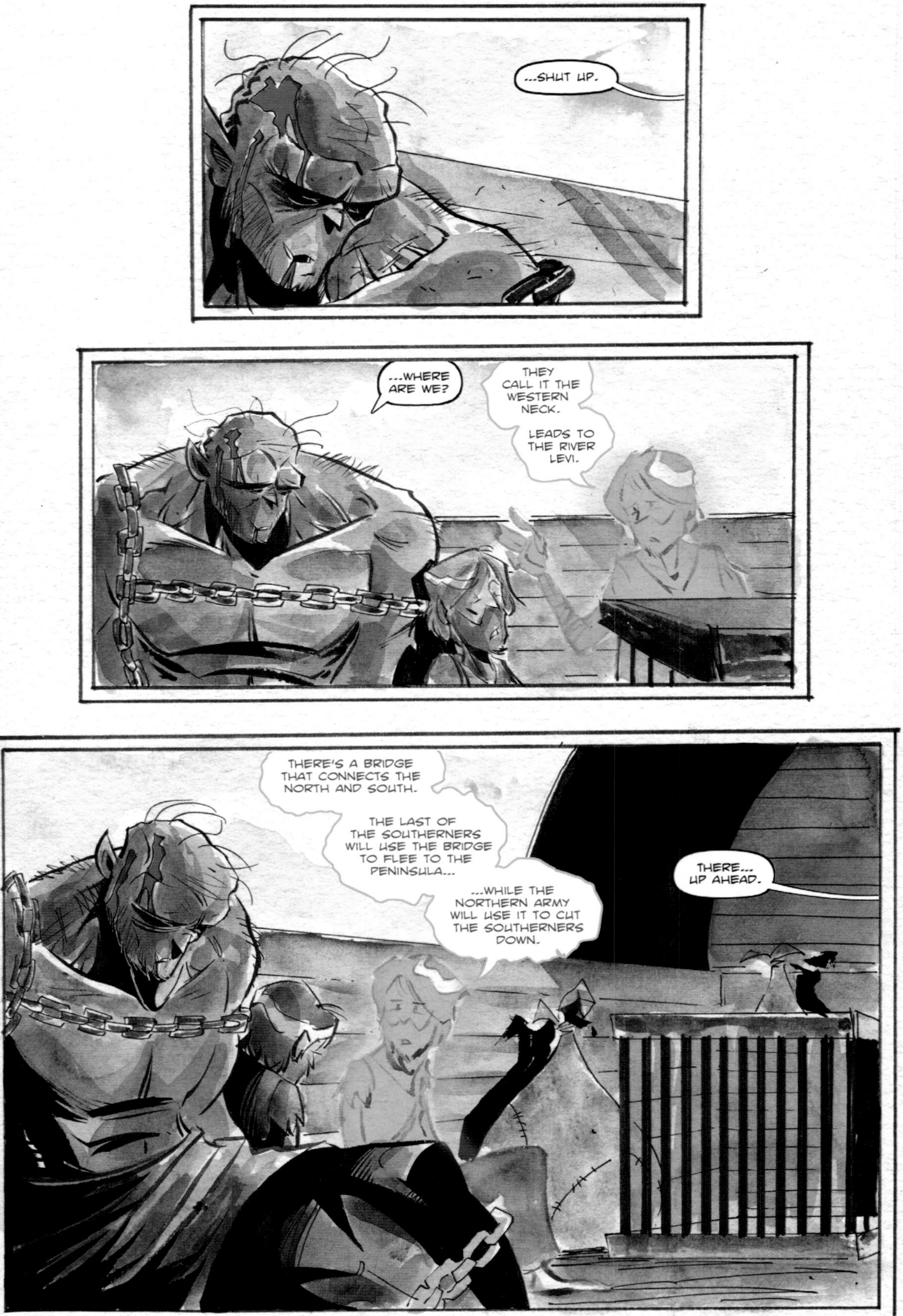
...SHUT UP.
...WHERE ARE WE?
THEY CALL IT THE WESTERN NECK.
LEADS TO THE RIVER LEVI.
THERE'S A BRIDGE THAT CONNECTS THE NORTH AND SOUTH.
THE LAST OF THE SOUTHERNERS WILL USE THE BRIDGE TO FLEE TO THE PENINSULA...
...WHILE THE NORTHERN ARMY WILL USE IT TO CUT THE SOUTHERNERS DOWN.
THERE... UP AHEAD.

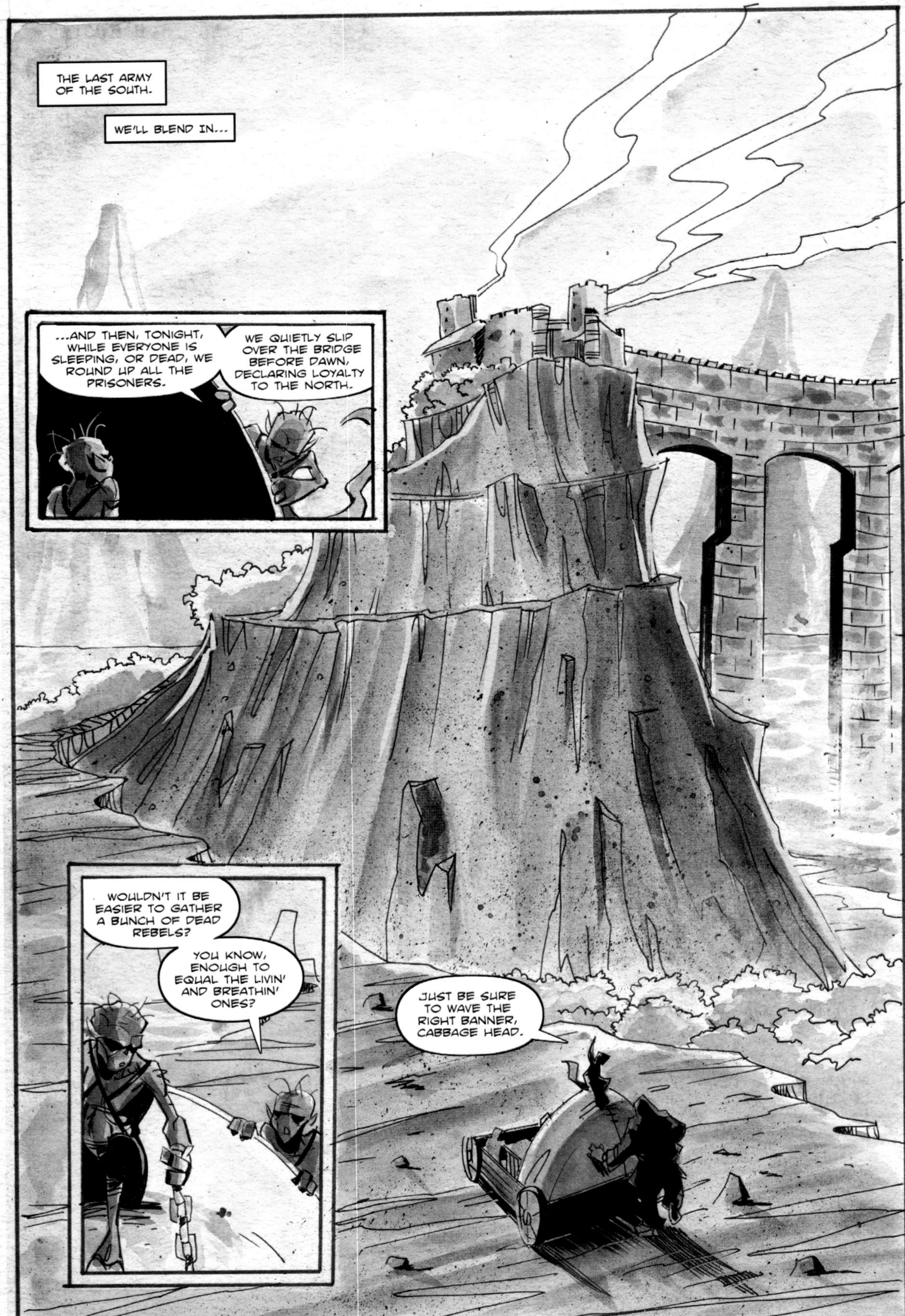

THE LAST ARMY OF THE SOUTH.
WE'LL BLEND IN...
...AND THEN, TONIGHT, WHILE EVERYONE IS SLEEPING, OR DEAD, WE ROUND UP ALL THE PRISONERS.
WE QUIETLY SLIP OVER THE BRIDGE BEFORE DAWN, DECLARING LOYALTY TO THE NORTH.
WOULDN'T IT BE EASIER TO GATHER A BUNCH OF DEAD REBELS?
YOU KNOW, ENOUGH TO EQUAL THE LIVIN' AND BREATHIN' ONES?
JUST BE SURE TO WAVE THE RIGHT BANNER, CABBAGE HEAD.

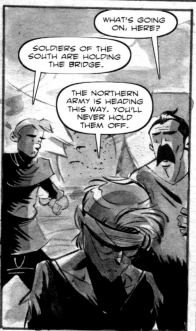

WHAT'S GOING ON, HERE?

SOLDIERS OF THE SOUTH ARE HOLDING THE BRIDGE.

THE NORTHERN ARMY IS HEADING THIS WAY. YOU'LL NEVER HOLD THEM OFF.

AYE... WE'RE ONLY HOLDING THEM LONG ENOUGH FOR THE WOMEN, CHILDREN AND ELDERLY TO FLEE TO SAFETY.

YOUR HUMANITY IS GOING TO GET YOU ALL KILLED.

BETTER TO DIE WITH IT THAN TO LIVE WITHOUT IT, AY?

THE ARMISTICE HAS BEGUN BUT WON'T LAST LONG!

HURRY TO THE BRIDGE!

THE FIGHT HAS BROKEN. IT IS TIME TO RETRIEVE THE INJURED AND THE DEAD.

COME!

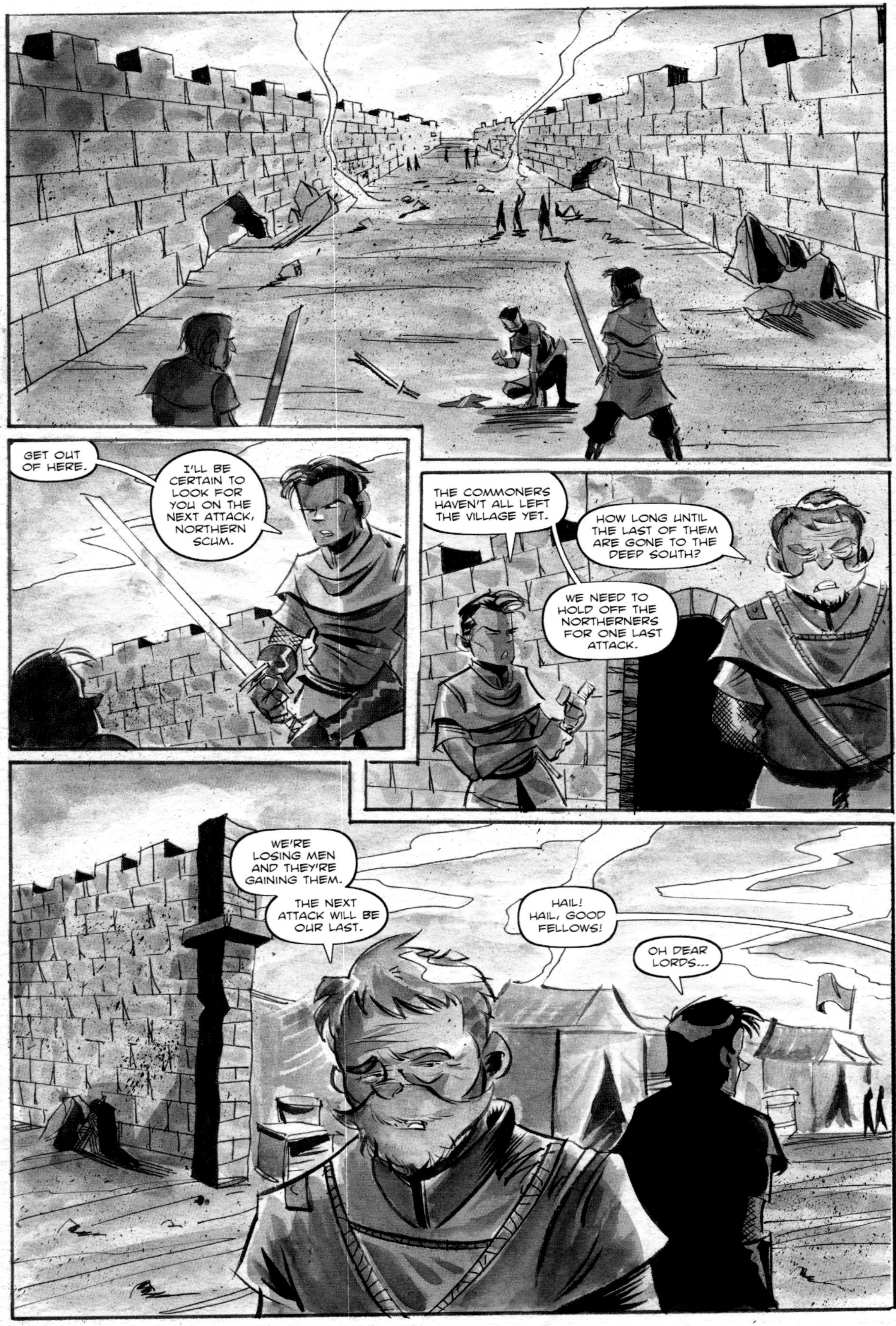
GET OUT OF HERE.
I'LL BE CERTAIN TO LOOK FOR YOU ON THE NEXT ATTACK, NORTHERN SCUM.
THE COMMONERS HAVEN'T ALL LEFT THE VILLAGE YET.
HOW LONG UNTIL THE LAST OF THEM ARE GONE TO THE DEEP SOUTH?
WE NEED TO HOLD OFF THE NORTHERNERS FOR ONE LAST ATTACK.
WE'RE LOSING MEN AND THEY'RE GAINING THEM.
THE NEXT ATTACK WILL BE OUR LAST.
HAIL! HAIL, GOOD FELLOWS!
OH DEAR LORDS...

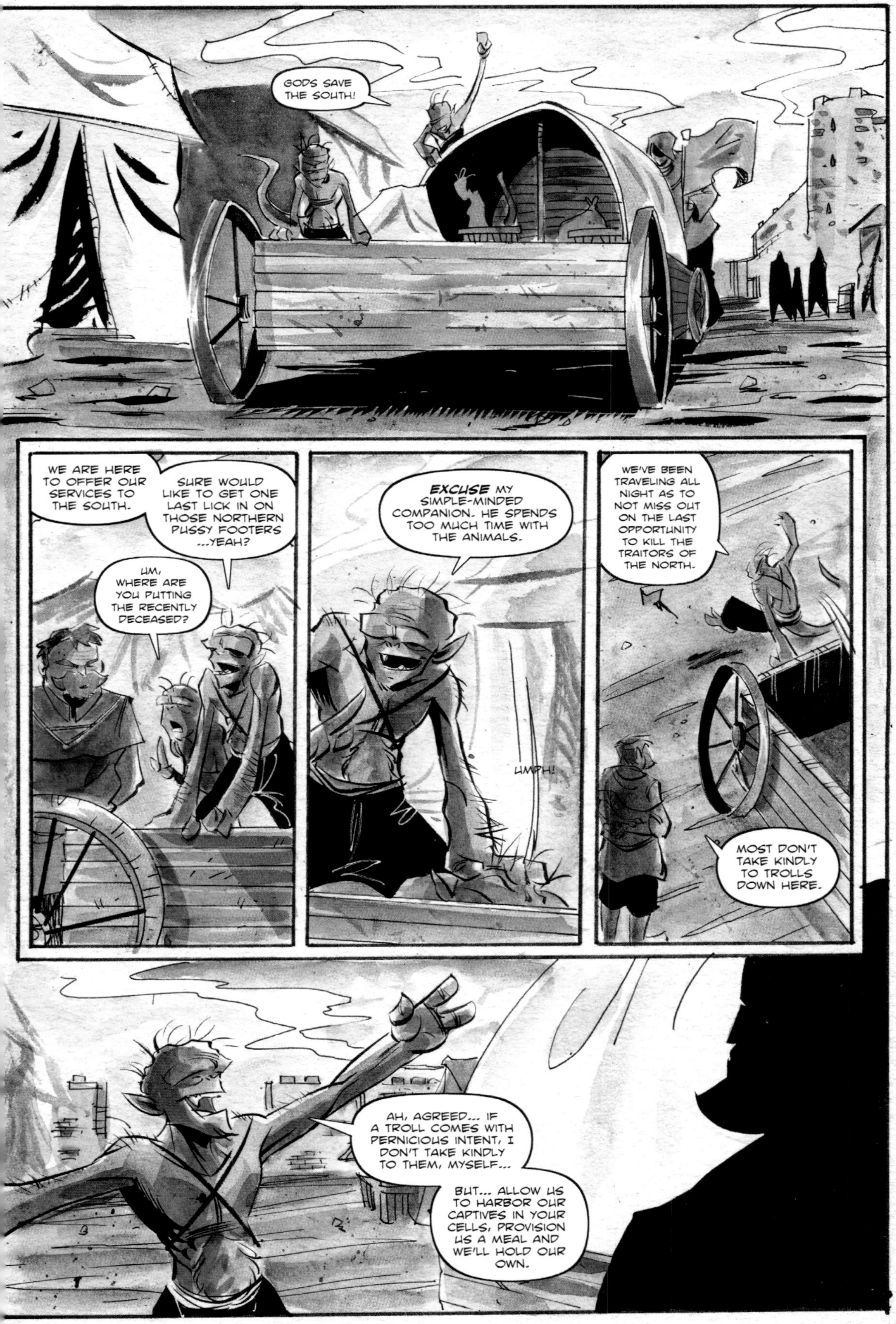
GODS SAVE THE SOUTH!
WE ARE HERE TO OFFER OUR SERVICES TO THE SOUTH.
SURE WOULD LIKE TO GET ONE LAST LICK IN ON THOSE NORTHERN PUSSY FOOTERS ...YEAH?
UM, WHERE ARE YOU PUTTING THE RECENTLY DECEASED?
EXCUSE MY SIMPLE-MINDED COMPANION. HE SPENDS TOO MUCH TIME WITH THE ANIMALS.
UMPH!
WE'VE BEEN TRAVELING ALL NIGHT AS TO NOT MISS OUT ON THE LAST OPPORTUNITY TO KILL THE TRAITORS OF THE NORTH.
MOST DON'T TAKE KINDLY TO TROLLS DOWN HERE.
AH, AGREED... IF A TROLL COMES WITH PERNICIOUS INTENT, I DON'T TAKE KINDLY TO THEM, MYSELF...
BUT... ALLOW US TO HARBOR OUR CAPTIVES IN YOUR CELLS, PROVISION US A MEAL AND WE'LL HOLD OUR OWN.

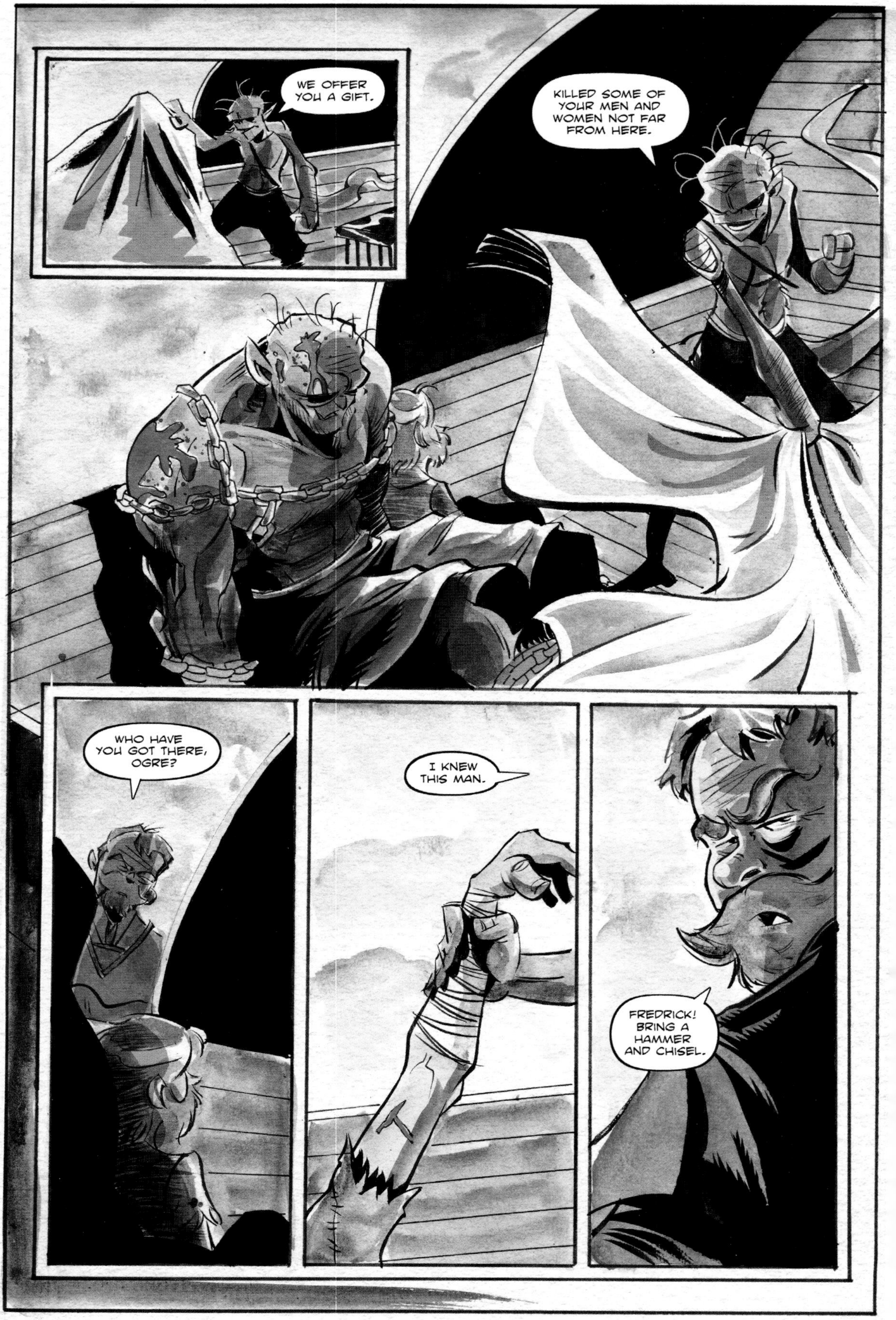
WE OFFER YOU A GIFT.
KILLED SOME OF YOUR MEN AND WOMEN NOT FAR FROM HERE.
WHO HAVE YOU GOT THERE, OGRE?
I KNEW THIS MAN.
FREDRICK! BRING A HAMMER AND CHISEL.

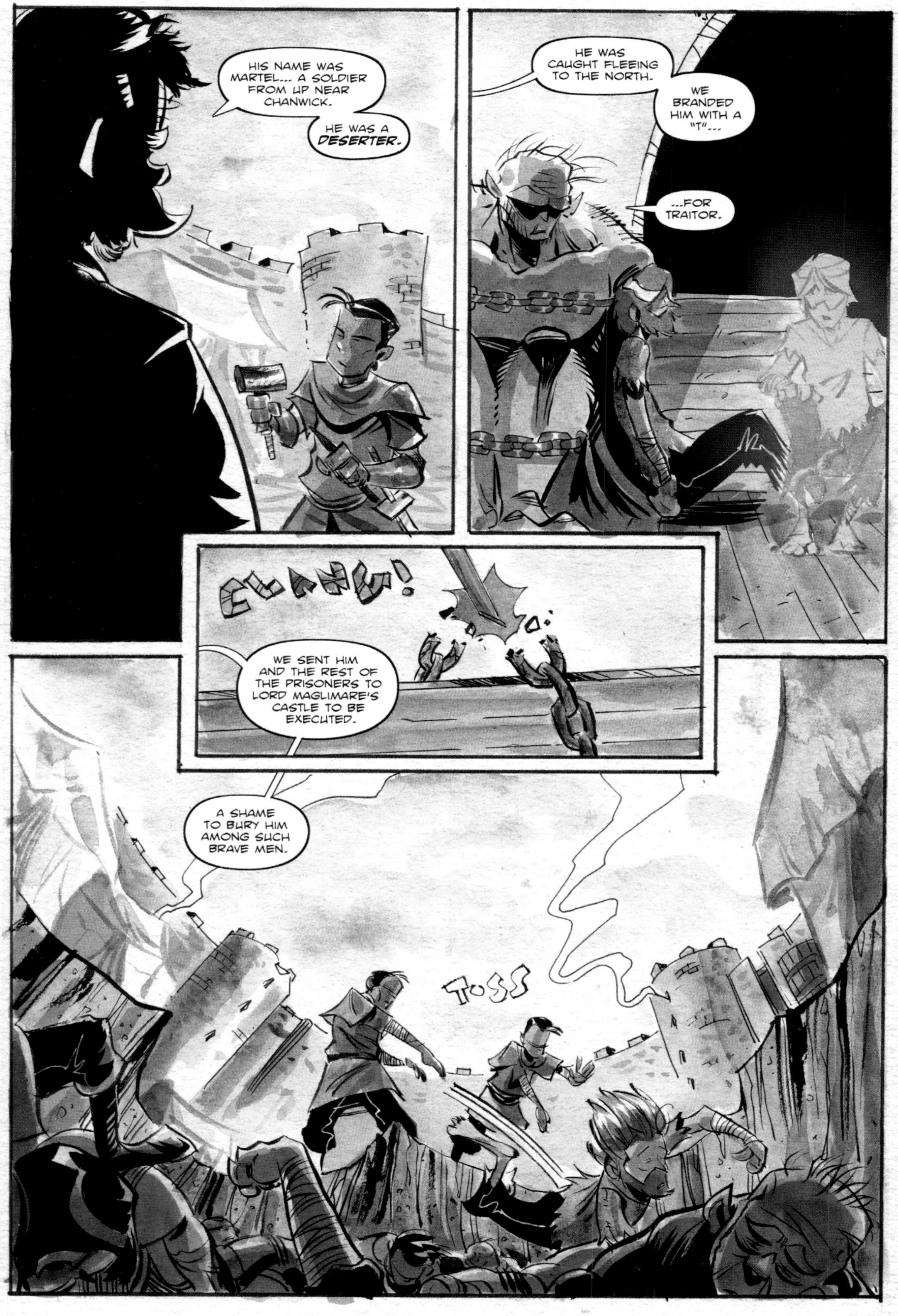
HIS NAME WAS MARTEL... A SOLDIER FROM UP NEAR CHANWICK.
HE WAS A DESERTER.
HE WAS CAUGHT FLEEING TO THE NORTH.
WE BRANDED HIM WITH A "T"...
...FOR TRAITOR.
CLANG!
WE SENT HIM AND THE REST OF THE PRISONERS TO LORD MAGLIMARE'S CASTLE TO BE EXECUTED.
A SHAME TO BURY HIM AMONG SUCH BRAVE MEN.
TOSS

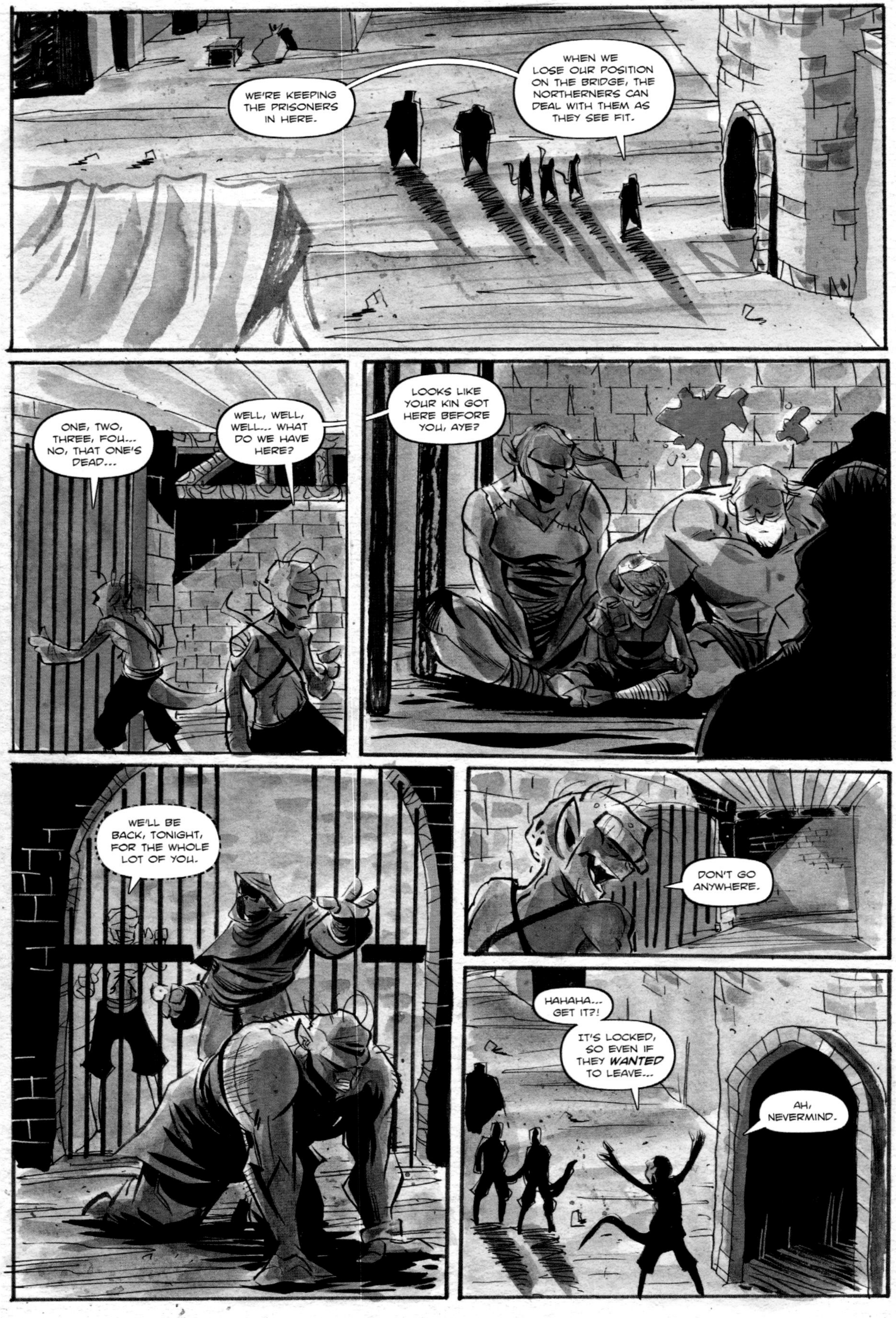
WE'RE KEEPING THE PRISONERS IN HERE.
WHEN WE LOSE OUR POSITION ON THE BRIDGE, THE NORTHERNERS CAN DEAL WITH THEM AS THEY SEE FIT.
ONE, TWO, THREE, FOU... NO, THAT ONE'S DEAD...
WELL, WELL, WELL... WHAT DO WE HAVE HERE?
LOOKS LIKE YOUR KIN GOT HERE BEFORE YOU, AYE?
WE'LL BE BACK, TONIGHT, FOR THE WHOLE LOT OF YOU.
DON'T GO ANYWHERE.
HAHAHA... GET IT?!
IT'S LOCKED, SO EVEN IF THEY *WANTED* TO LEAVE...
AH, NEVERMIND.

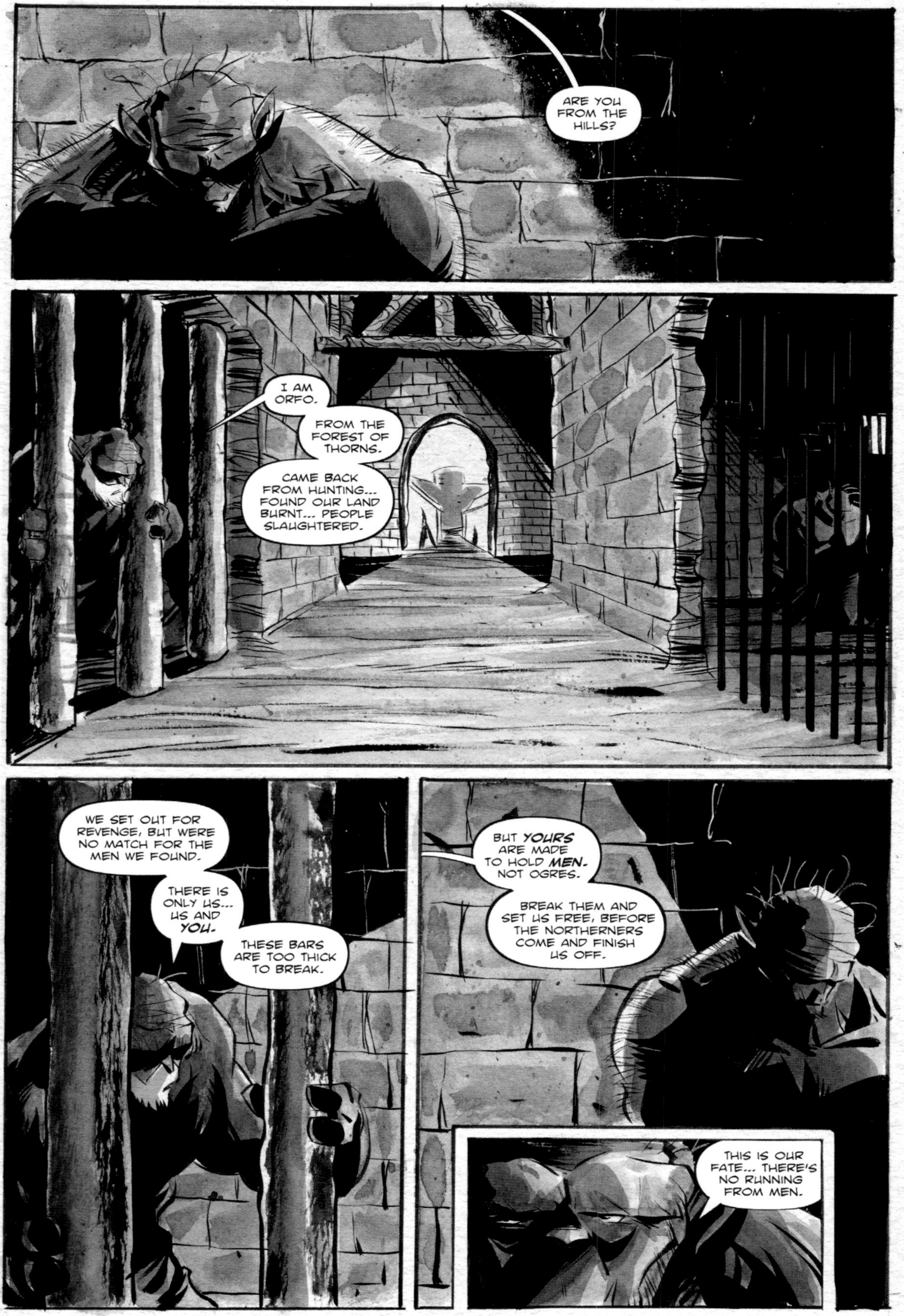
ARE YOU FROM THE HILLS?
I AM ORFO.
FROM THE FOREST OF THORNS.
CAME BACK FROM HUNTING... FOUND OUR LAND BURNT... PEOPLE SLAUGHTERED.
WE SET OUT FOR REVENGE, BUT WERE NO MATCH FOR THE MEN WE FOUND.
THERE IS ONLY US... US AND YOU.
THESE BARS ARE TOO THICK TO BREAK.
BUT YOURS ARE MADE TO HOLD MEN. NOT OGRES.
BREAK THEM AND SET US FREE, BEFORE THE NORTHERNERS COME AND FINISH US OFF.
THIS IS OUR FATE... THERE'S NO RUNNING FROM MEN.

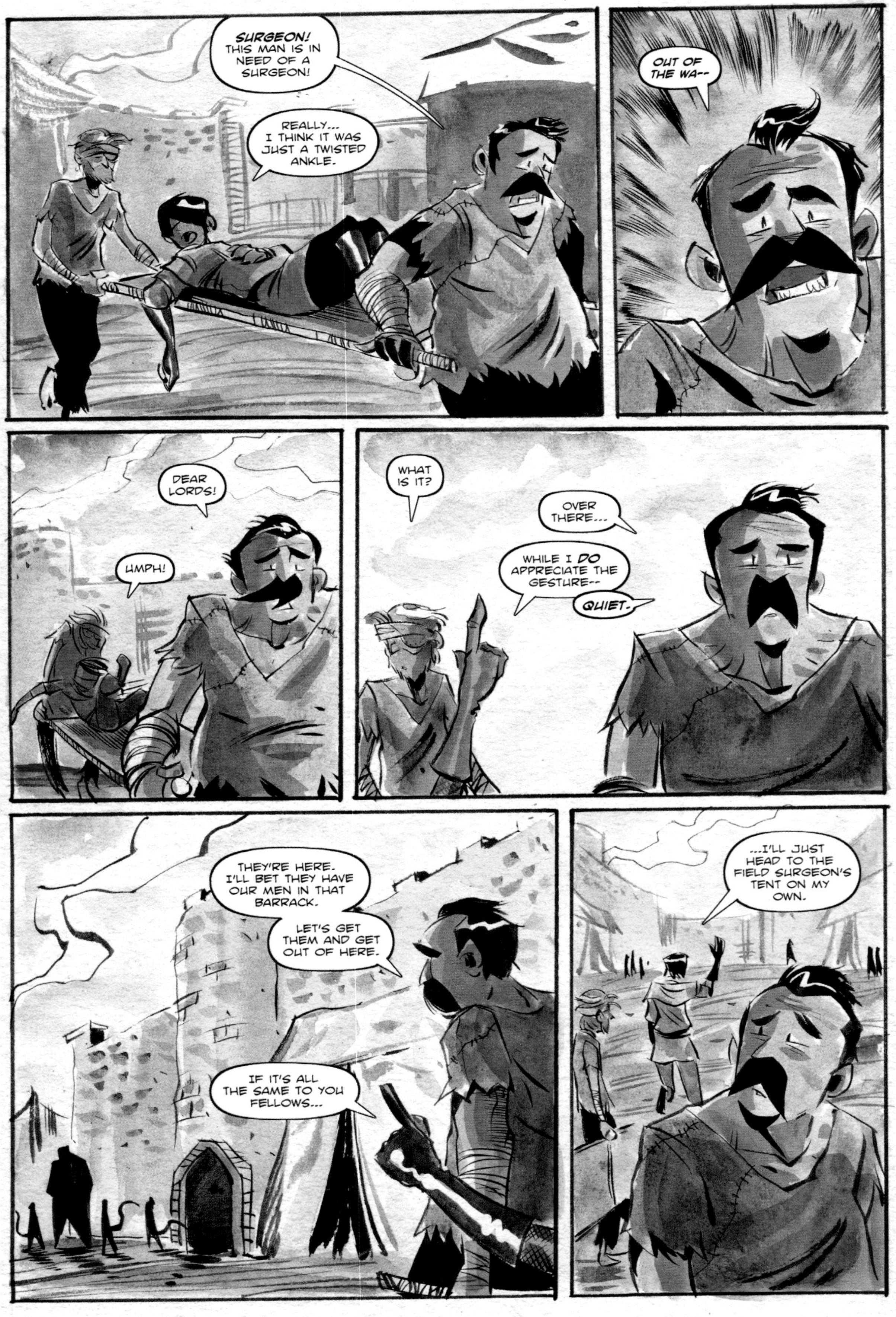
SURGEON! THIS MAN IS IN NEED OF A SURGEON!
REALLY... I THINK IT WAS JUST A TWISTED ANKLE.
OUT OF THE WA--
DEAR LORDS!
UMPH!
WHAT IS IT?
OVER THERE...
WHILE I DO APPRECIATE THE GESTURE--
QUIET.
THEY'RE HERE. I'LL BET THEY HAVE OUR MEN IN THAT BARRACK.
LET'S GET THEM AND GET OUT OF HERE.
IF IT'S ALL THE SAME TO YOU FELLOWS...
...I'LL JUST HEAD TO THE FIELD SURGEON'S TENT ON MY OWN.

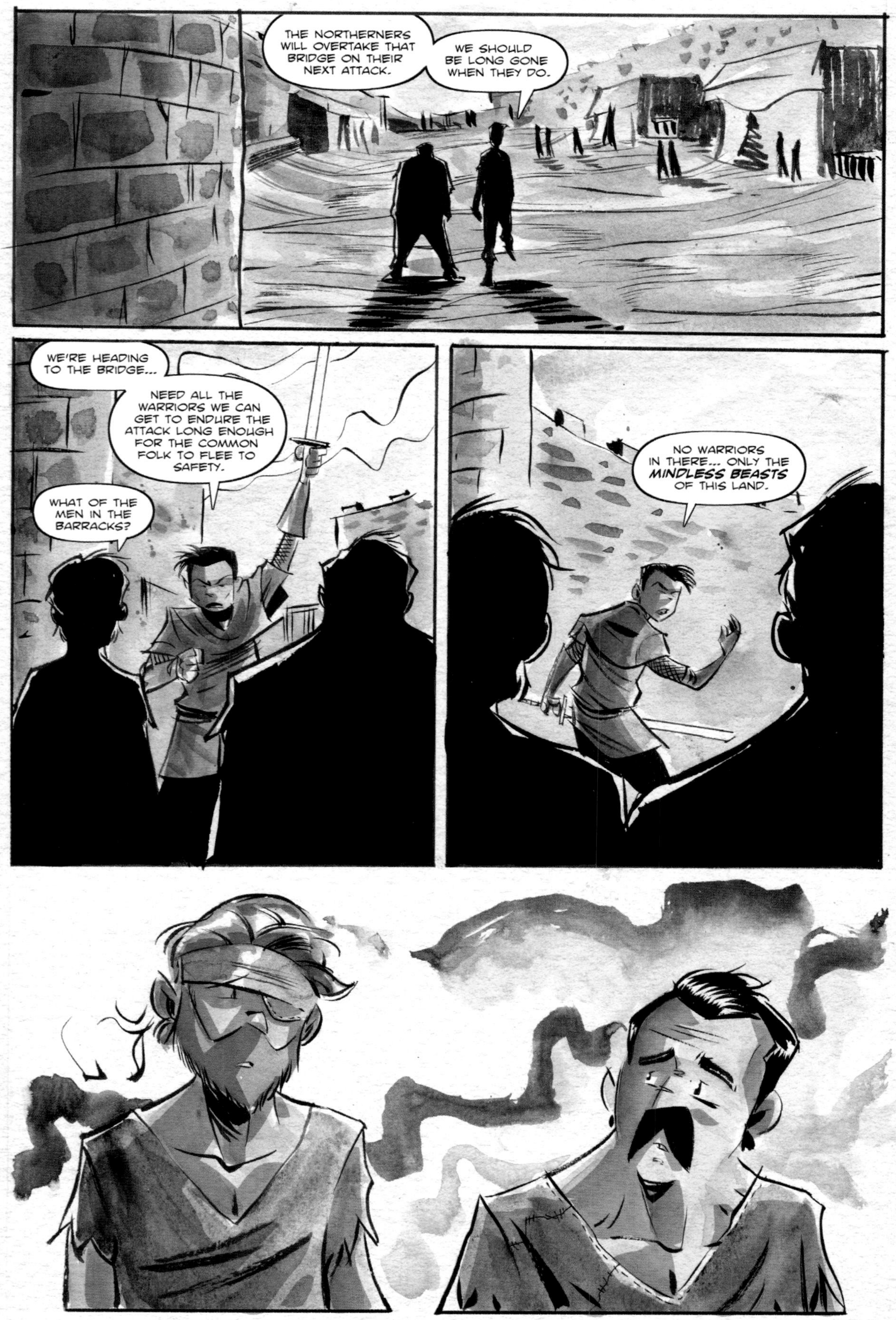
THE NORTHERNERS WILL OVERTAKE THAT BRIDGE ON THEIR NEXT ATTACK.
WE SHOULD BE LONG GONE WHEN THEY DO.
WE'RE HEADING TO THE BRIDGE...
NEED ALL THE WARRIORS WE CAN GET TO ENDURE THE ATTACK LONG ENOUGH FOR THE COMMON FOLK TO FLEE TO SAFETY.
WHAT OF THE MEN IN THE BARRACKS?
NO WARRIORS IN THERE... ONLY THE ***MINDLESS BEASTS*** OF THIS LAND.

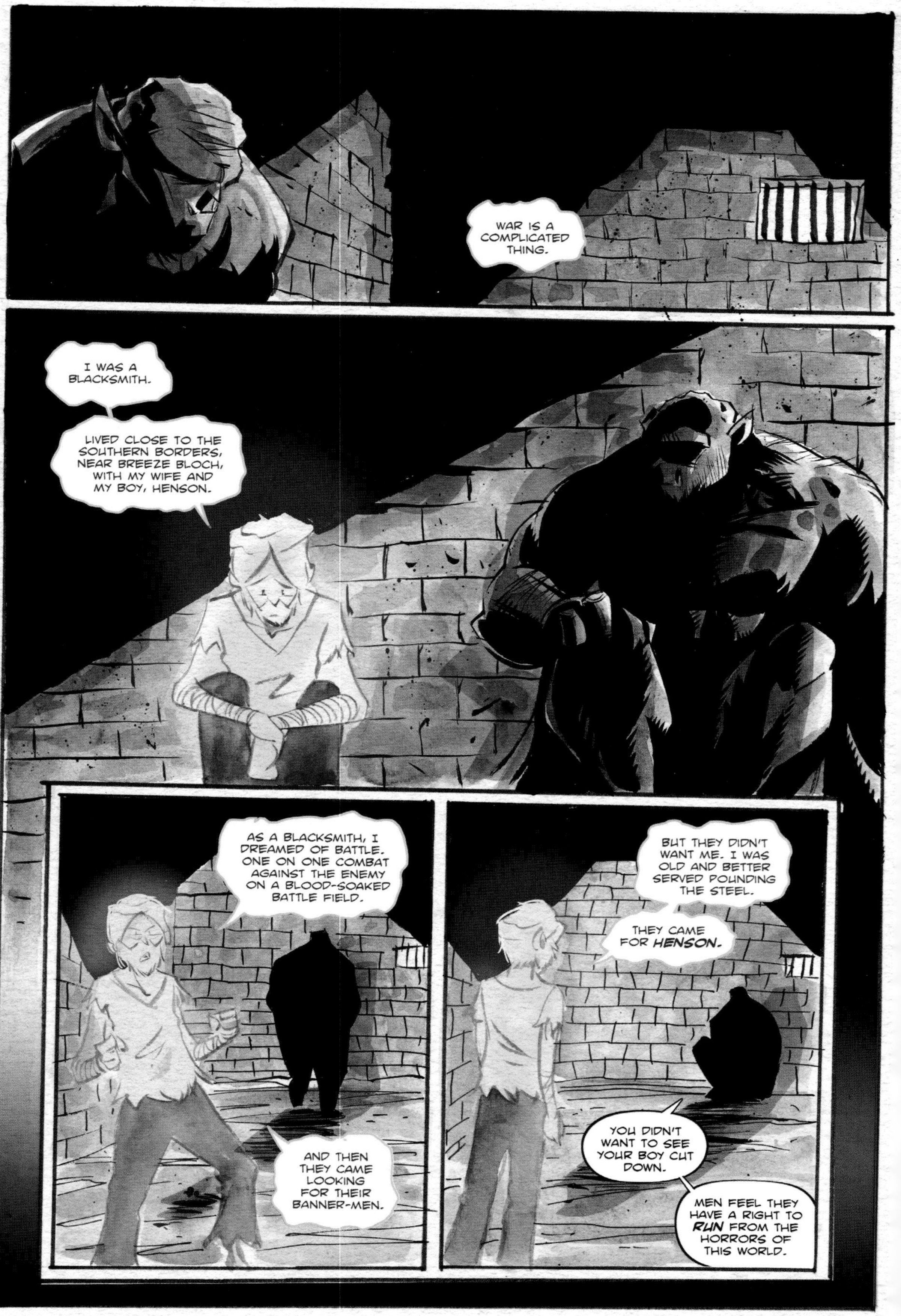
WAR IS A COMPLICATED THING.
I WAS A BLACKSMITH.
LIVED CLOSE TO THE SOUTHERN BORDERS, NEAR BREEZE BLOCH, WITH MY WIFE AND MY BOY, HENSON.
AS A BLACKSMITH, I DREAMED OF BATTLE. ONE ON ONE COMBAT AGAINST THE ENEMY ON A BLOOD-SOAKED BATTLE FIELD.
AND THEN THEY CAME LOOKING FOR THEIR BANNER-MEN.
BUT THEY DIDN'T WANT ME. I WAS OLD AND BETTER SERVED POUNDING THE STEEL.
THEY CAME FOR ***HENSON.***
YOU DIDN'T WANT TO SEE YOUR BOY CUT DOWN.
MEN FEEL THEY HAVE A RIGHT TO ***RUN*** FROM THE HORRORS OF THIS WORLD.

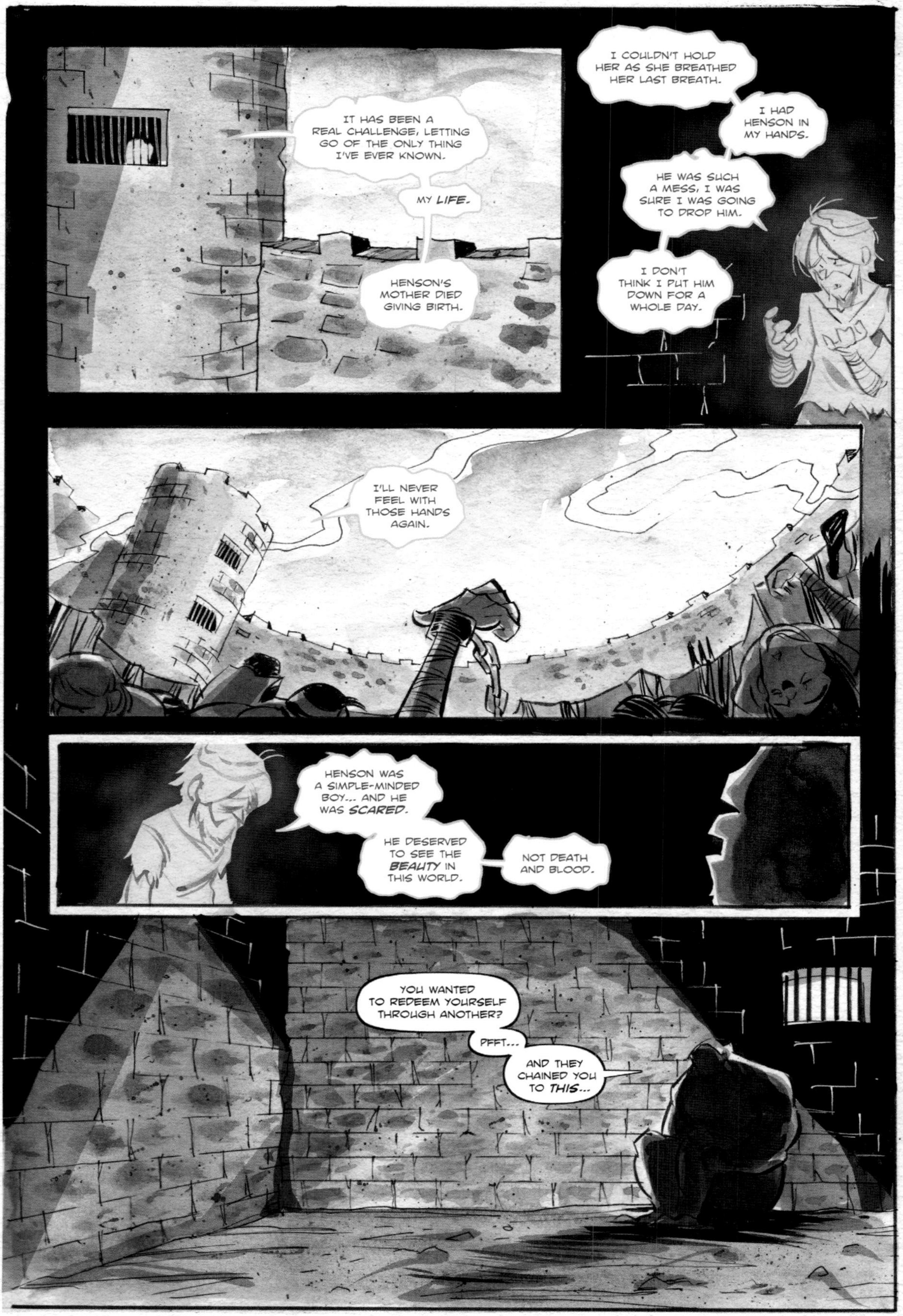

IT HAS BEEN A REAL CHALLENGE, LETTING GO OF THE ONLY THING I'VE EVER KNOWN.
MY *LIFE.*
HENSON'S MOTHER DIED GIVING BIRTH.
I COULDN'T HOLD HER AS SHE BREATHED HER LAST BREATH.
I HAD HENSON IN MY HANDS.
HE WAS SUCH A MESS, I WAS SURE I WAS GOING TO DROP HIM.
I DON'T THINK I PUT HIM DOWN FOR A WHOLE DAY.
I'LL NEVER FEEL WITH THOSE HANDS AGAIN.
HENSON WAS A SIMPLE-MINDED BOY... AND HE WAS *SCARED.*
HE DESERVED TO SEE THE *BEAUTY* IN THIS WORLD.
NOT DEATH AND BLOOD.
YOU WANTED TO REDEEM YOURSELF THROUGH ANOTHER?
PFFT...
AND THEY CHAINED YOU TO *THIS*...

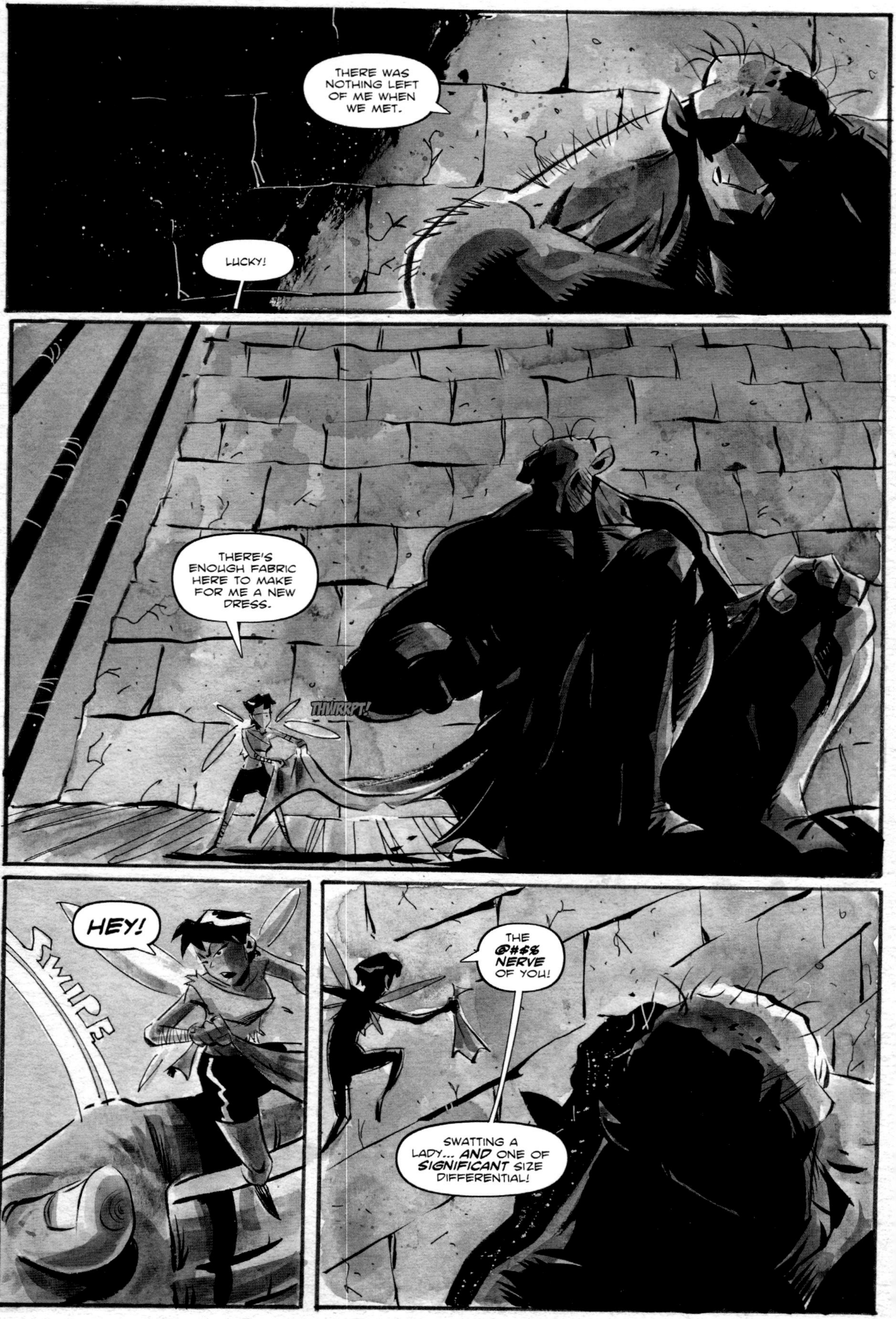

THERE WAS NOTHING LEFT OF ME WHEN WE MET.
LUCKY!
THERE'S ENOUGH FABRIC HERE TO MAKE FOR ME A NEW DRESS.
THWIRRPT!
HEY!
SWIPE
THE @#$% NERVE OF YOU!
SWATTING A LADY... AND ONE OF SIGNIFICANT SIZE DIFFERENTIAL!

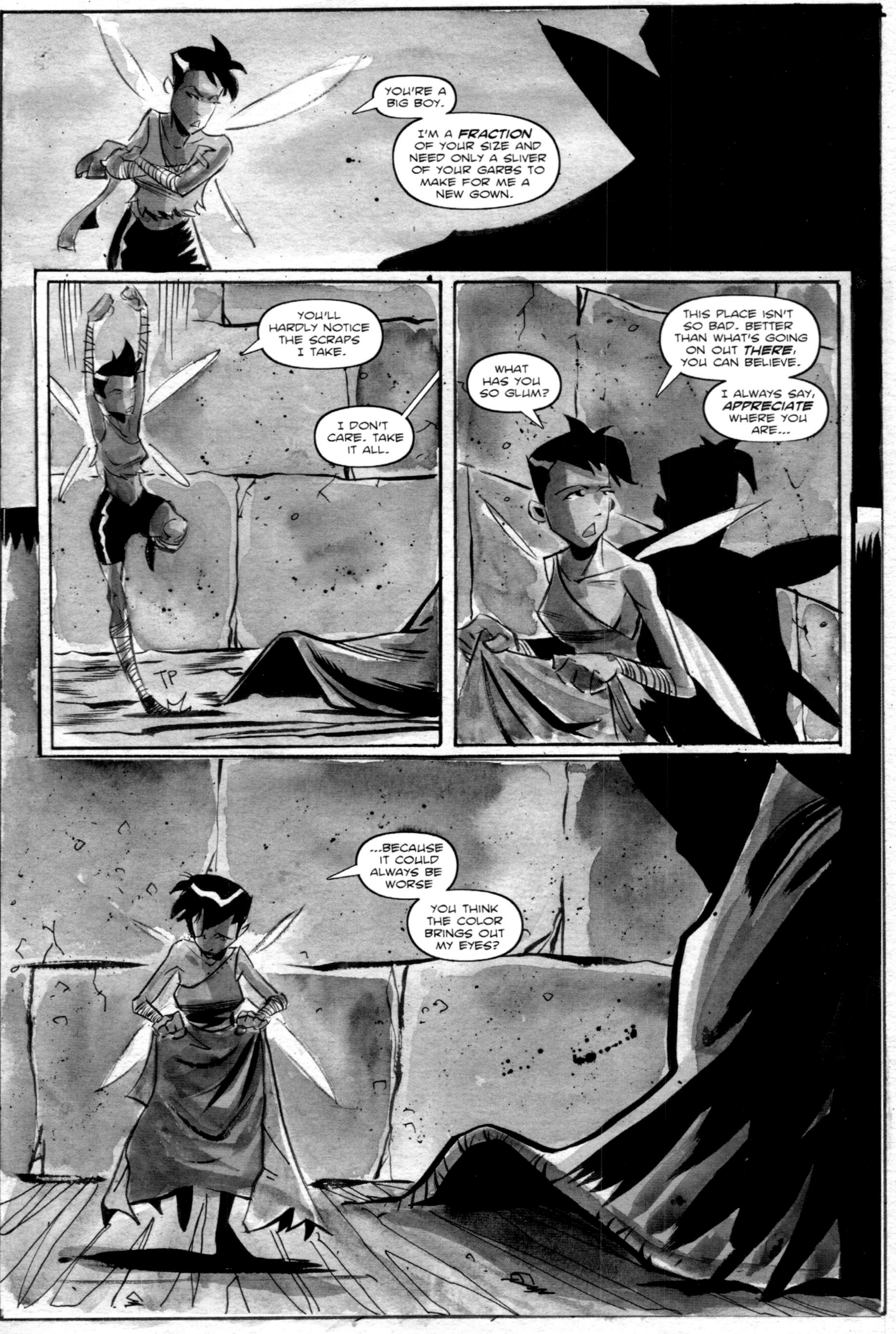
YOU'RE A BIG BOY.
I'M A FRACTION OF YOUR SIZE AND NEED ONLY A SLIVER OF YOUR GARBS TO MAKE FOR ME A NEW GOWN.
YOU'LL HARDLY NOTICE THE SCRAPS I TAKE.
I DON'T CARE. TAKE IT ALL.
WHAT HAS YOU SO GLUM?
THIS PLACE ISN'T SO BAD. BETTER THAN WHAT'S GOING ON OUT THERE, YOU CAN BELIEVE.
I ALWAYS SAY, APPRECIATE WHERE YOU ARE...
...BECAUSE IT COULD ALWAYS BE WORSE
YOU THINK THE COLOR BRINGS OUT MY EYES?

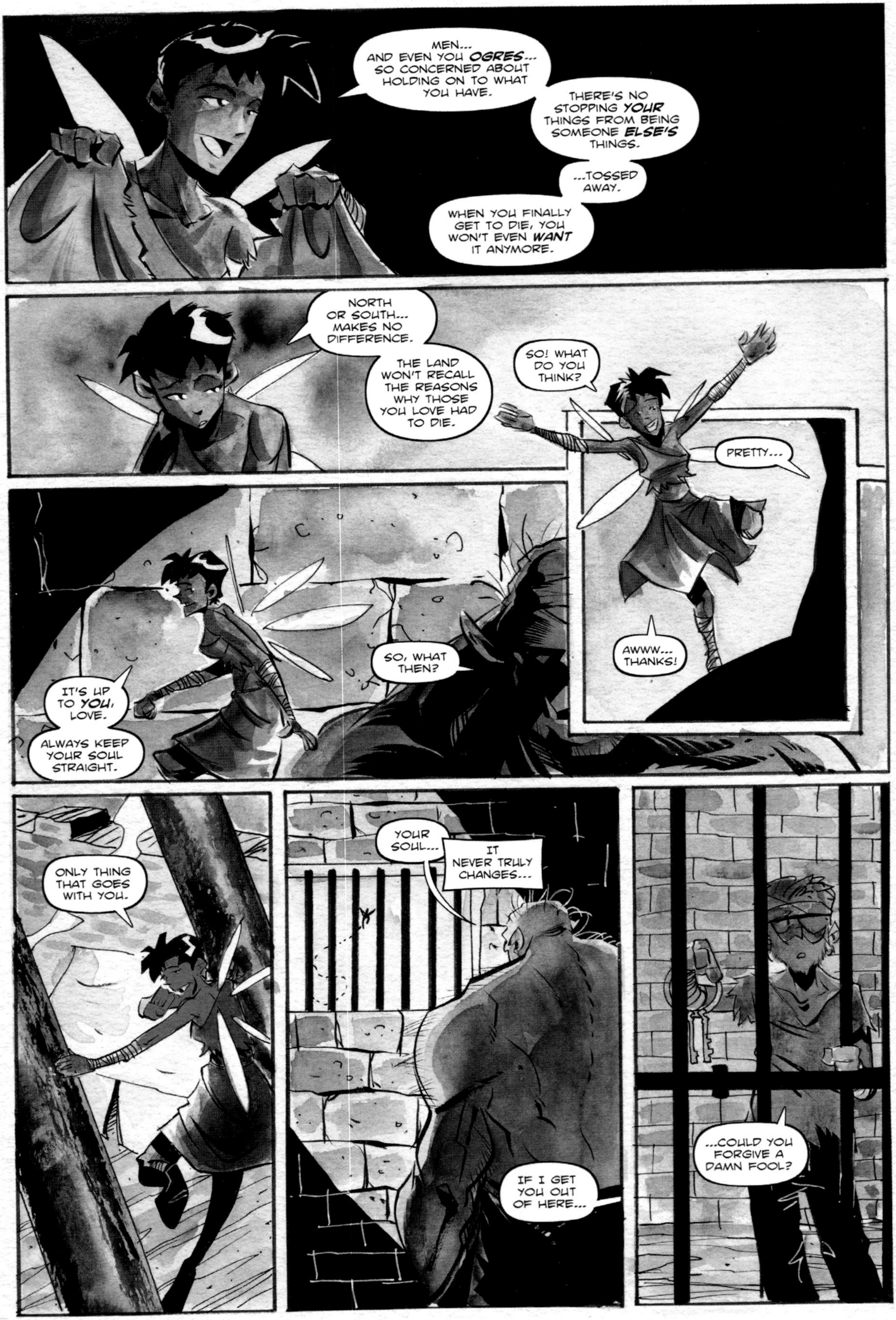
MEN... AND EVEN YOU OGRES... SO CONCERNED ABOUT HOLDING ON TO WHAT YOU HAVE.
THERE'S NO STOPPING YOUR THINGS FROM BEING SOMEONE ELSE'S THINGS.
...TOSSED AWAY.
WHEN YOU FINALLY GET TO DIE, YOU WON'T EVEN WANT IT ANYMORE.
NORTH OR SOUTH... MAKES NO DIFFERENCE.
THE LAND WON'T RECALL THE REASONS WHY THOSE YOU LOVE HAD TO DIE.
SO! WHAT DO YOU THINK?
PRETTY...
AWWW... THANKS!
SO, WHAT THEN?
IT'S UP TO YOU, LOVE.
ALWAYS KEEP YOUR SOUL STRAIGHT.
ONLY THING THAT GOES WITH YOU.
YOUR SOUL...
IT NEVER TRULY CHANGES...
IF I GET YOU OUT OF HERE...
...COULD YOU FORGIVE A DAMN FOOL?

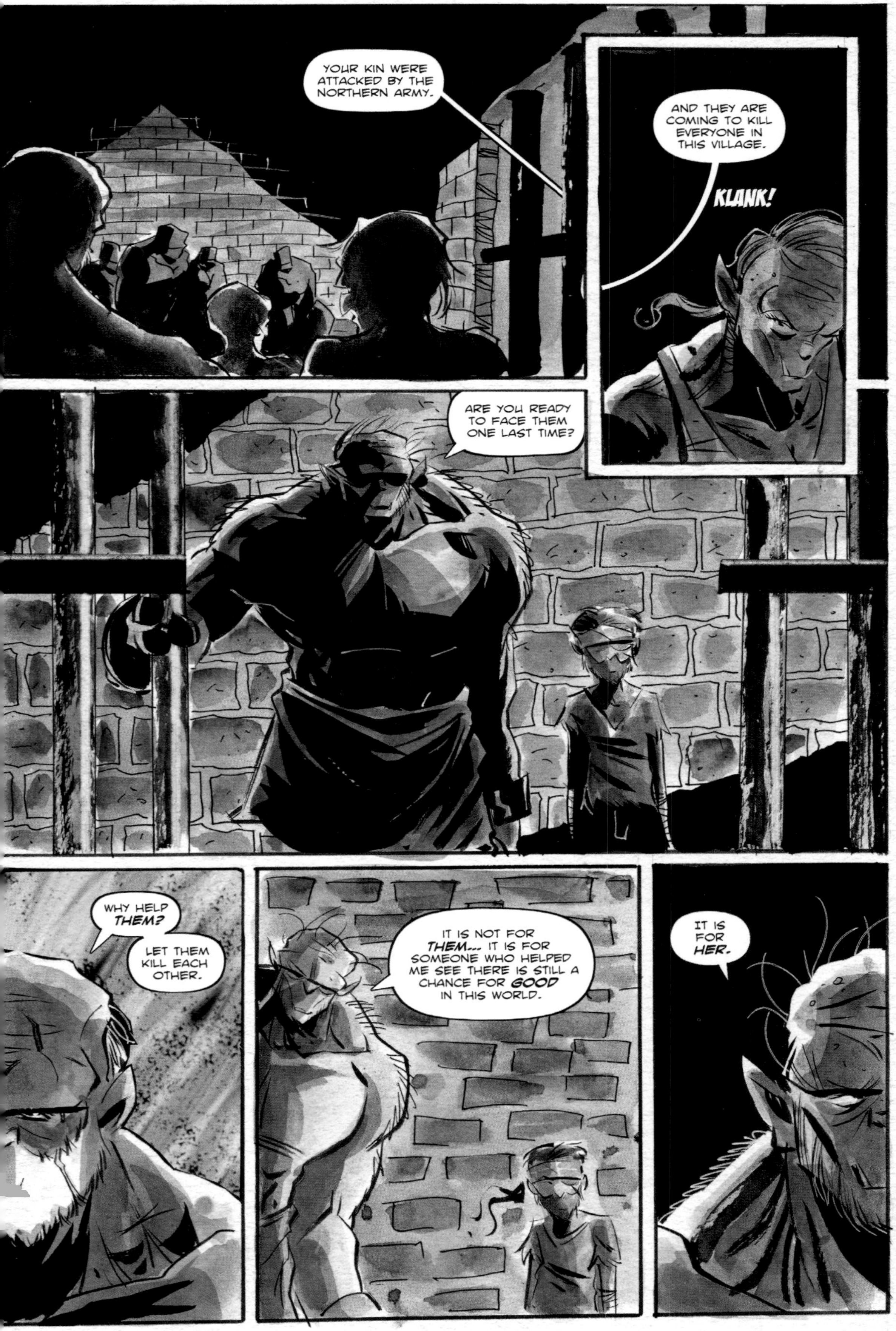
YOUR KIN WERE ATTACKED BY THE NORTHERN ARMY.
AND THEY ARE COMING TO KILL EVERYONE IN THIS VILLAGE.
KLANK!
ARE YOU READY TO FACE THEM ONE LAST TIME?
WHY HELP THEM?
LET THEM KILL EACH OTHER.
IT IS NOT FOR THEM... IT IS FOR SOMEONE WHO HELPED ME SEE THERE IS STILL A CHANCE FOR GOOD IN THIS WORLD.
IT IS FOR HER.

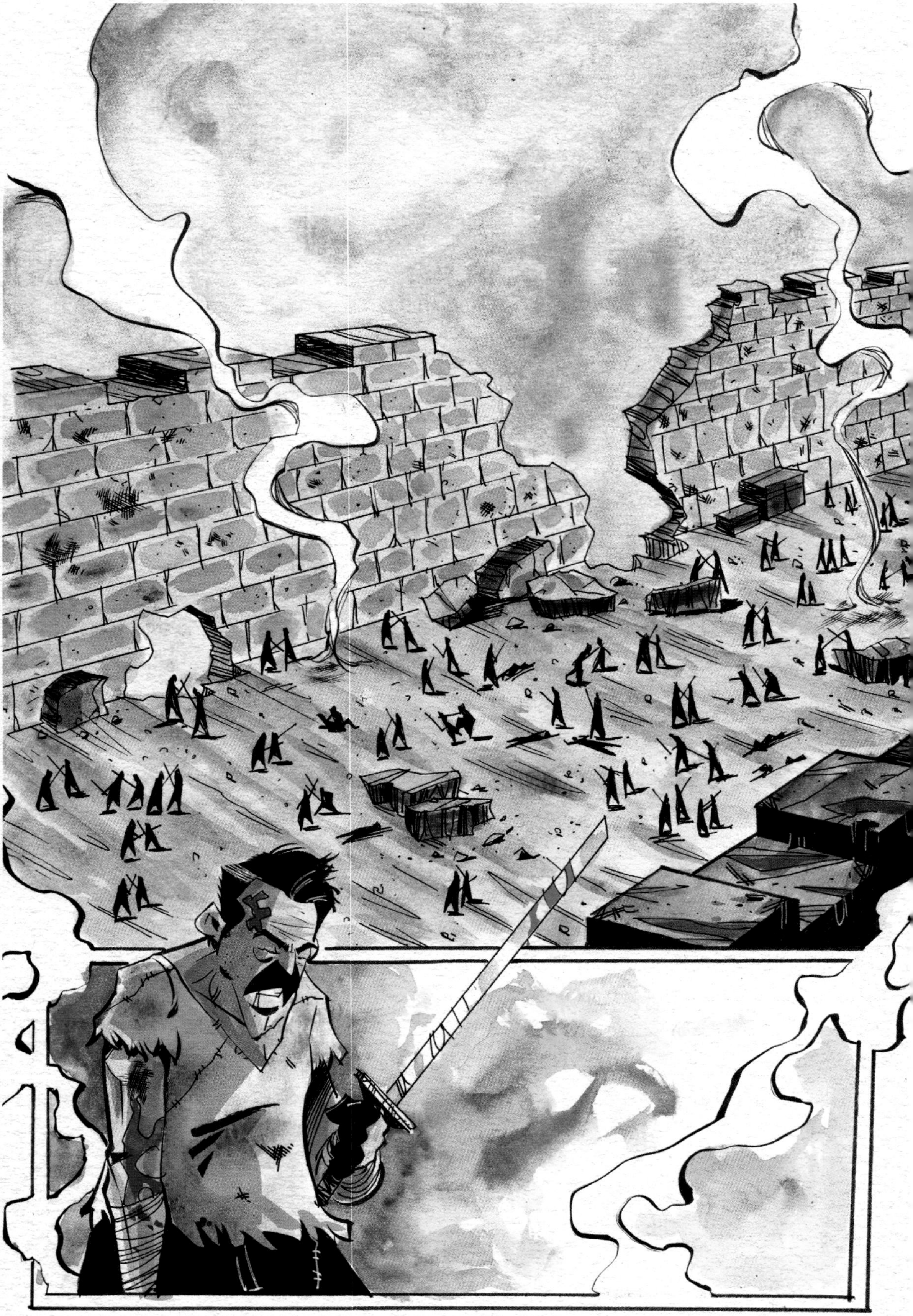

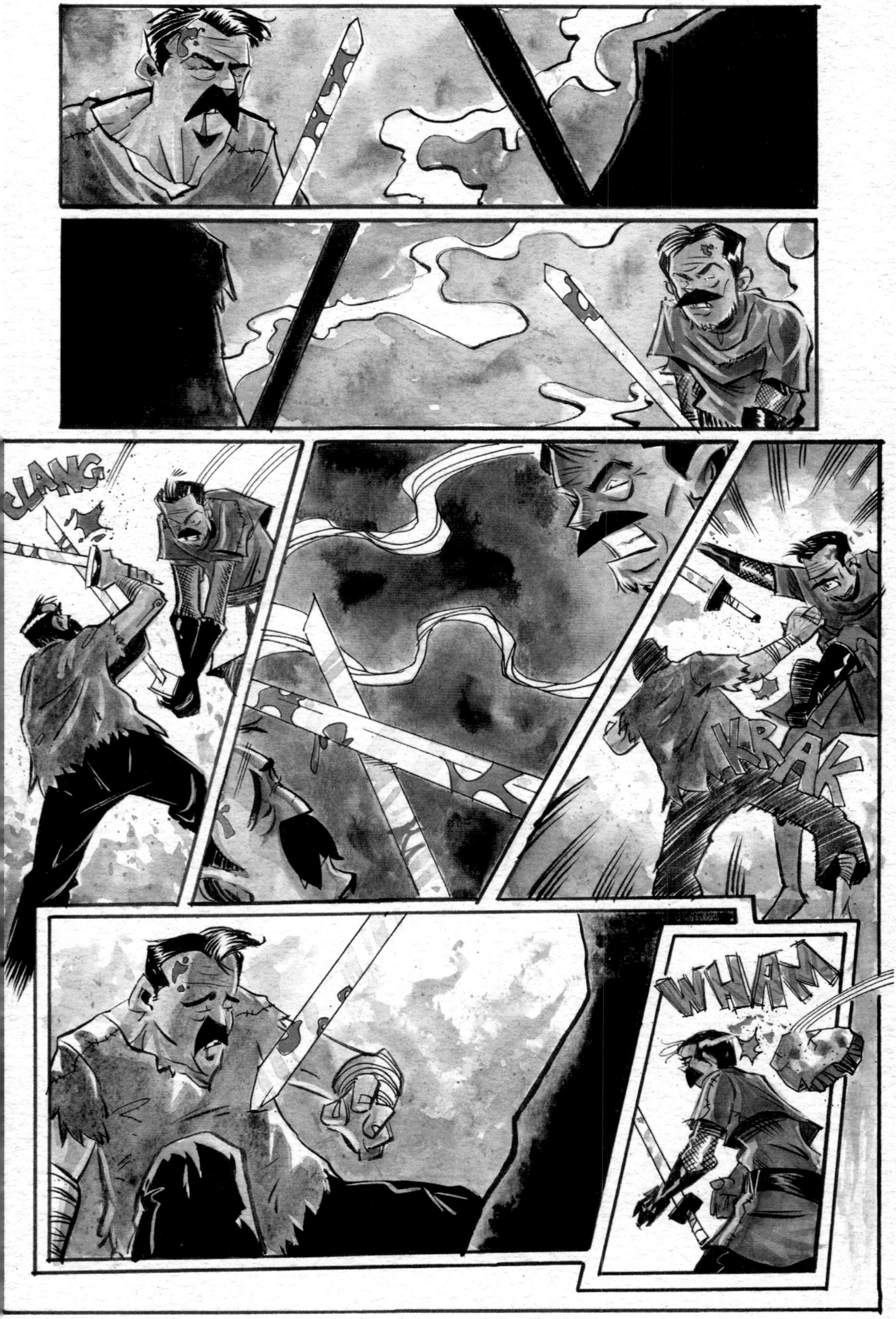
CLANG
KRAK
WHAM

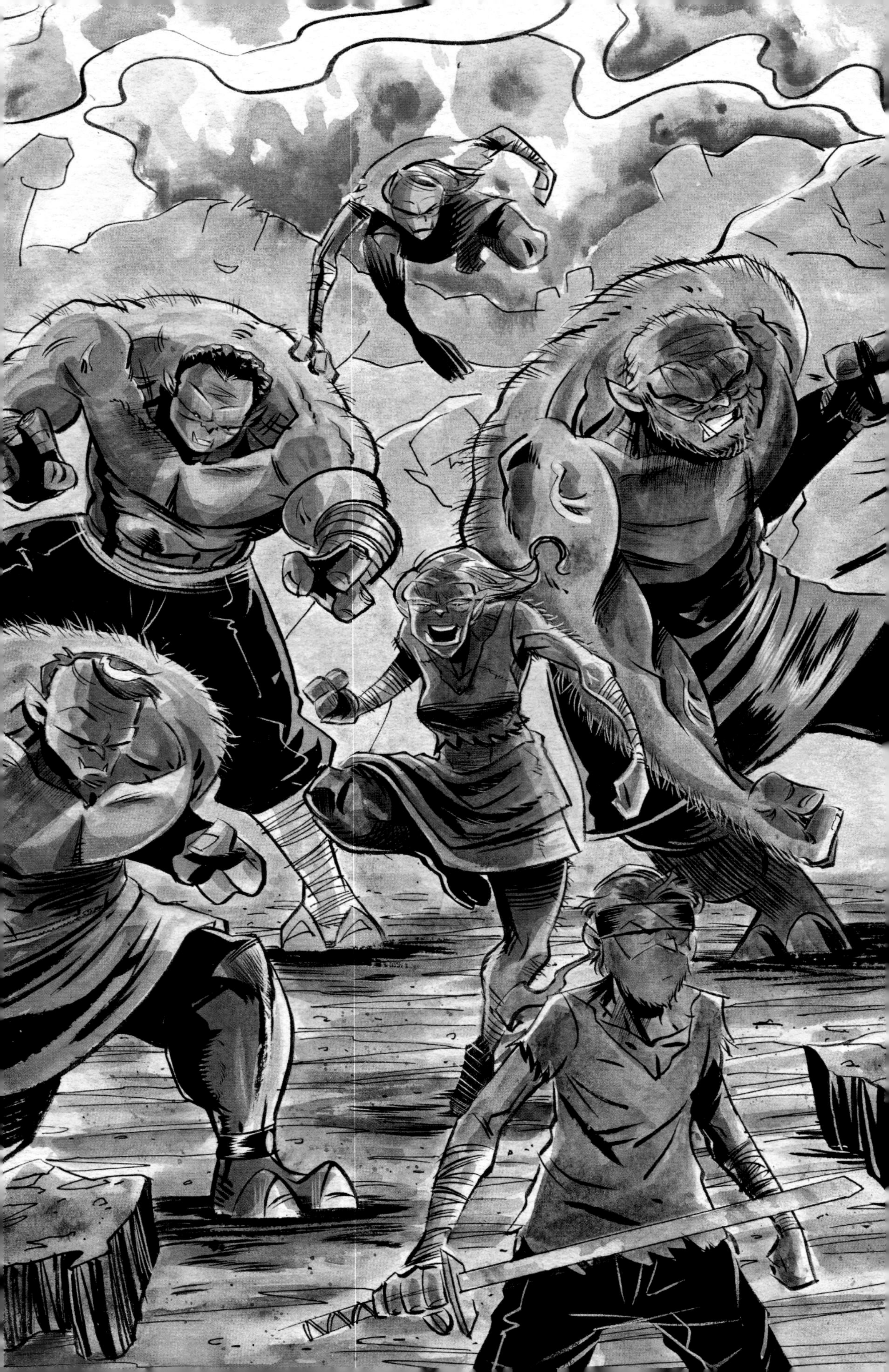

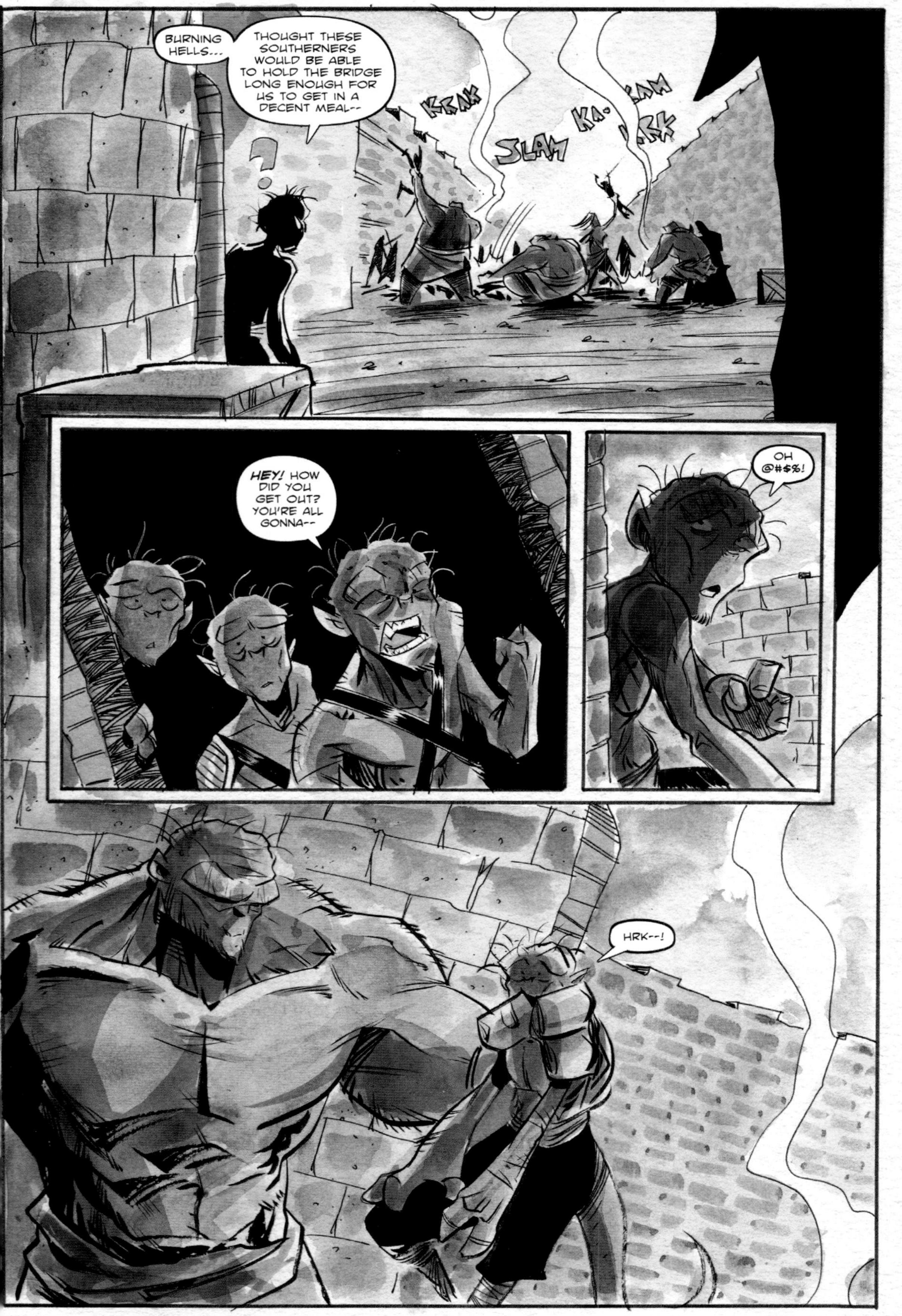
BURNING HELLS...
THOUGHT THESE SOUTHERNERS WOULD BE ABLE TO HOLD THE BRIDGE LONG ENOUGH FOR US TO GET IN A DECENT MEAL--
KRAK
SLAM
KA-
?
HEY! HOW DID YOU GET OUT? YOU'RE ALL GONNA--
OH @#$%!
HRK--!

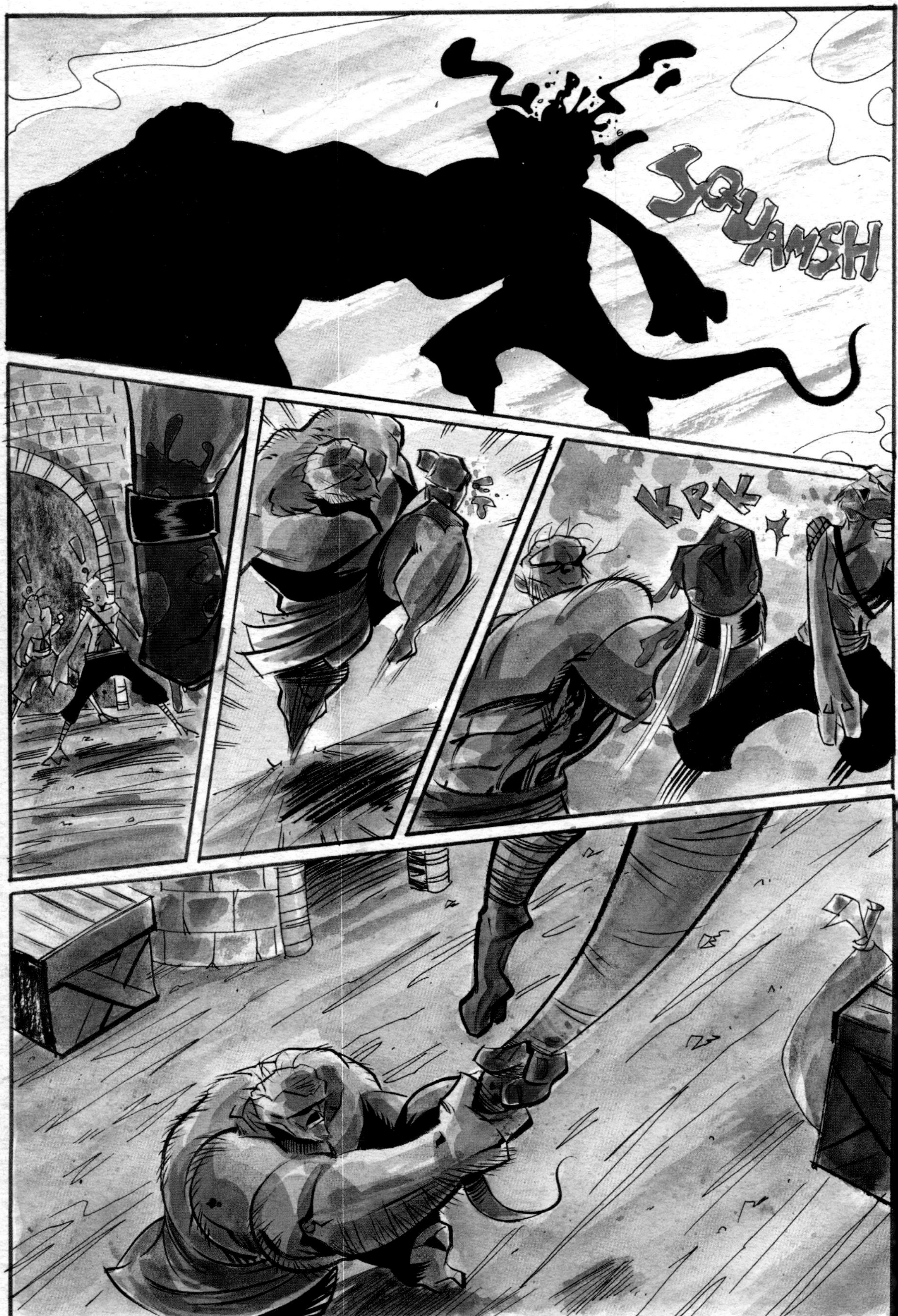
SQUAMSH
KRK

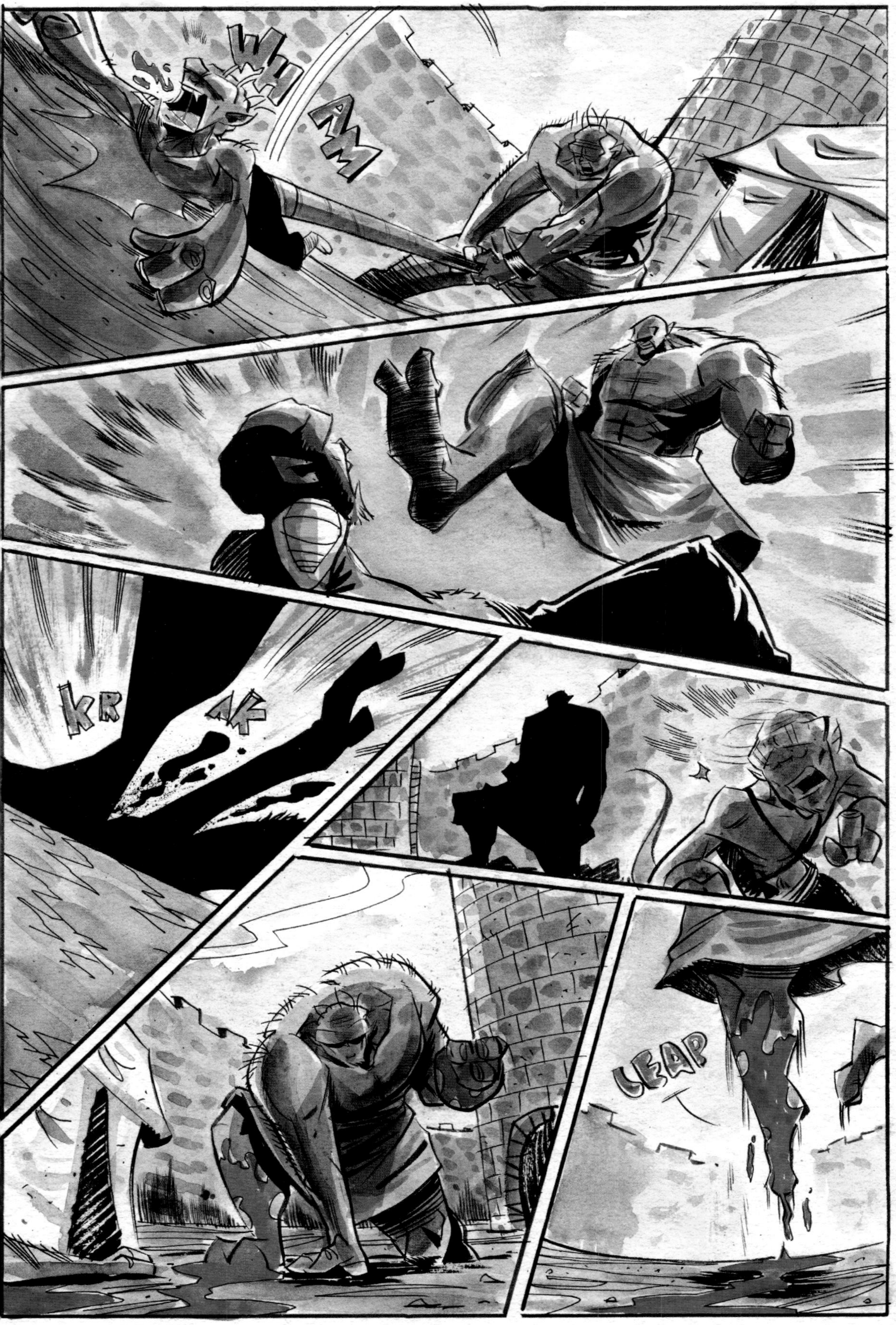
WHAM
KRAK
LEAP

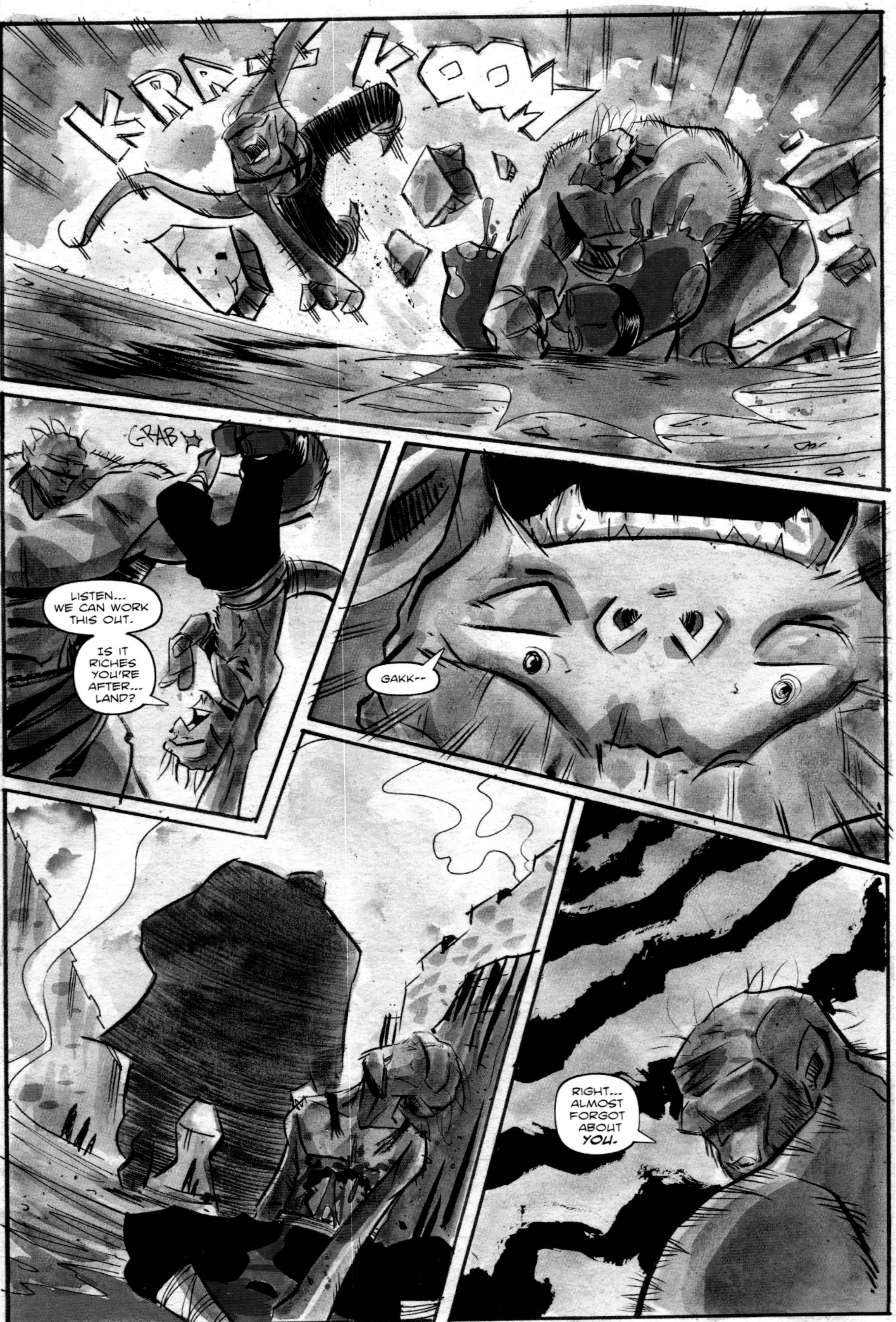
KRA-KOOM
GRAB
LISTEN... WE CAN WORK THIS OUT.
IS IT RICHES YOU'RE AFTER... LAND?
GAKK--
RIGHT... ALMOST FORGOT ABOUT *YOU*.

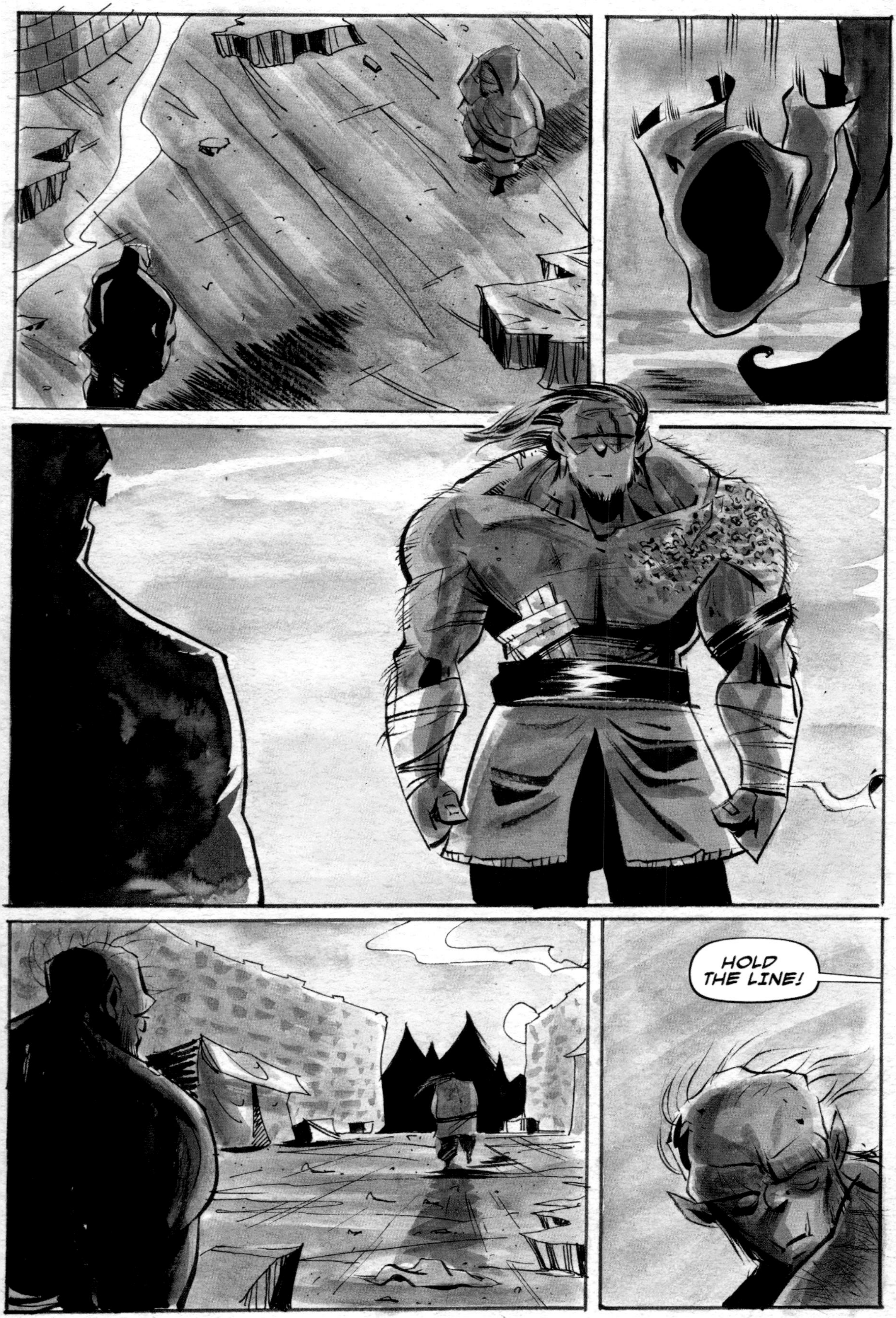
HOLD THE LINE!

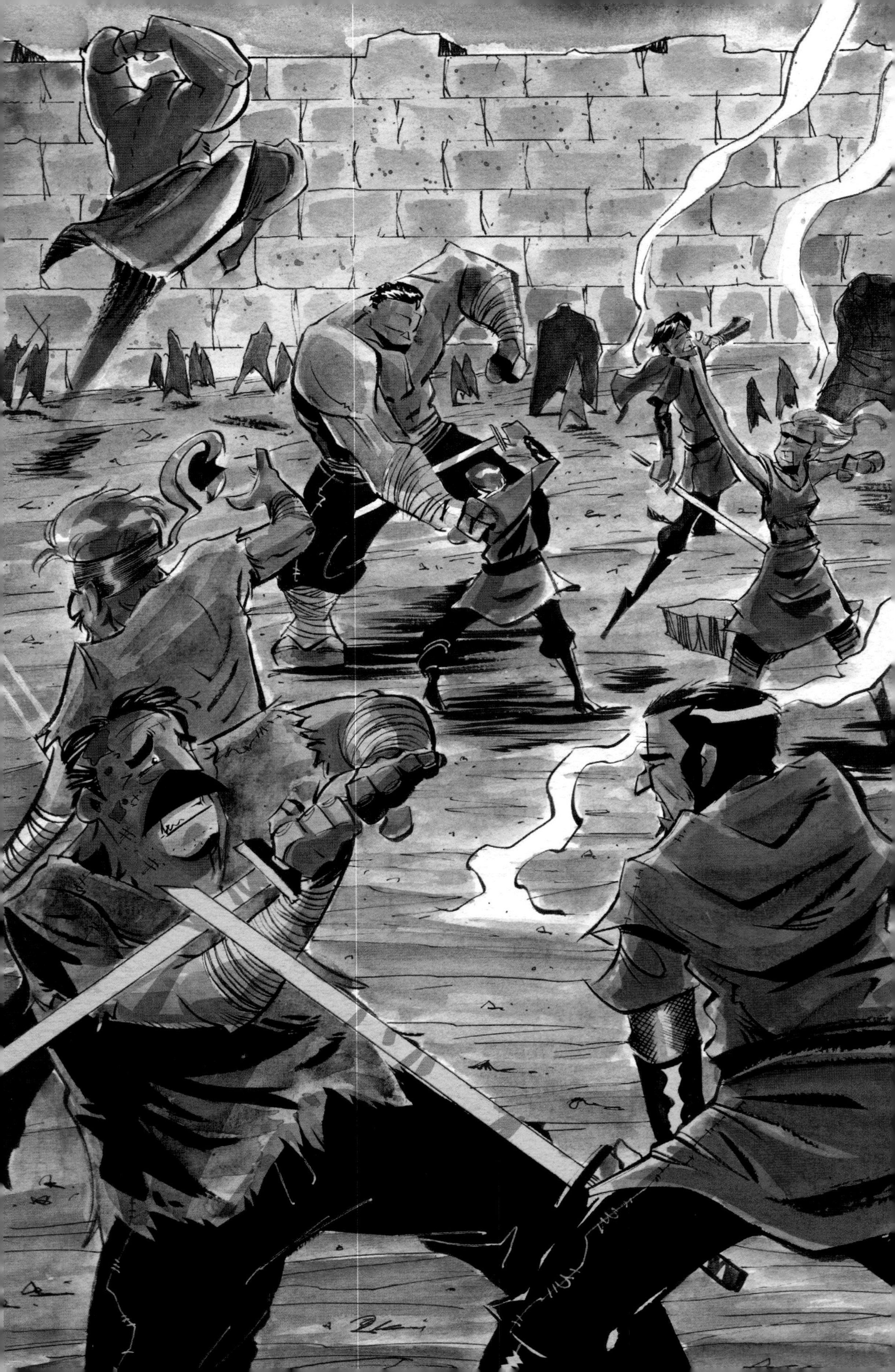

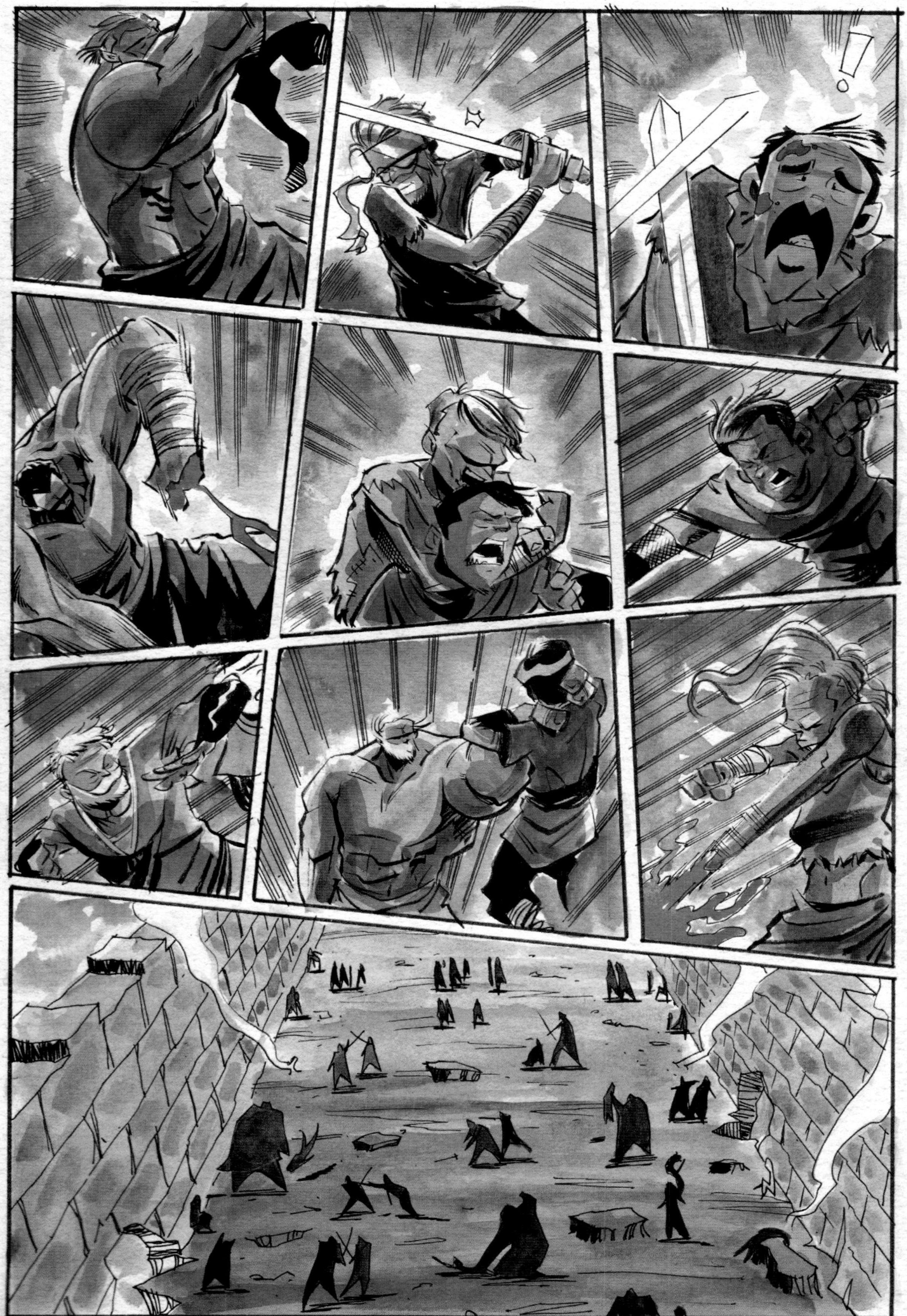
!

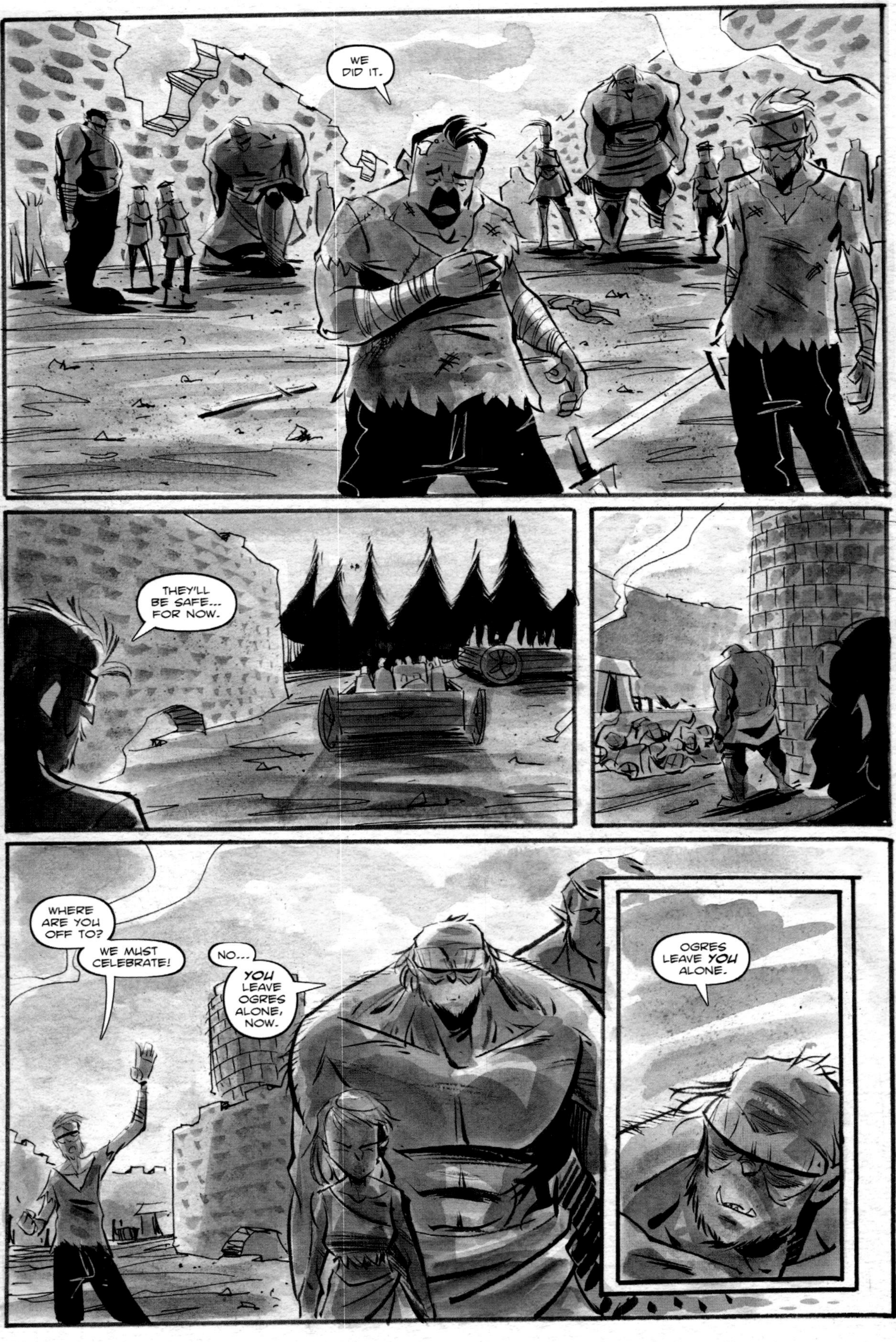
WE DID IT.
THEY'LL BE SAFE... FOR NOW.
WHERE ARE YOU OFF TO?
WE MUST CELEBRATE!
NO...
YOU LEAVE OGRES ALONE, NOW.
OGRES LEAVE YOU ALONE.

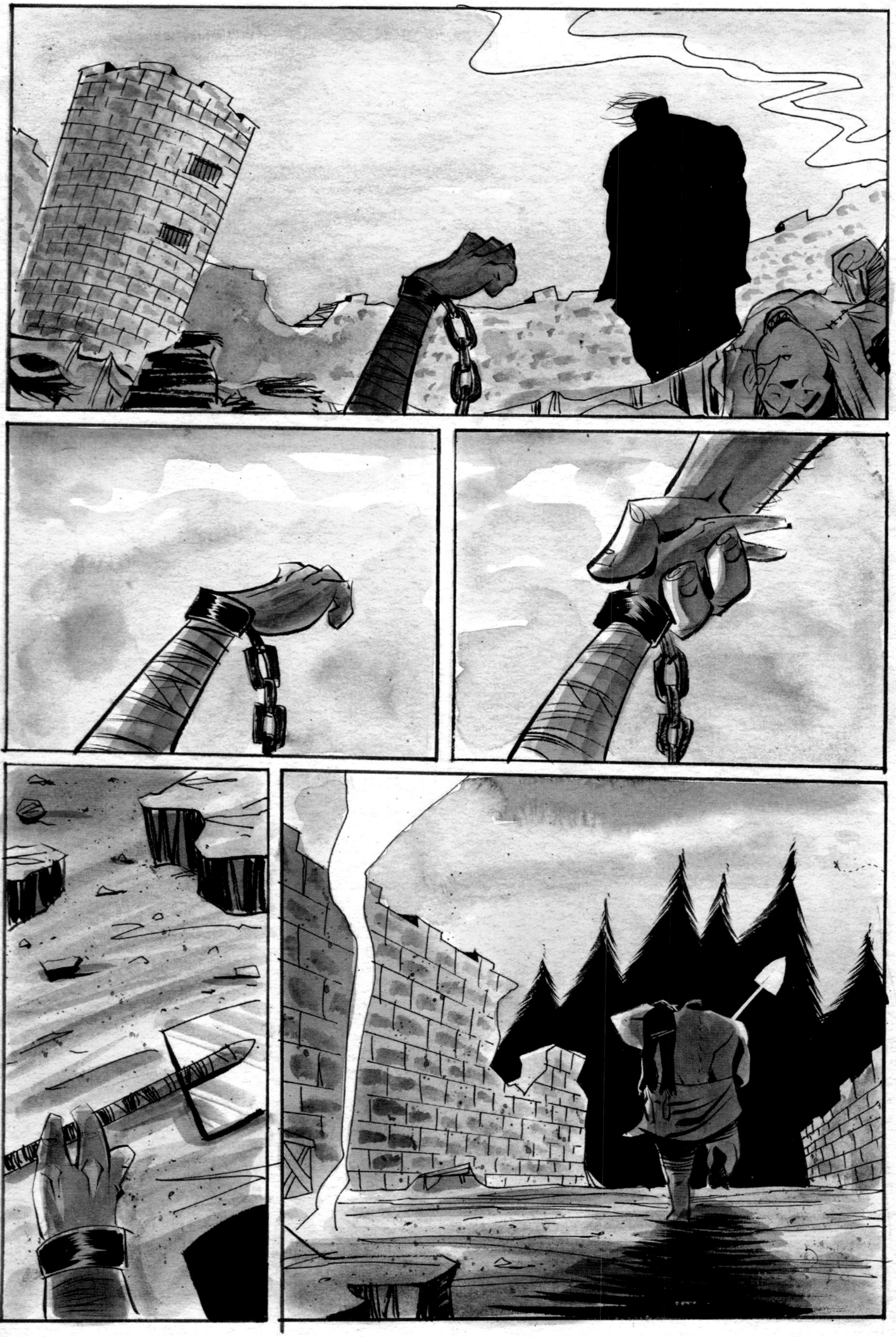

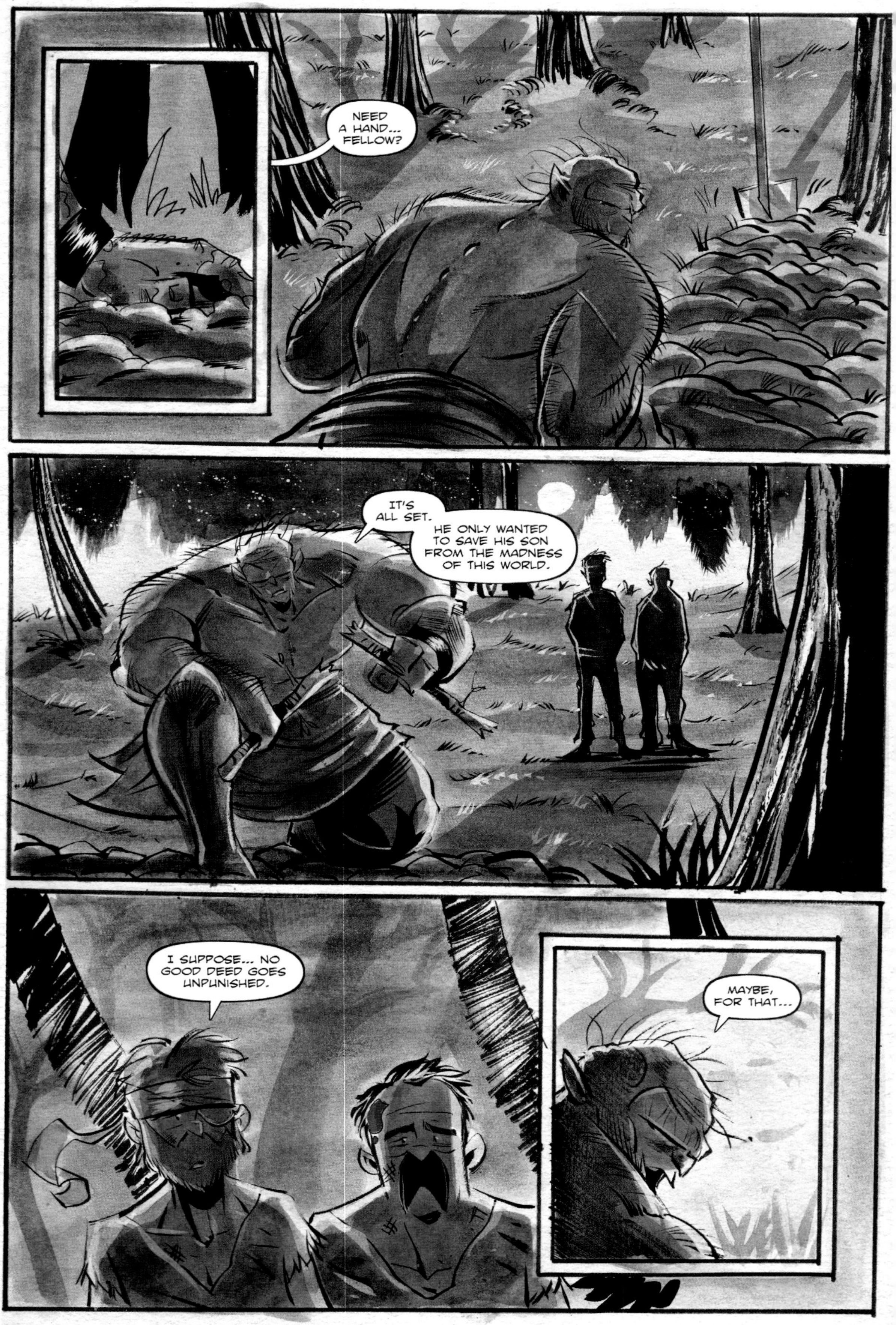
NEED A HAND... FELLOW?
IT'S ALL SET.
HE ONLY WANTED TO SAVE HIS SON FROM THE MADNESS OF THIS WORLD.
I SUPPOSE... NO GOOD DEED GOES UNPUNISHED.
MAYBE, FOR THAT...

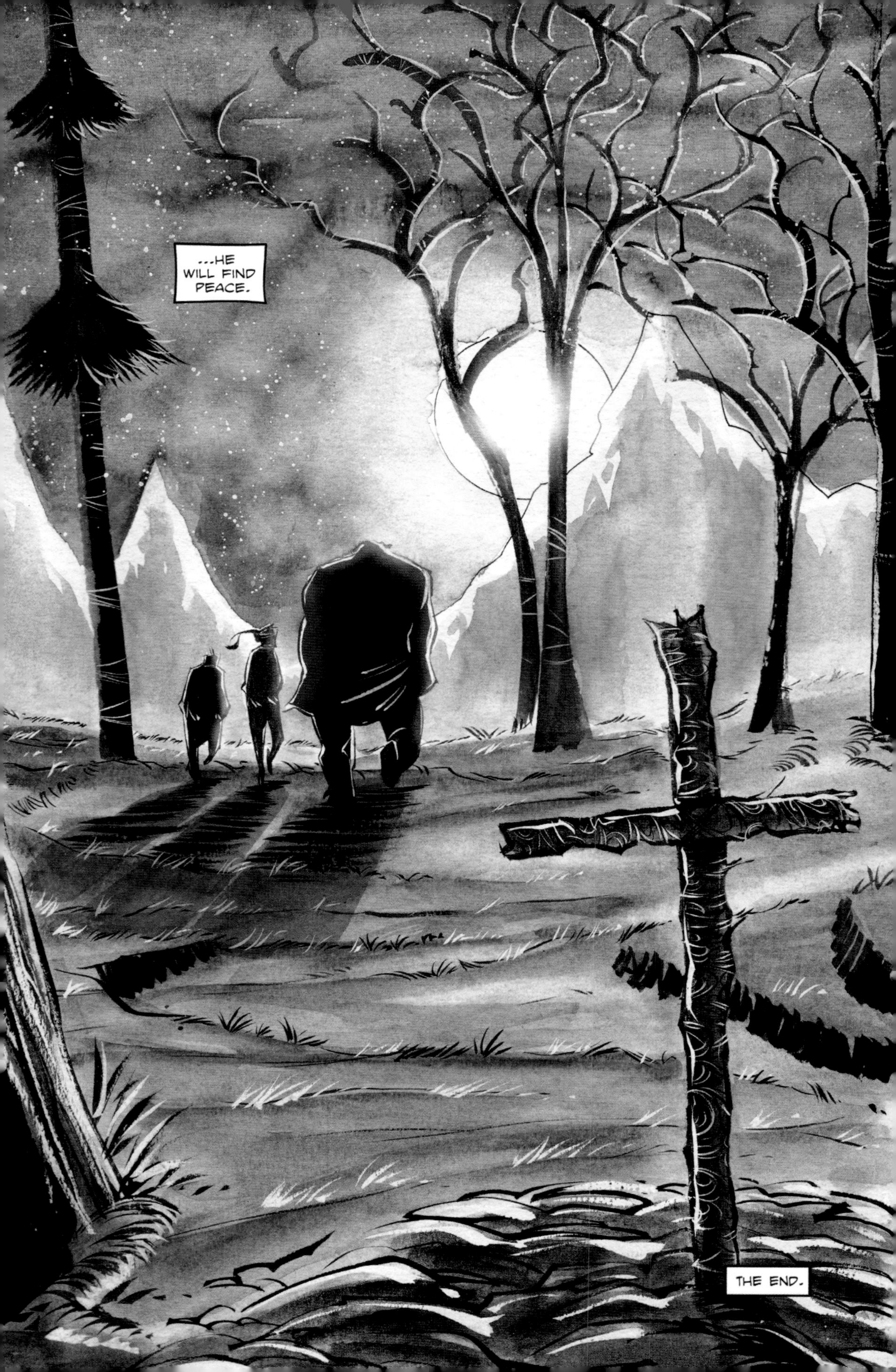
...HE WILL FIND PEACE.
THE END.

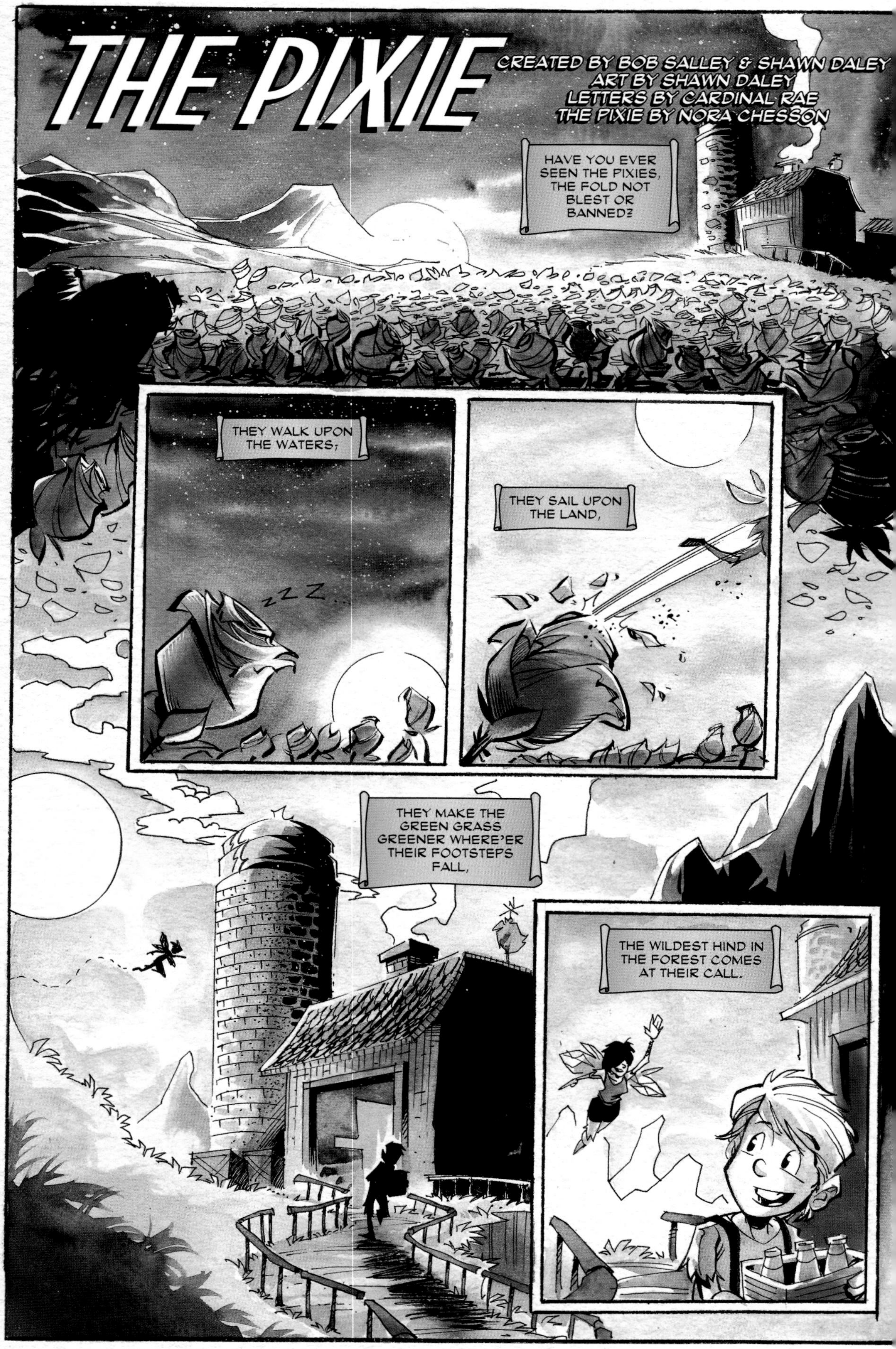
THE PIXIE
CREATED BY BOB SALLEY & SHAWN DALEY
ART BY SHAWN DALEY
LETTERS BY CARDINAL RAE
THE PIXIE BY NORA CHESSON
HAVE YOU EVER SEEN THE PIXIES, THE FOLD NOT BLEST OR BANNED?
THEY WALK UPON THE WATERS;
ZZZ...
THEY SAIL UPON THE LAND,
THEY MAKE THE GREEN GRASS GREENER WHERE'ER THEIR FOOTSTEPS FALL,
THE WILDEST HIND IN THE FOREST COMES AT THEIR CALL.

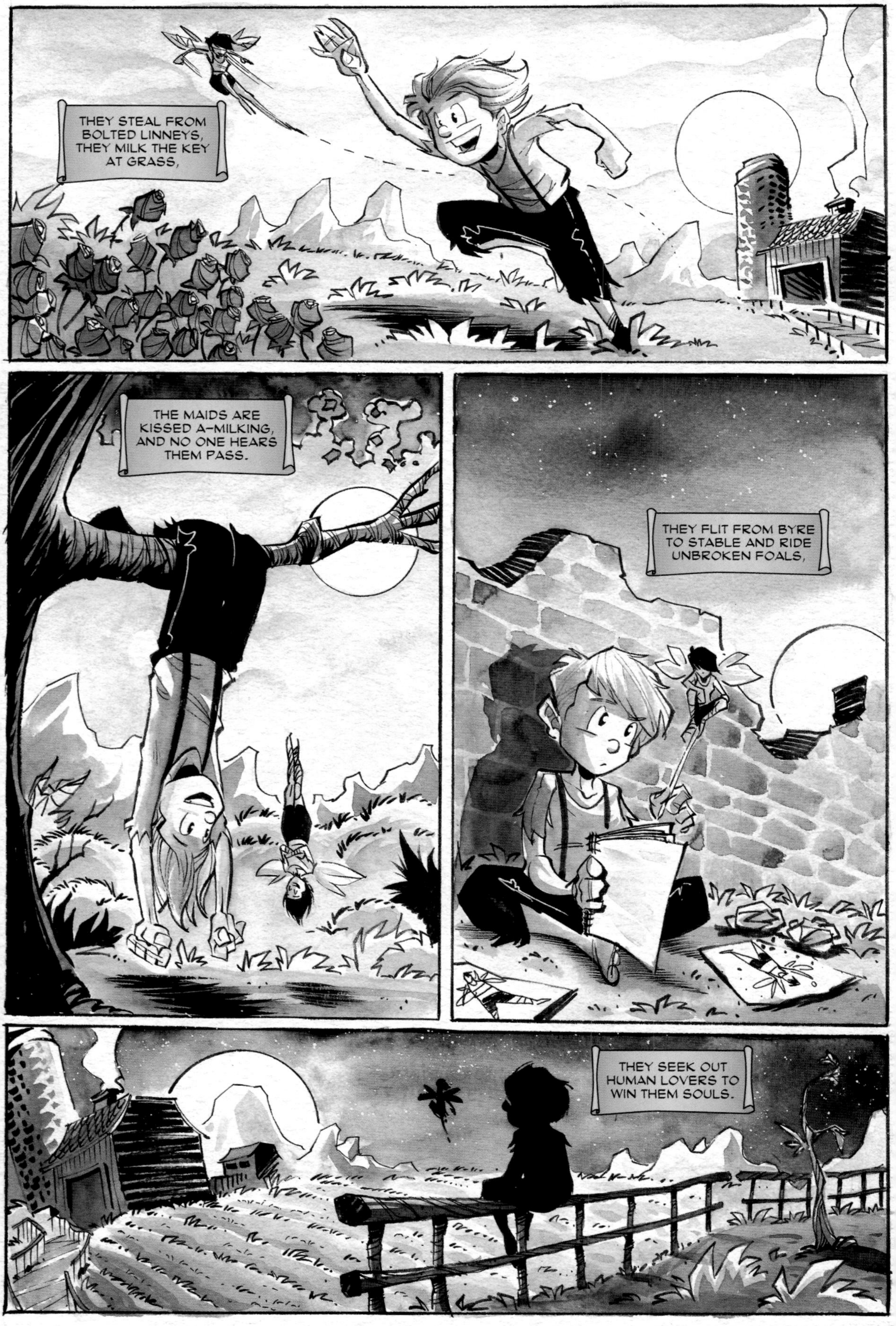
THEY STEAL FROM BOLTED LINNEYS, THEY MILK THE KEY AT GRASS,
THE MAIDS ARE KISSED A-MILKING, AND NO ONE HEARS THEM PASS.
THEY FLIT FROM BYRE TO STABLE AND RIDE UNBROKEN FOALS,
THEY SEEK OUT HUMAN LOVERS TO WIN THEM SOULS.

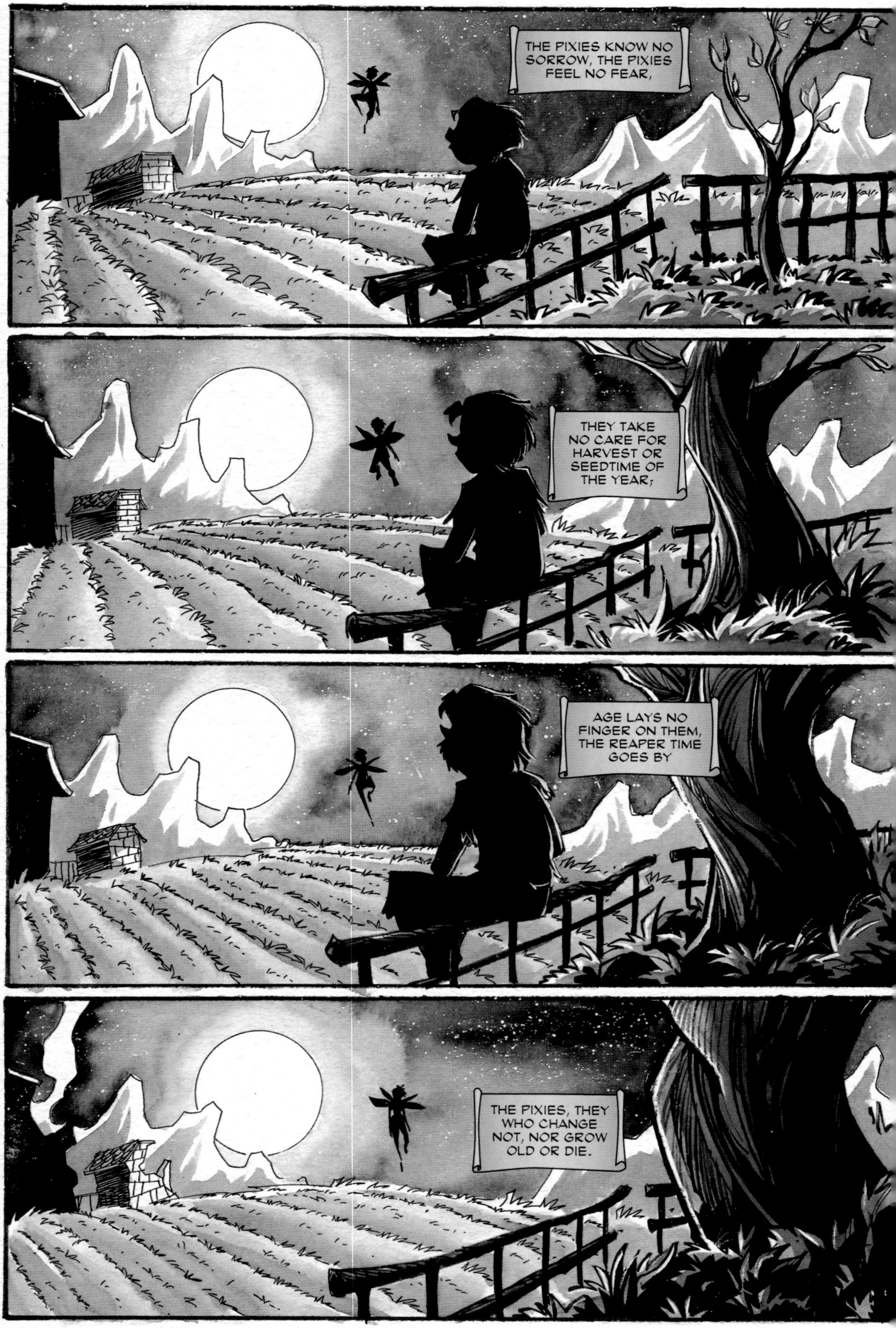
THE PIXIES KNOW NO SORROW, THE PIXIES FEEL NO FEAR,
THEY TAKE NO CARE FOR HARVEST OR SEEDTIME OF THE YEAR;
AGE LAYS NO FINGER ON THEM, THE REAPER TIME GOES BY
THE PIXIES, THEY WHO CHANGE NOT, NOR GROW OLD OR DIE.

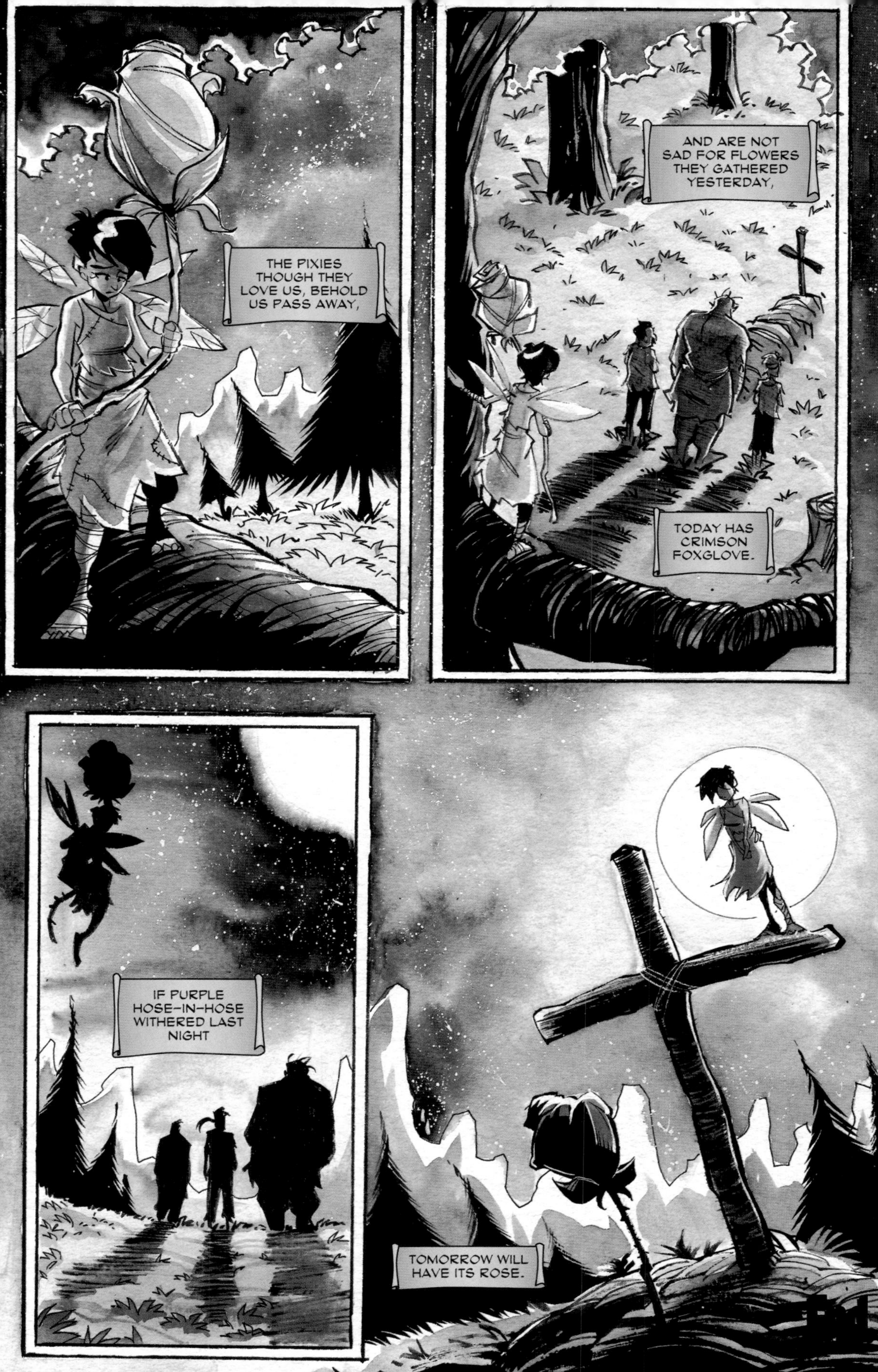
THE PIXIES THOUGH THEY LOVE US, BEHOLD US PASS AWAY,
AND ARE NOT SAD FOR FLOWERS THEY GATHERED YESTERDAY,
TODAY HAS CRIMSON FOXGLOVE.
IF PURPLE HOSE-IN-HOSE WITHERED LAST NIGHT
TOMORROW WILL HAVE ITS ROSE.

Ogre #1 2nd Printing Variant Cover by Katie Cook.

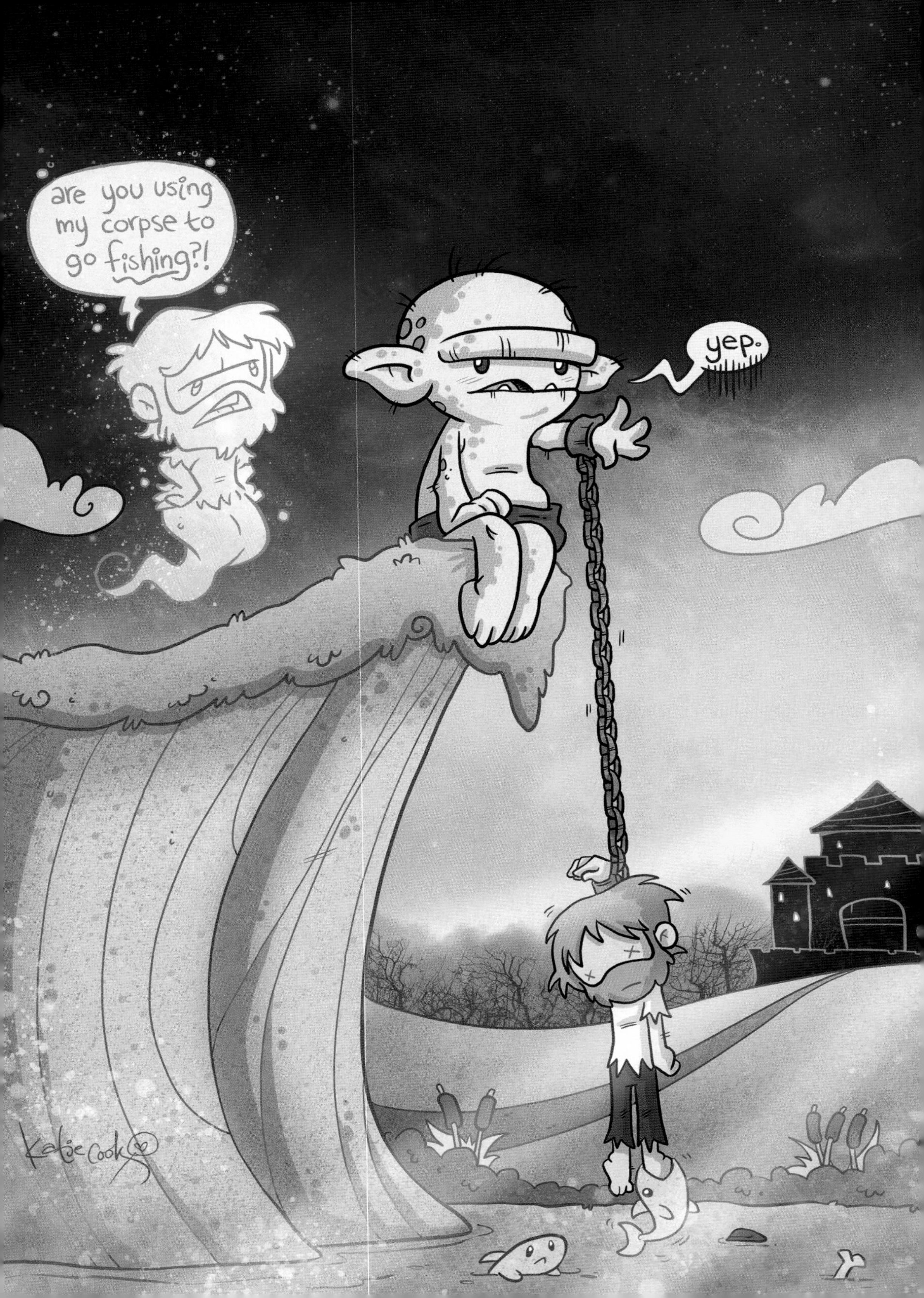
are you using my corpse to go fishing?!
yep.
Katie Cook

Ogre #1 variant cover by Jay Fosgitt for Black Cape Comics.

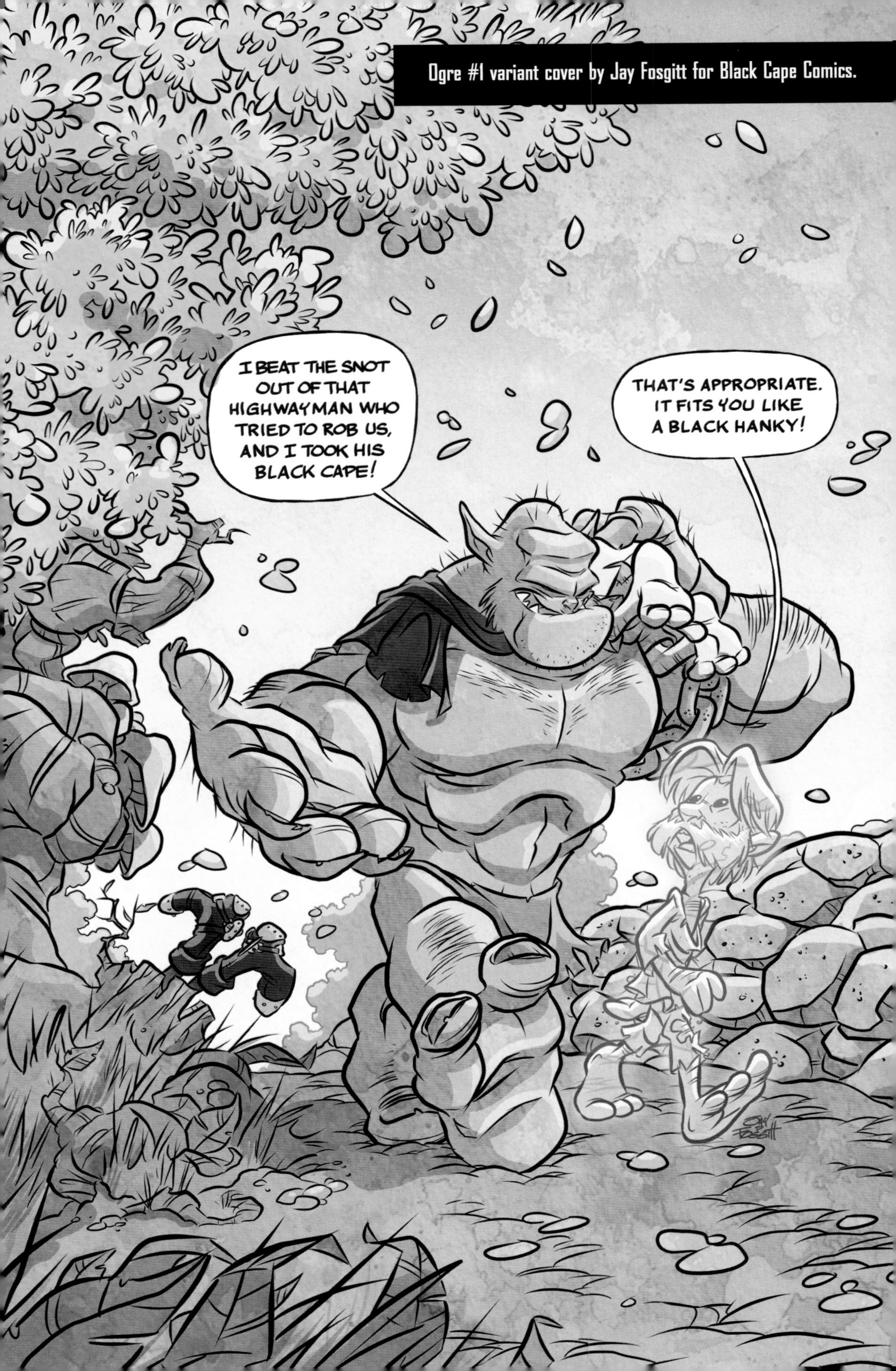
I BEAT THE SNOT OUT OF THAT HIGHWAYMAN WHO TRIED TO ROB US, AND I TOOK HIS BLACK CAPE!
THAT'S APPROPRIATE. IT FITS YOU LIKE A BLACK HANKY!

Ogre #2 variant cover by Jay Fosgitt for Black Cape Comics.

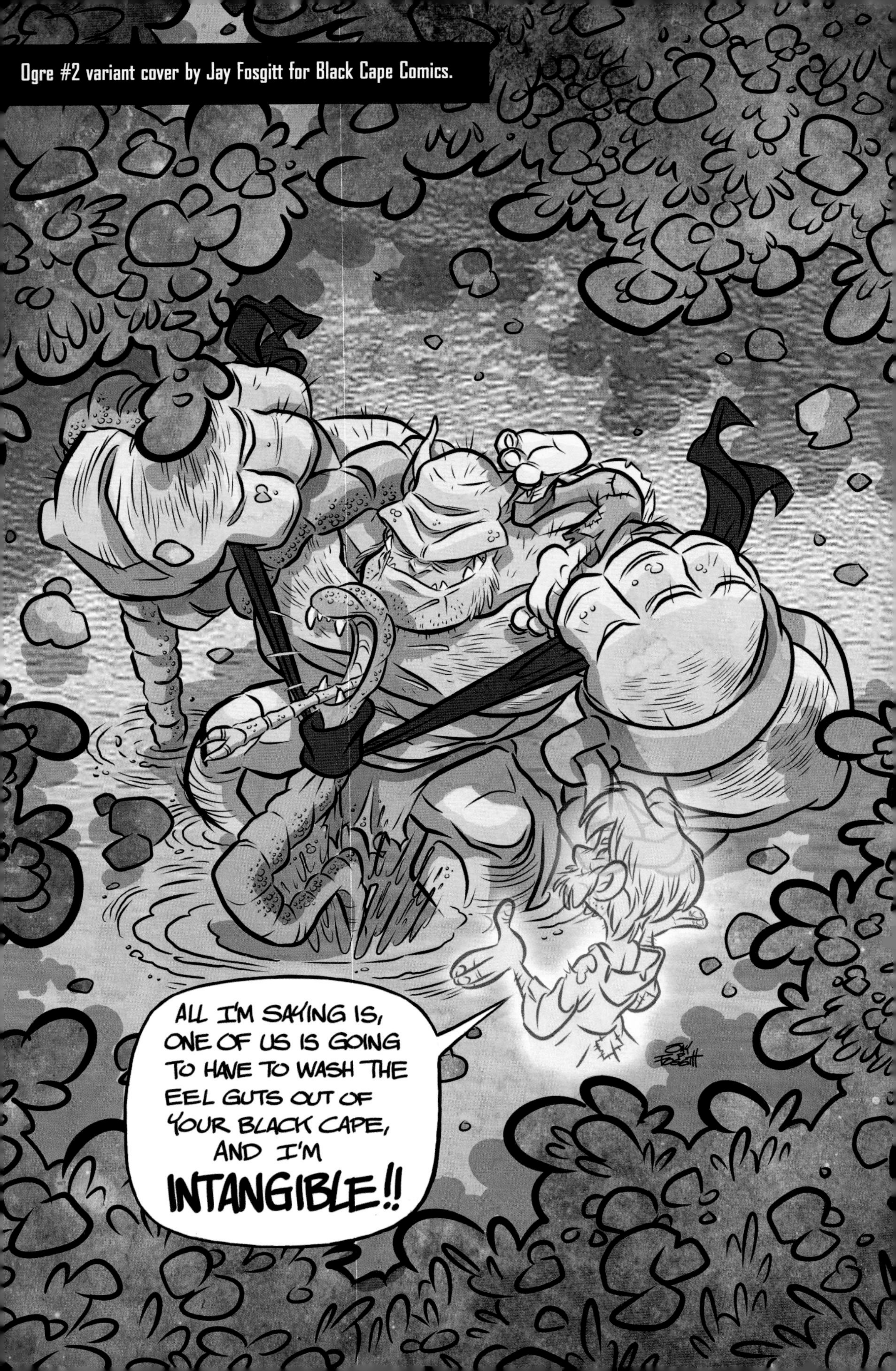
ALL I'M SAYING IS, ONE OF US IS GOING TO HAVE TO WASH THE EEL GUTS OUT OF YOUR BLACK CAPE, AND I'M INTANGIBLE!!

Ogre #3 variant cover by Jay Fosgitt for Black Cape Comics.

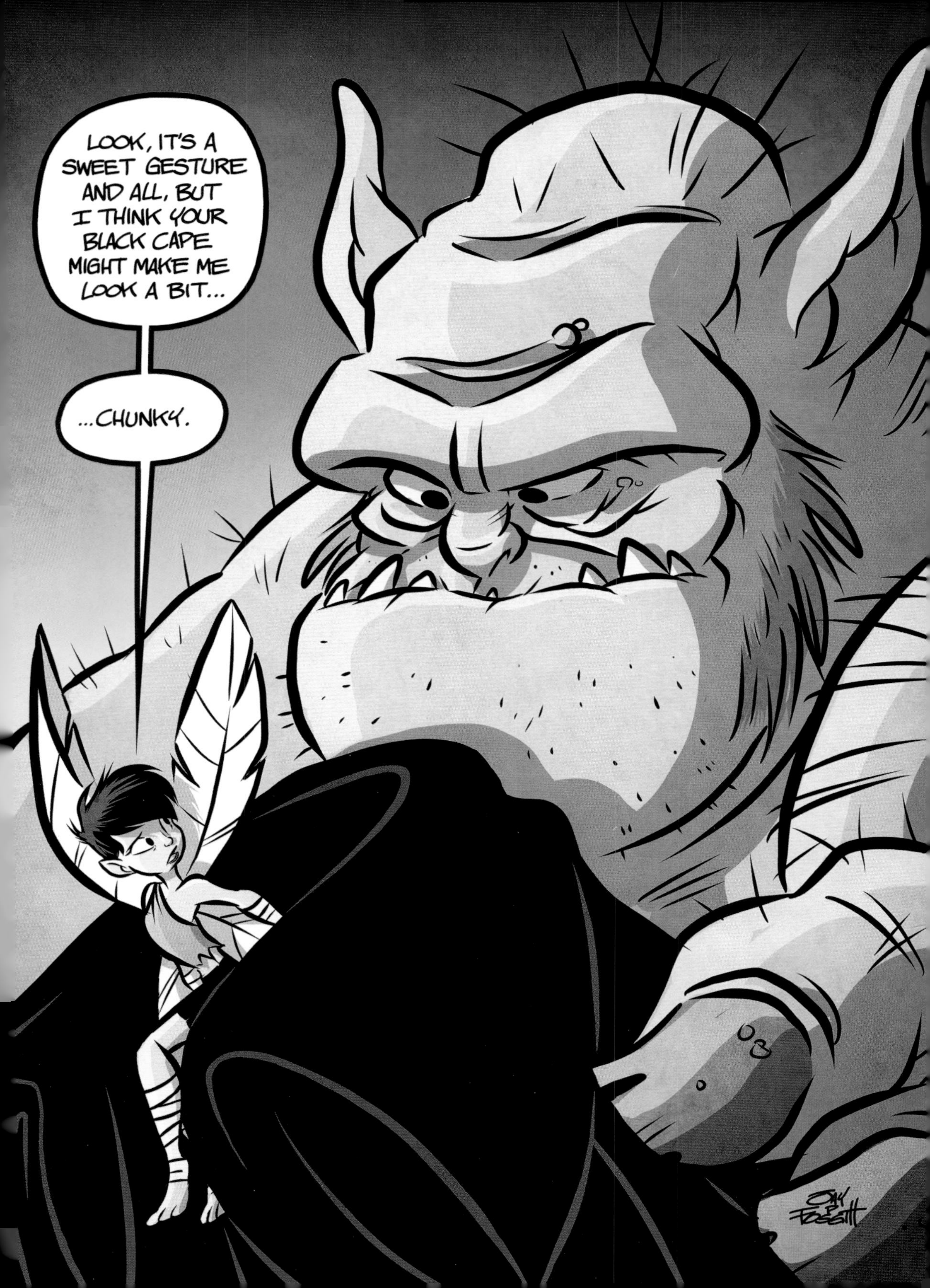
LOOK, IT'S A SWEET GESTURE AND ALL, BUT I THINK YOUR BLACK CAPE MIGHT MAKE ME LOOK A BIT...
...CHUNKY.

Ogre #1, 2 & 3 connecting variant covers by Shawn Daley for Exchange Collectibles.

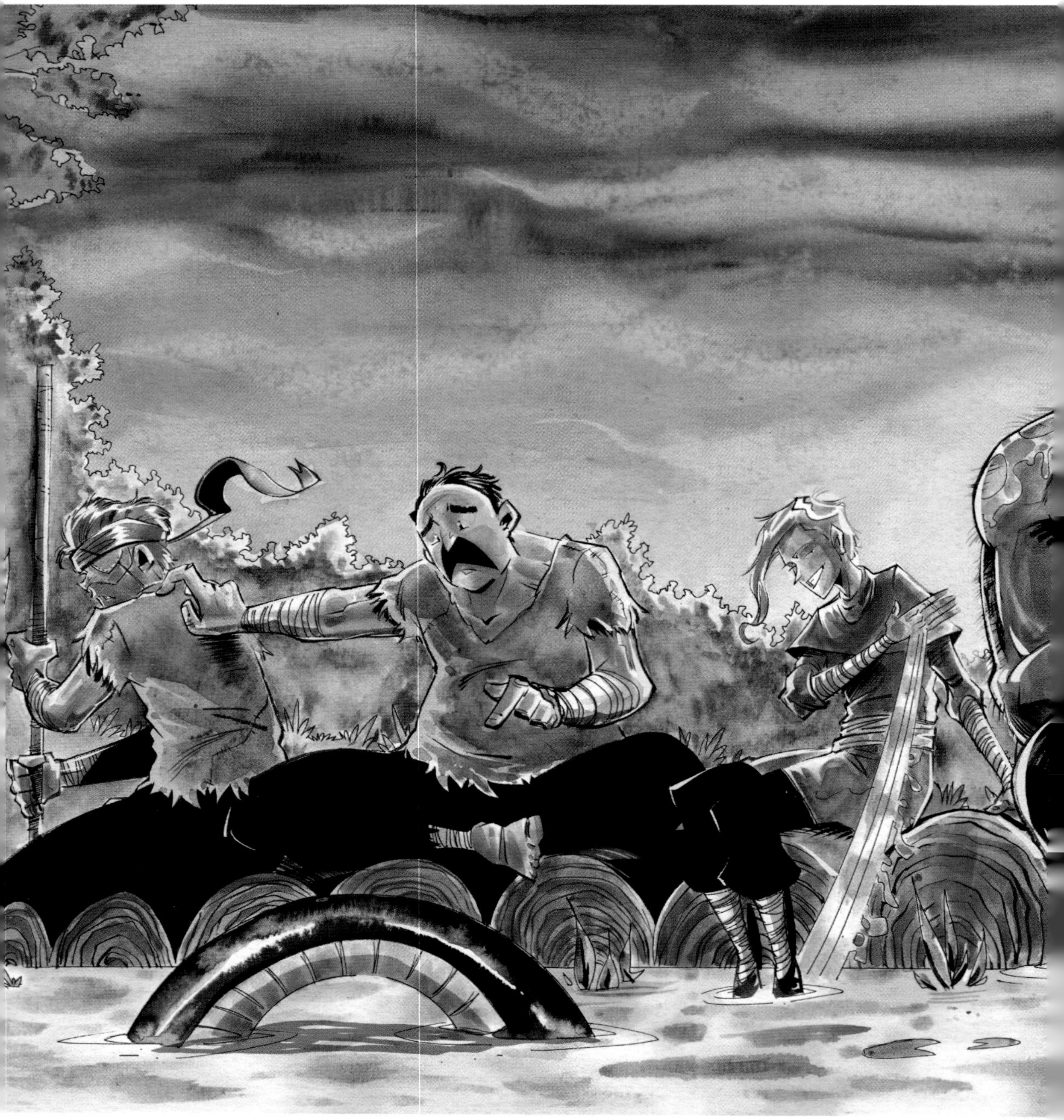

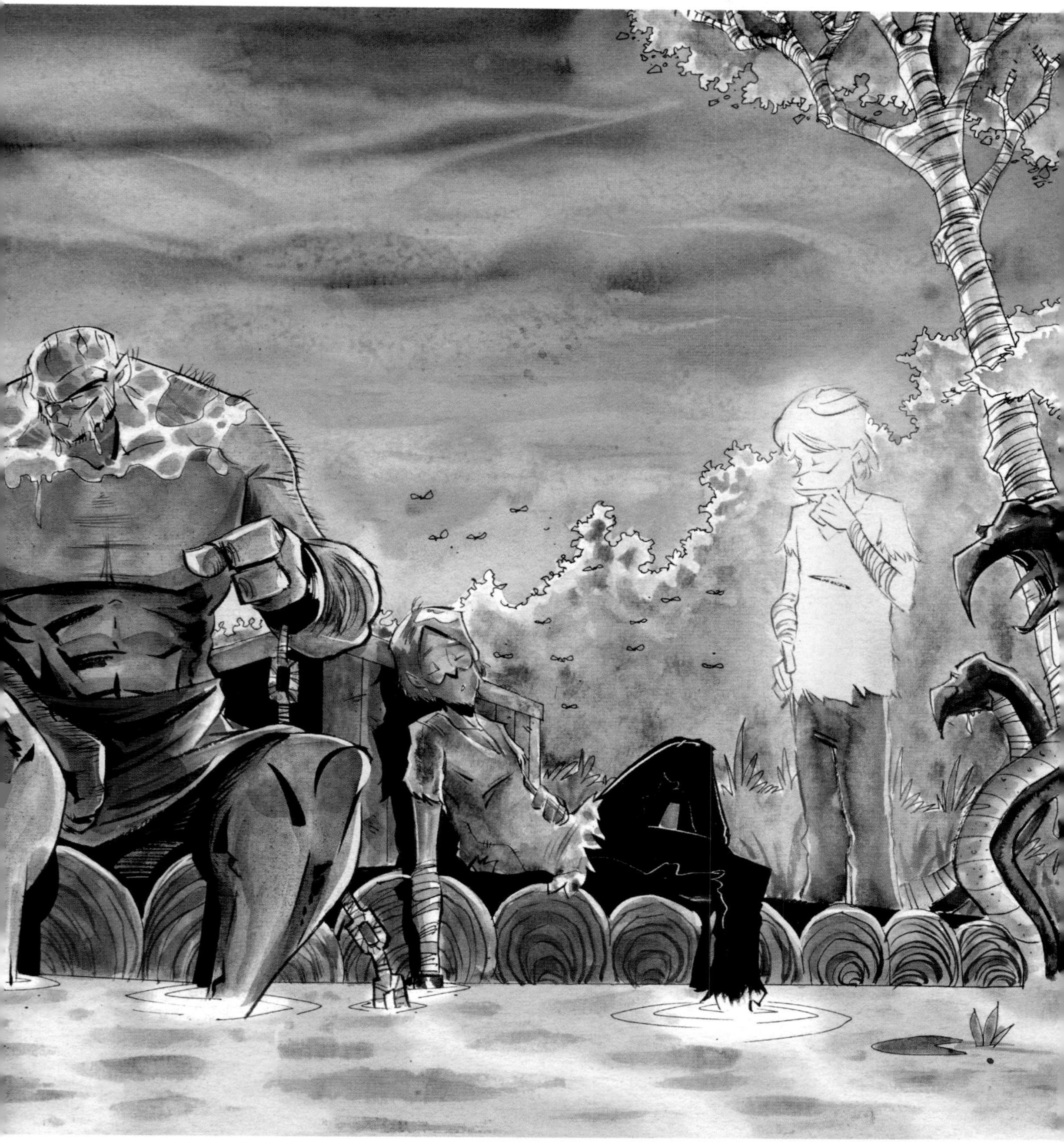

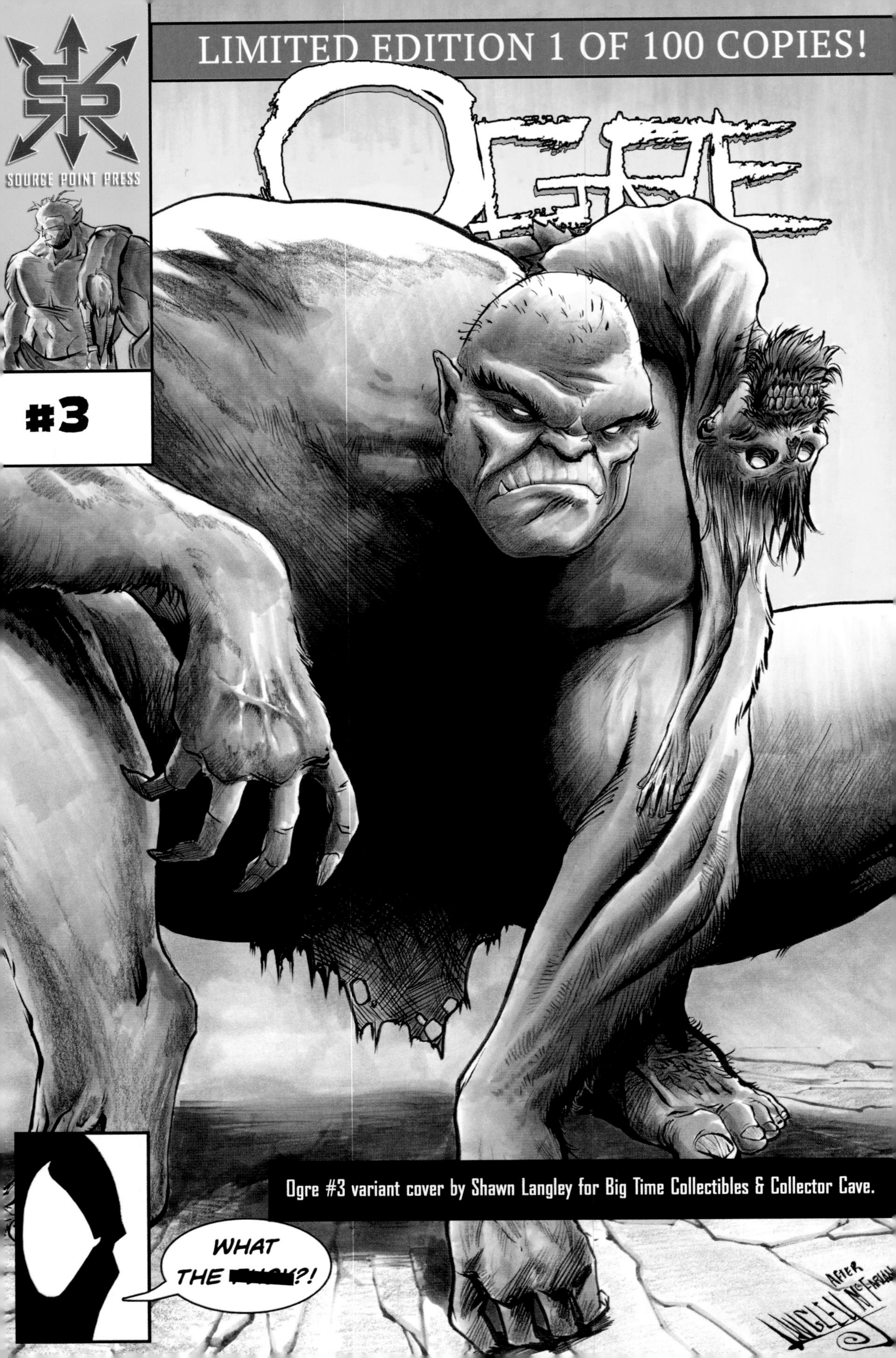
LIMITED EDITION 1 OF 100 COPIES!
OGRE
SOURCE POINT PRESS
#3
Ogre #3 variant cover by Shawn Langley for Big Time Collectibles & Collector Cave.
WHAT THE [redacted]?!

Ogre #3 variant cover by Shawn Daley for the Indie Spotlight Series.

OGRE PIN-UP ARTWORK BY STAN YAK.

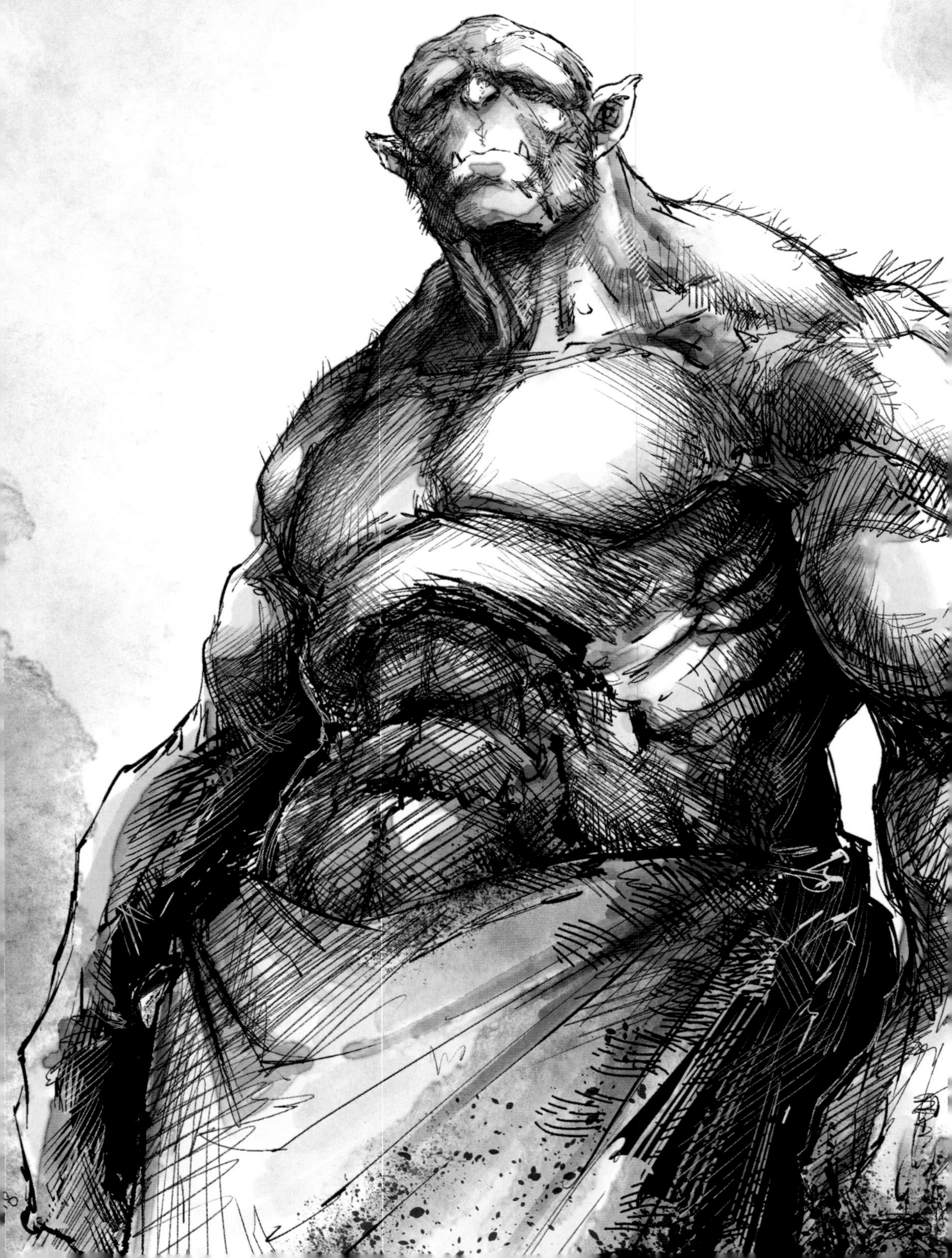

PAGE PROCESS

HERE'S A LOOK AT THE PAGE PROCESS FROM LAYOUTS TO INKS, SEEN BELOW IS THE FIRST STEP OF THE PROCESS AFTER RECEIVING THE SCRIPT. THESE LAYOUTS ARE QUICK SKETCHES, AND MAKE SURE THAT THE PAGE FLOWS PROPERLY WHEN IT COMES TO DRAWING IT. I CONSIDER A FEW DIFFERENT THINGS WHEN LAYING OUT A PAGE:

- HOW MUCH ROOM WILL BE NEEDED FOR DIALOGUE AND CAPTIONS?
- WHICH 'CAMERA ANGLE' BALANCES BOTH CLARITY AND THEME?
- WHAT ELEMENTS CAN BE USED AS 'ANCHORS' TO DRAW THE EYE THROUGH THE PAGE?
- IS THE PAGE COMPOSITION DYNAMIC AND INTERESTING?
- DOES THIS PAGE TRANSITION CLEARLY INTO AND OUT OF THE PAGES BEFORE AND AFTER IT?

I SOMETIMES TAKE A LITTLE LONGER THAN I LIKE WITH LAYOUTS, OVERTHINKING THEIR PRODUCTION. MANY TIMES, I'VE LAYED OUT A PAGE THREE OR FOUR TIMES BEFORE DECIDING ON WHICH TO USE FOR PENCILS. AND ALMOST EVERY TIME, I END UP CHOOSING MY FIRST DESIGN. THERE'S NOTHING WRONG WITH TRYING OUT A NUMBER OF IDEAS AND CIRCLING BACK TO THE ORIGINAL. I RECOMMEND TRYING NOT TO OVERTHINK YOUR LAYOUTS. DON'T FEEL BAD ABOUT KEEPING YOUR FIRST TAKES. I WAS TAUGHT THAT THE FIRST TAKE IS THE OBVIOUS ONE, AND THEREFORE LIKELY THE MOST UNINTERESTING. OVER THE YEARS, I'M NOT SURE I CAN COMPLETELY AGREE WITH THAT. IN THAT, THE OBVIOUS CHOICE ISN'T NECESSARILY THE LESS INTERESTING CHOICE. NEVER SACRIFICE CLARITY FOR FLOURISH, UNLESS FOR THEMATIC REASONS.

WHEN THE SOUTHERN COWARDS RETREAT FROM THEIR CASTLE, THIS WILL BE THEIR ONLY WAY OUT.
THIS WILL BE WHERE WE FINISH THEM.
DEATH TO THE SOUTH.
ANY SURVIVORS WILL BE CUT DOWN BY THAT NORTHERN FLANK.
COME... IT'S NO LONGER OUR PROBLEM.
KEEP GOING UNTIL YOU REACH THE FIELDS.
OVER THE HILLS YOU'LL COME TO THE CAVES OF EAST. YOU'LL FIND HOME THEIR.
THANK YOU.

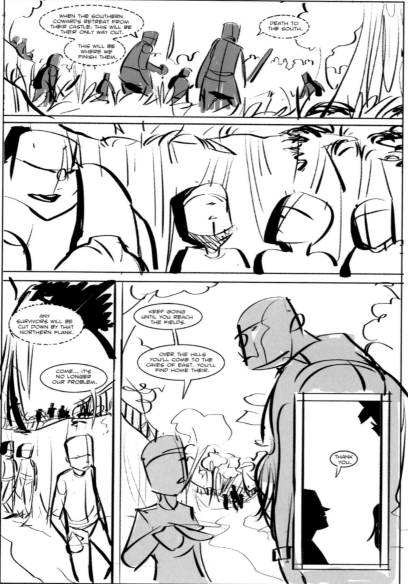

I TOOK A ROUGH PASS AT LETTERING RIGHT INTO THE LAYOUTS, IN ORDER TO MAKE SURE THAT THE DIALOGUE WOULD FIT PROPERLY.

ORIGINALLY, THE SCRIPT FOR THIS PAGE WAS SIX PANELS. WORKING WITH BOB IS ALWAYS A GREAT TIME, AS HE DOESN'T MIND WHEN I MAKE SOME SLIGHT STORYTELLING ALTERATIONS BY COMBINING PANELS WHEN IT CAN BE DONE.

THE LAST PANEL WAS PUT IN SILHOUETTE LAST MINUTE, AND THE OTHER CHARACTERS WERE REMOVED FROM THE BACKGROUND.

THIS WAS DONE FOR IMPACT. I WANTED SHON AND OGRE TO BE ALONE TOGETHER, JUST FOR A MOMENT - ENOUGH TIME TO SAY "THANK YOU".

IN OUR WORLD, IT'S ODD FOR A HUMAN TO SHOW KINDNESS TO AN OGRE. THOUGH IT'S A SMALL PANEL, ENOUGH ROOM TO BE CONSIDERED A SIDE-NOTE, IT ALSO STANDS OUT FROM THE OTHERS, AND ALMOST TAKE PLACE WITHIN A MOOD OF ITS OWN.

THIS IS MOSTLY DUE TO ITS SIMPLICITY. THOUGH IT WOULD STILL WORK PERFECTLY FINE WITH OTHER CHARACTERS IN THE BACKGROUND, OR WITH VISIBLE, DETAILED EXPRESSIONS, IT WOULDN'T FEEL ANY DIFFERENT THAN THE REST OF THE PAGE.

USE SIMPLICITY AS A TOOL TO CREATE CONTRAST AND IMPACT.

PENCILS

EVERYTHING WAS PENCILED ON 11X17 PIECES OF WATERCOLOUR PAPER. THE PENCILS ARE USUALLY VERY QUICK SKETCHES, NOT MUCH MORE DETAILED THAN THE LAYOUTS.

WHEN PENCILLING, I FOCUS ON A FEW ASPECTS:

CHARACTER EXPRESSIONS
THESE NEED TO BE CLEAR, MOVING INTO THE INKING PHASE. A CHARACTER'S EXPRESSION NEEDS TO SAY AS MUCH ABOUT THEIR FEELINGS AS THE DIALOGUE DOES, AND SOMETIMES EVEN MORE.

BASIC CLOTHING FOLDS
I USED TO DRAW DETAILED FOLDS INTO CLOTHING DURING PENCILS, BUT NOW I MOSTLY KEEP IT SIMPLE BY DRAWING ONLY THE IMPORTANT FOLDS THAT OCCUR AT CERTAIN ANCHOR POINTS LIKE THE ELBOWS, UNDER ARMS, AND CHEST. I TEND TO ADD MORE DURING INKS, IF NEEDED.

STRAIGHT LINES VS CURVED LINES
OGRE HAS A RIGID PERSONALITY AT FIRST GLANCE. I TRIED TO REFLECT THAT IN HIS DESIGN BY USING STRAIGHT LINES TO CONSTRUCT HIM. SOMEONE MORE COMPASSIONATE LIKE SHON HAS MORE CURVES LINES. HITTING THESE LINES DURING PENCILING MAKES FOR A SMOOTH INKING EXPERIENCE.

INKS

I INKED THIS BOOK WITH A WINSOR & NEWTON ARTIST'S WATERCOLOUR SABLE BRUSH, AND SOME CROW QUILL NIB PENS. THE CHARACTERS WERE ALL INKED BY BRUSH, AND THE ENVIRONMENTS WERE INKED WITH THE PENS. THIS ALLOWS THE CHARACTERS OCCUPY A DIFFERENT LINE WEIGHT THAN THE ENVIRONMENT, HELPING THEM STAND OUT.

WHEN INKING, I FOCUS ON A FEW ASPECTS:

LINE WEIGHT
LINE WEIGHT AND QUALITY ARE WHAT CREATE DYNAMICS IN LINEWORK. A SHAKY THIN LINE SAYS SOMETHING COMPLETELY DIFFERENT THAN A THICK, RUGGED BRUSH STROKE. BECOMING FAMILIAR WITH YOUR INKING TOOLS IS THE BEST WAY TO FIGURE OUT WHICH LINE WEIGHTS WORK FOR YOUR STORYTELLING.

TEXTURES
THE HATCHING ON OGRE'S SHOULDER IN PANEL FOUR CREATE A HAIR TEXTURE, WHILE THE DOTS AND SPECKLES ON THE CLIFFSIDE REPRESENT A DIRTY, SANDY TEXTURE. THERE ARE COUNTLESS TECHNIQUES TO CREATE TEXTURES WITH INK, AND EXPERIMENTING IS ALWAYS A BLAST.

SHADOW / SPOT BLACKS
SOLID BLACK SECTIONS OF INK IS A GREAT WAY NOT JUST TO CREATE SHADOW, BUT TO CREATE DEPTH AND DYNAMICS IN A PANEL. IT CAN ALSO BE USED TO DRAW ATTENTION WHERE NEEDED. THE FIGURES IN PANEL ONE ARE CLEARLY ESTABLISH BECAUSE THEY'RE IN SILHOUETTE. IT'S CLEAR HOW MANY THERE ARE, AND WHERE THEY EXIST ON THE PAGE.

CONCEPTS

THE INITIAL DESIGN FOR OGRE SAW A GOOD NUMBER OF CHANGES BEFORE BECOMING THE DESIGN USED IN THE BOOK. WE DROPPED THE WRIST TAPE, FIGURING THE IRON CUFFS HE WORE WOULD BE BUSY ENOUGH FOR ARMWEAR. HE ORIGINALLY HAD ONE ONE CLOUDY EYE, AS WELL AS AN EARRING, WHICH WAS GOING TO BE A BRIGHT GOLD COLOUR. I WANTED HIM TO HAVE ONE SMALL BRIGHT, COLOURFUL ASPECT TO HIS DESIGN AS A NOD TO HIS HIDDEN KINDNESS AND HOPE. BUT I FIGURED THAT, AS A PRISONER, HE WOULDN'T OWN ANY PRECIOUS VALUABLES, AS THEY'D BE TAKEN AWAY WHEN HE WAS CAPTURED.

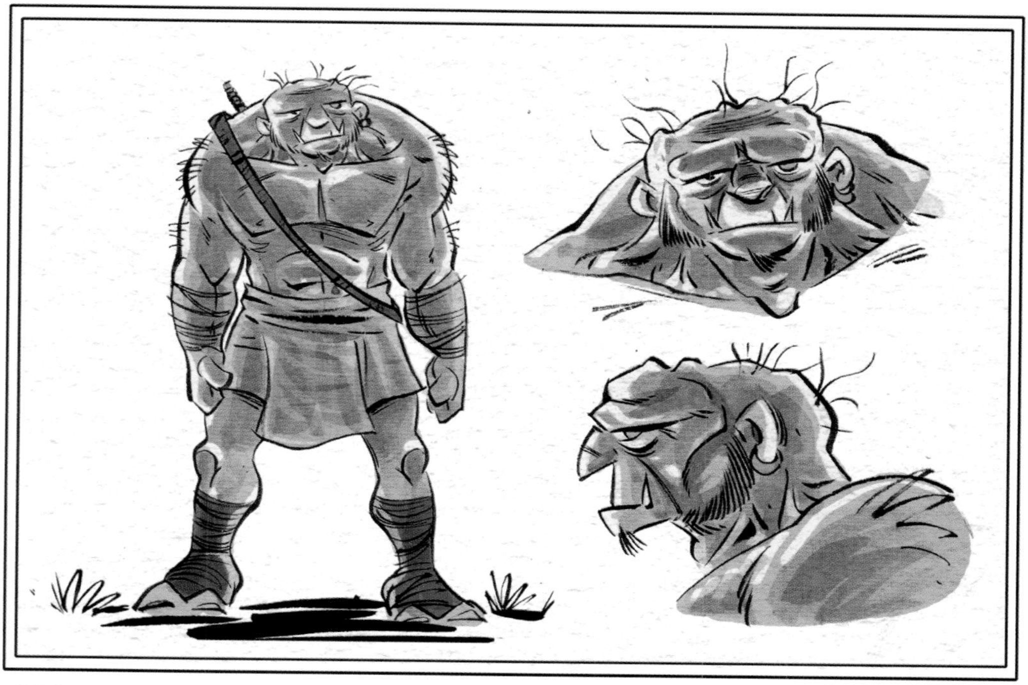

MARTEL WAS BASED OFF OF MY FAVOURITE CHARACTER FROM MY FAVOURITE ERA OF A FAVOURITE FRANCHISE. THE TRANSLUCENT BLUE GHOST EFFECT WAS ALSO A NOD TO ALL OF THE ABOVE. HE WAS ALWAYS MY FAVOURITE CHARACTER TO DRAW. HE WAS NEVER INKED - HE WAS ALWAYS DRAWN IN USING INDIGO WATERCOLOUR, WHICH IS MY FAVOURITE SHADE OF PAINT TO USE DUE TO ITS VERSATILITY. MARTEL HAS A BEARD AND, FOR THE RECORD, BEARDED CHARACTERS WILL ALWAYS BE AMONGST MY FAVOURITE CHARACTERS TO DRAW. HIS DESIGN DIDN'T CHANGE MUCH AT ALL, LOOKING BACK AT IT, WITH THE EXCEPTION OF A MORE TATTERED SHIRT.

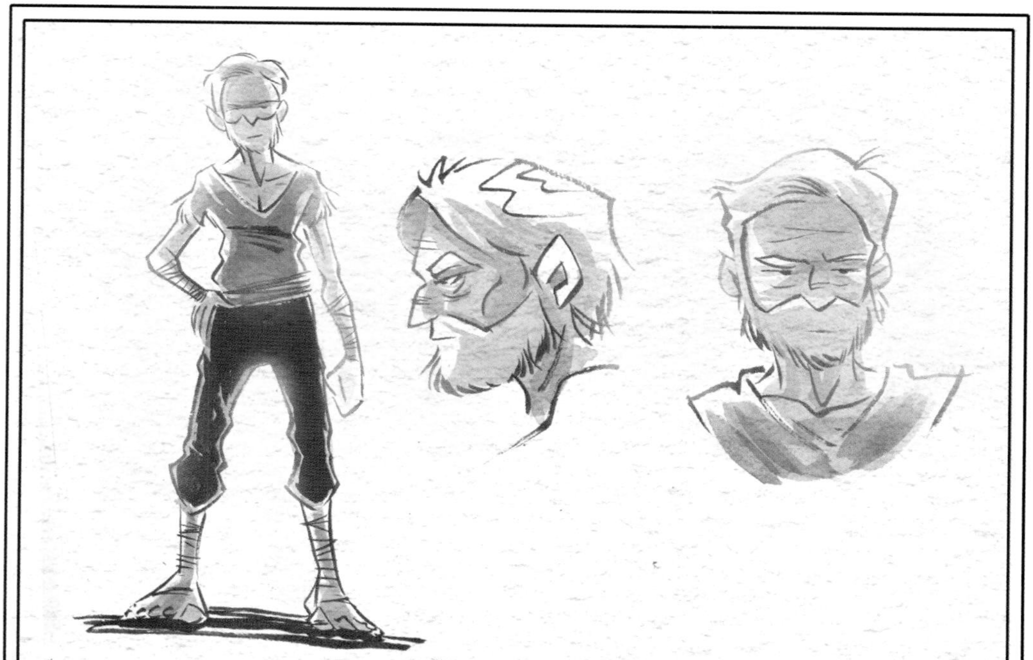

COVER CONCEPTS

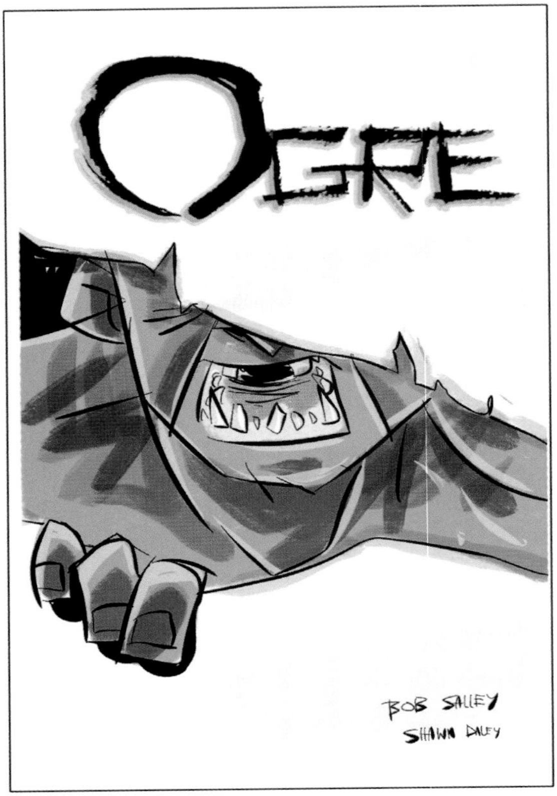
OGRE
BOB SALLEY
SHAWN DALEY

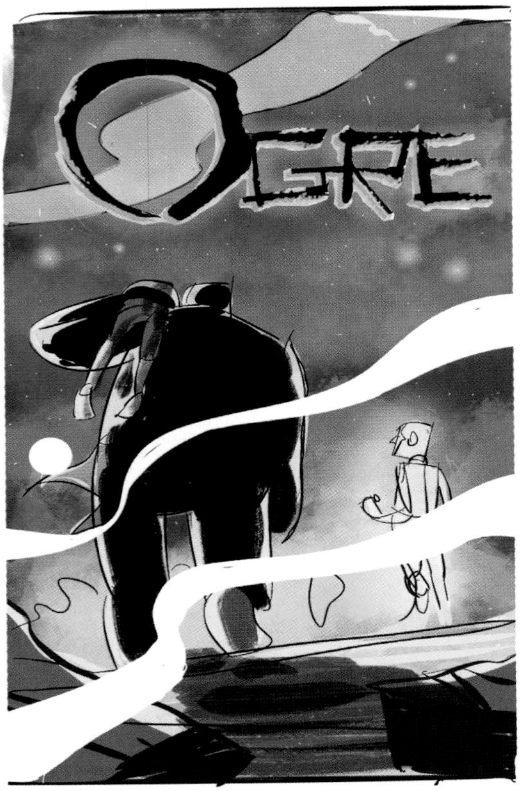
OGRE

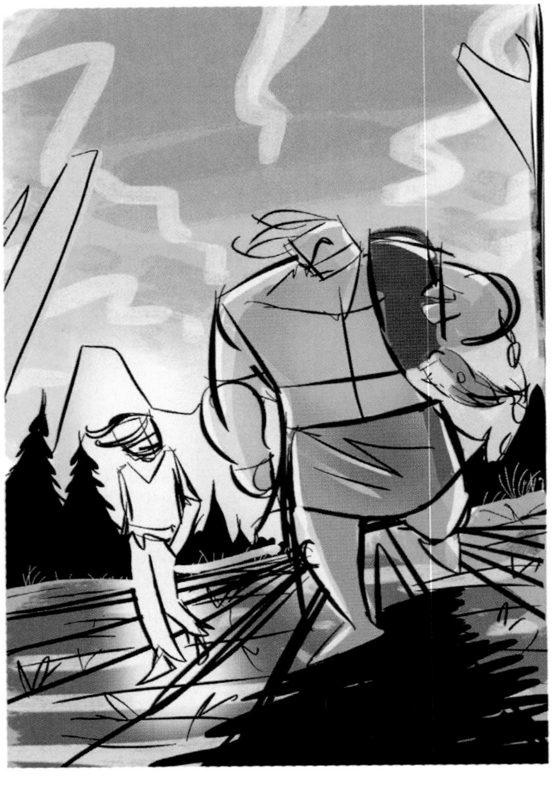

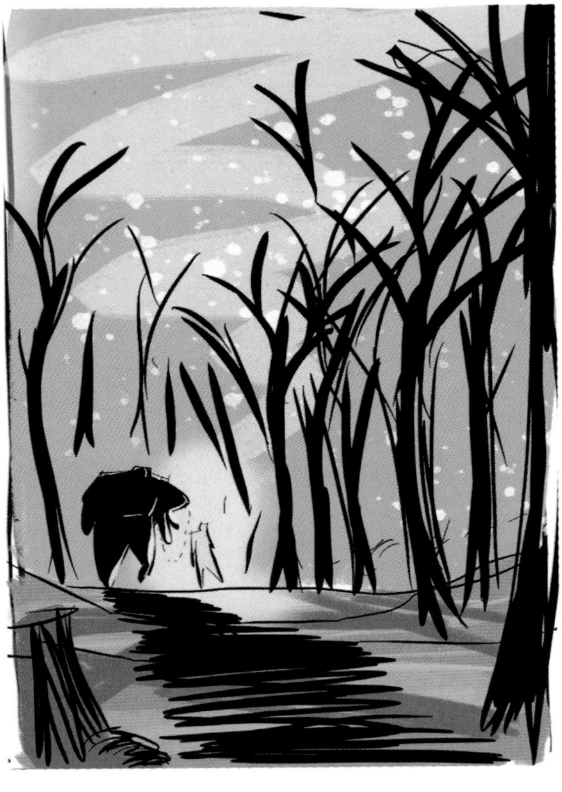

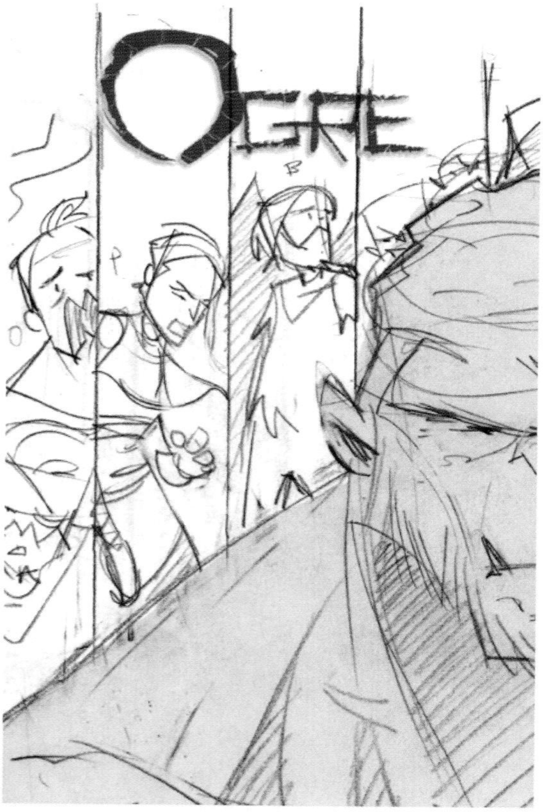
OGRE

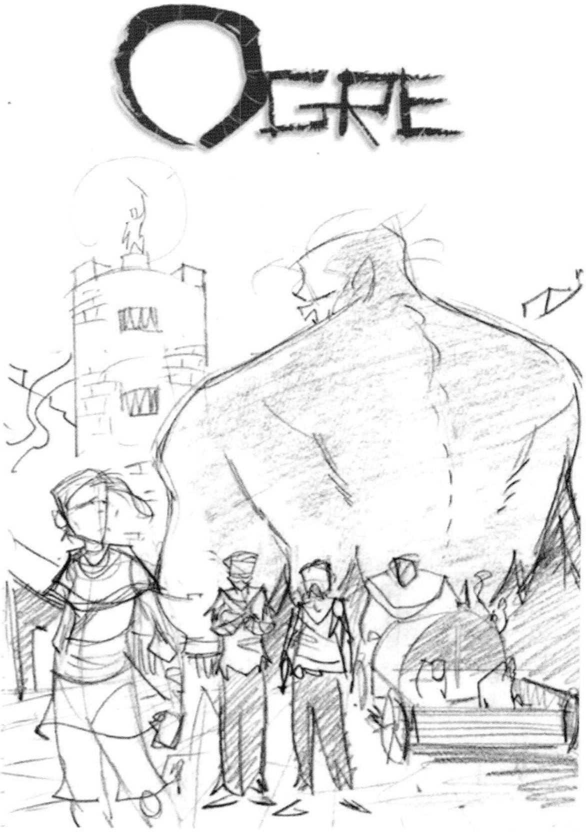
OGRE

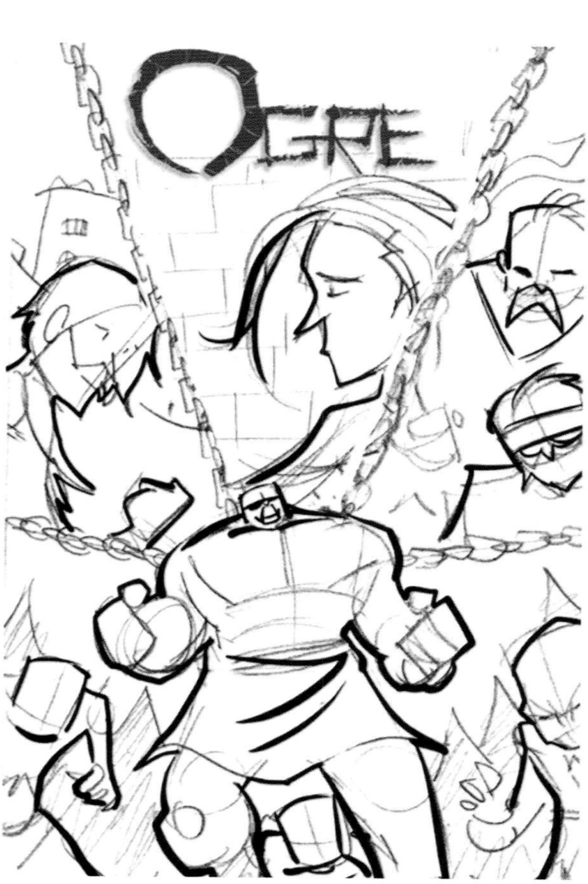
OGRE

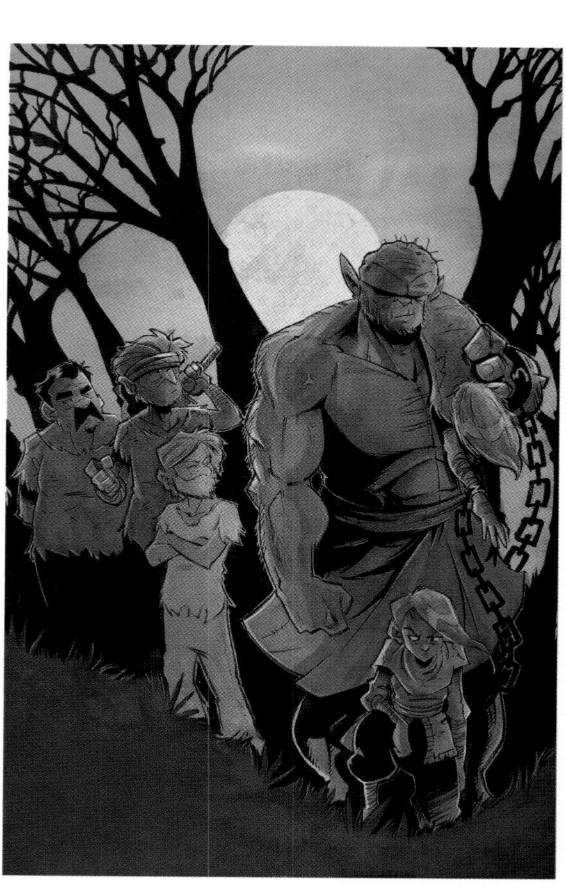

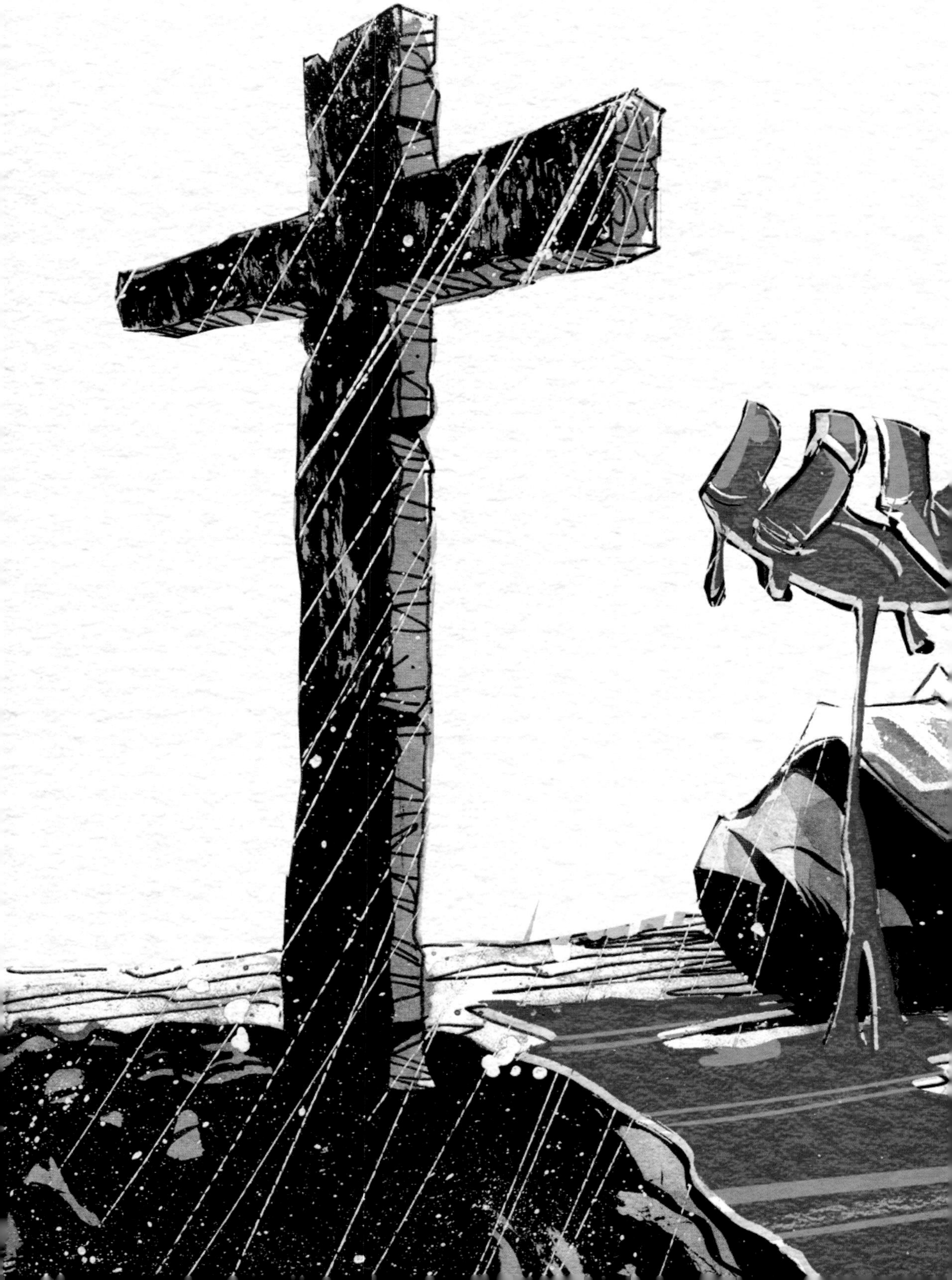

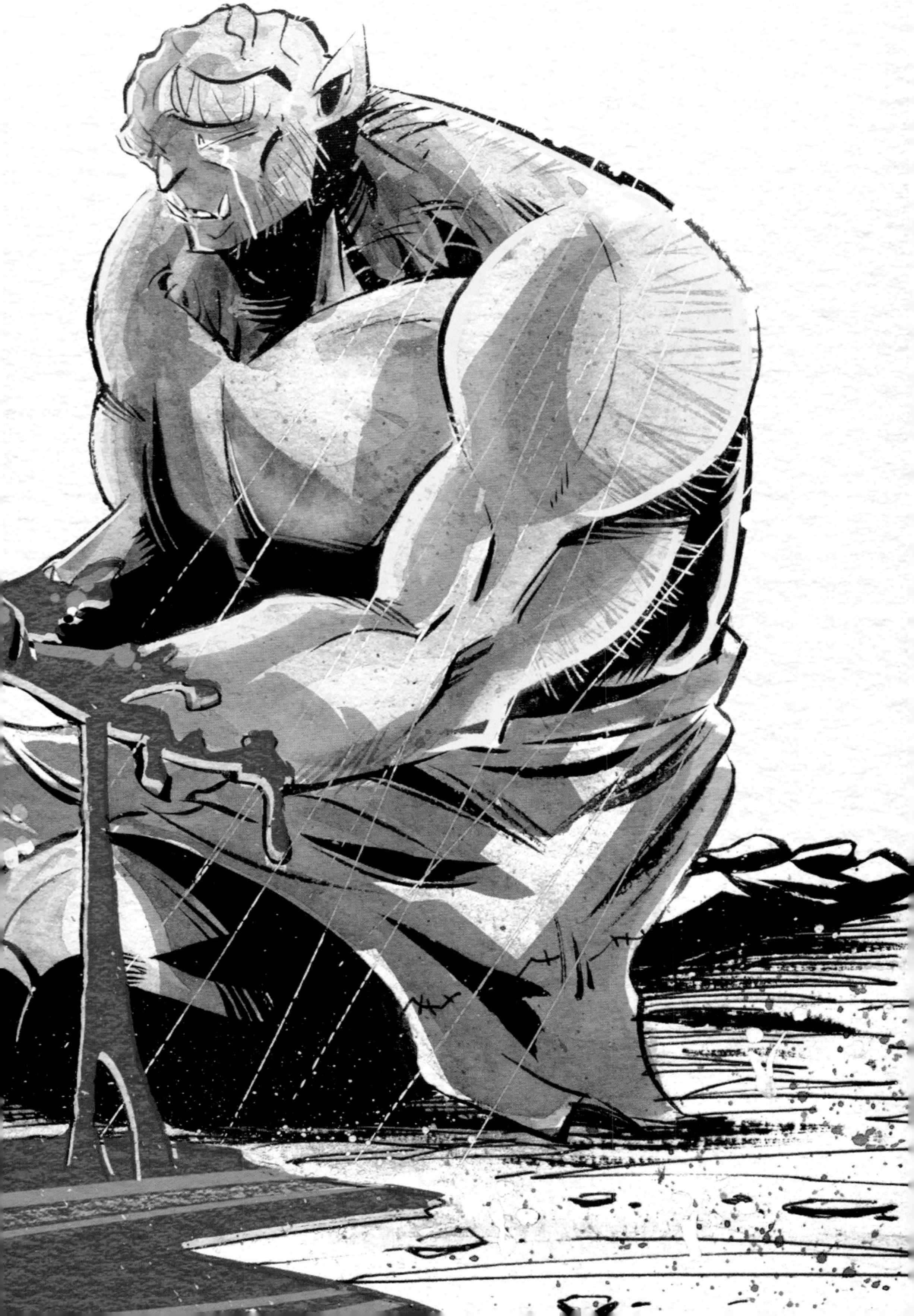

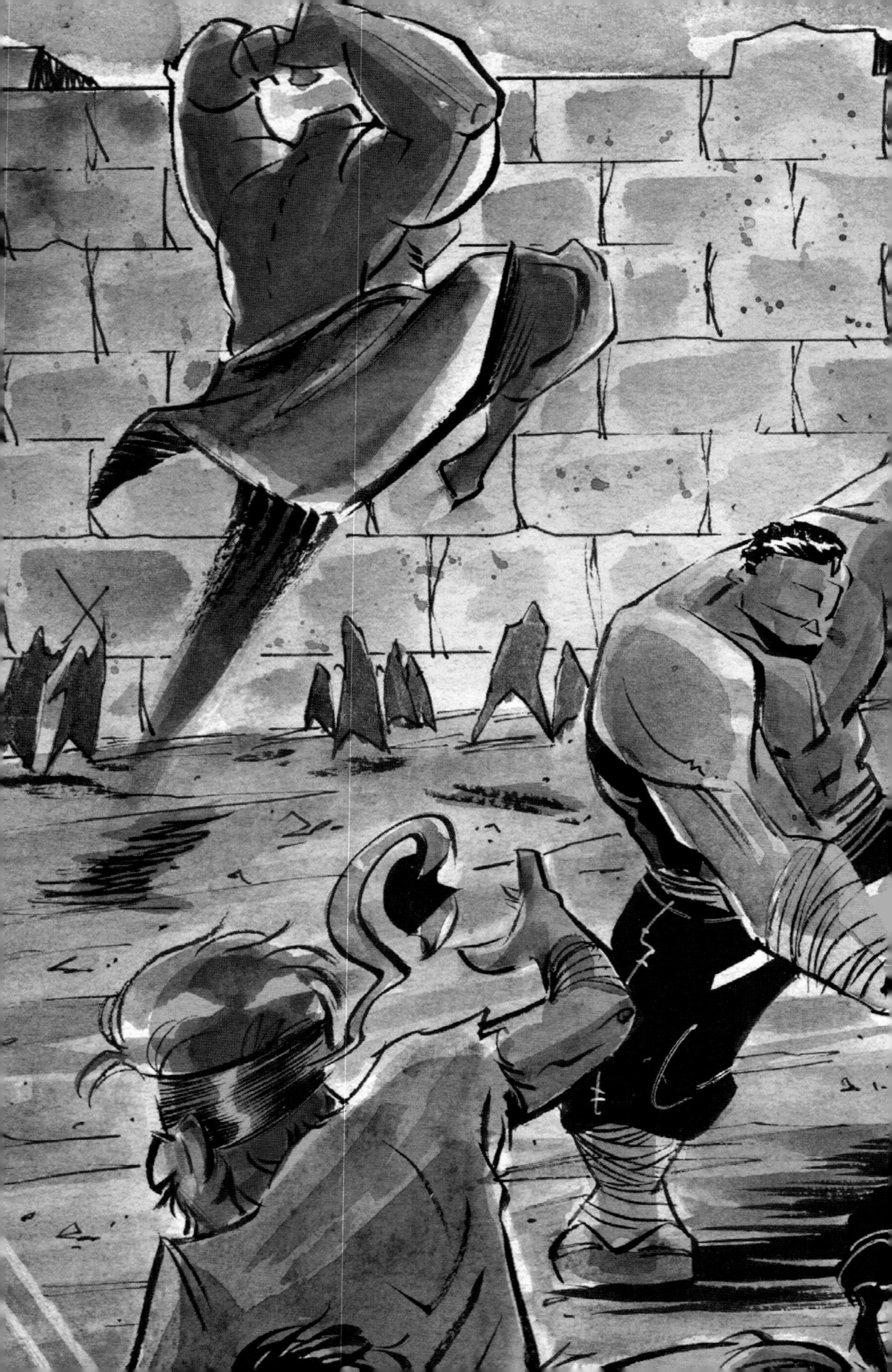